THE STORY

OF THE

AUGUSTA

NATIONAL

GOLF CLUB

THE STORY

OF THE

AUGUSTA

NATIONAL

GOLF CLUB

By Clifford Roberts

1976

DOUBLEDAY & COMPANY, INC.

GARDEN CITY, NEW YORK

ISBN: 0-385-11543-1
Library of Congress Catalog Card Number 75–38170

*To the Staff of the Augusta
National Golf Club and the
Masters Tournament Organization.*

Contents

THE STORY

OF THE

AUGUSTA

NATIONAL

GOLF CLUB

AUGUSTA NATIONAL GOLF CLUB

ORIGINAL PLANNING
1930
ROBERT TYRE JONES, JR. AND CLIFFORD ROBERTS

ORGANIZATION COMMITTEE
1931
CLIFFORD ROBERTS, CHAIRMAN; ROBERT TYRE JONES, JR.
ALFRED SEVERIN BOURNE, GRANTLAND RICE, WILLIAM C. WATT

GOLF COURSE DESIGN
1931
DOCTOR ALISTER MACKENZIE AND ROBERT TYRE JONES, JR.

FIRST OFFICERS
1932
ROBERT TYRE JONES, JR. PRESIDENT; CLIFFORD ROBERTS, EXECUTIVE COMMITTEE CHAIRMAN
ALFRED SEVERIN BOURNE, VICE PRESIDENT; MELVIN A. TRAYLOR, VICE PRESIDENT
CHARLES H. SABIN, TREASURER; FIELDING WALLACE, SECRETARY

OTHERS ESPECIALLY ACTIVE DURING CLUB'S FORMATIVE PERIOD

HARRY M. ATKINSON, ATLANTA	ROBERT P. JONES, ATLANTA
THOMAS BARRETT, JR., AUGUSTA	W. ALTON JONES, NEW YORK CITY
A. G. BEANE, NEW YORK CITY	RUSSELL LAW, NEW YORK CITY
LOUIS A. BERCKMANS, AUGUSTA	WALTON H. MARSHALL, NEW YORK CITY
WILLIAM C. BREED, NEW YORK CITY	LEWIS B. MAYTAG, COLORADO SPRINGS
J. FREDERIC BYERS, PITTSBURGH	JAY R. MONROE, ORANGE N. J.
HENRY P. CROWELL, CHICAGO	ALLAN M. PERKINS, GREENWICH
JEROME A. FRANKLIN, AUGUSTA	WILLIAM H. WALLACE, JR., NEW YORK CITY
J. G. GILFILLAN, LEROY, N. Y.	THOMAS B. YUILLE, NEW YORK CITY
JOHN W. HERBERT, NEW YORK CITY	SCOTT B. APPLEBY, WASHINGTON
LANSING B. LEE, AUGUSTA	FRANCIS E. DRURY, CLEVELAND
GEORGE M. OATES, NEW YORK CITY	B. B. TAGGART, NEW YORK CITY

This plaque commemorating the formative years of the club is located in the front hallway of the clubhouse.

Introduction

Several of our members have suggested during recent years that I write a book about the Augusta National Golf Club, one which would be a part of the club's records, with copies available to the present membership and to new members in future years.

The idea appealed to me from the start, but when the subject first arose I had just finished a very considerable amount of effort in preparing information for Columbia University. This information pertains to General Eisenhower and is to be made available after a period of years to history students. The experience gave me some idea of the extent of the research effort that would be required for a book about the Augusta National. My association with the General covered a period of twenty-one years, but I had been involved with our golf club in Augusta more than twice that long. Accordingly, I doubt that I would ever have done anything about the proposal except for the insistence of Sam M. Fleming, of Nashville, an active club member. It was Sam who contended that I had an obligation to write the history of the Augusta National, and he very generously offered to supply a professional writer, a special secretary, and recording equipment. All of this I declined, but I did promise to try to write the story, and this is my beginning. What follows was written during the period 1973–75.

There is an abundance of good material because so many fine and interesting people have been involved. My problem is whether to tell the complete story of the events that seem important to me, and thereby risk writing something too long to hold a reader's interest, or to seek popularity among the members by just hitting the high spots.

Another problem is to write about the club without appearing to overemphasize what might be termed the noncompetitive golfing career of Robert Tyre Jones, Jr. Bob influenced directly or indirectly every phase of the development of the Augusta National. It was his leadership position in the world of golf that made possible the organization of the club and the subsequent introduction of the Masters Tournament. It is my belief, as I shall later try to illustrate, that he probably did as much on a world-wide basis to promote the popularity of the game through the operation of the Masters as

1

Augusta National Golf Club

he ever did as a player. However, I shall not undertake in this book to describe the play of the Masters Tournament over the years, as this has already been fully and ably documented by professional writers and commentators.

During the forty-year period when Bob and I were closely consulting with each other, I invariably felt that I had benefited by having heard his views. Starting with the year 1948, when Bob became crippled, I made doubly certain that he was kept informed on all developments. Almost to the time of his death, in 1971, I sought his views on policy, especially if it had anything to do with public relations. Bob possessed a sixth sense of knowing just how and what to say in difficult situations, especially if the news media were involved. This was due in part to his exceptional command of the English language, which allowed him to express himself clearly and in a manner that left no doubt about complete sincerity. Few men in any walk of life ever attained the degree of international popularity accorded to Bob. It was predicated on modest bearing, gentlemanly conduct, sportsmanship of the highest order, and integrity. It would be impossible for me to write an accurate account of our club at Augusta without making Bob the central theme.

Before writing a line, I am quite aware that my book will deal with a number of personalities. It is the membership that makes a club, rather than the other way around. Our roster has borne the names of many influential men. More importantly, from our club's standpoint, has been the high percentage of easy-to-like and interesting members who generate enjoyable companionship. There has always been a common bond throughout the membership, which can be attributed to a genuine devotion to the game of golf plus a concern for its best interests.

I know next to nothing about the proper way to construct a readable book, and I shall make no effort to learn. Time is running out, as I was born in 1894. Gathering the needed factual material, dates, etc., requires considerable research work, so if I am ever to finish the book it must be in simple words and in my usual manner of expressing myself. I will, however, adopt the professional custom of telling the reader something about the author.

During all of my adult years I have been active in just one field, that of finance. Beginning in 1919, my headquarters had always been on Wall Street, until in recent years I changed to an uptown address in the General Motors Building at 767 Fifth Avenue. I have known two lean periods, one following the 1929 crash and another during World War II. On the whole, however, I have fared reasonably well, despite never having been willing to make an all-out effort. The making of lots of money never seemed as important as traveling extensively and retaining some independence, which, with the consent of my partners and associates, I have been able to do. This policy led me into several minor and two major nonprofit activities. The two major endeavors could be classified as golf and politics. Arising out of a close friendship with General Eisenhower, I was for a period of nine years intensely interested and active in his involvement in the political world. Even after his death I have continued to give much time and effort to his affairs, first as a trustee of his estate, and secondly, but more importantly, as a helper for several memorial projects bearing his name. I do not expect ever to finish my Eisenhower chores, and would not like it any other way so long as I am able to lend a hand.

Robert Tyre Jones, Jr., was the other great person who led me into a major altruistic undertaking—although it would perhaps be more honest for me to say I walked into both endeavors with my eyes wide open. The main point, regardless, is that the basis of my association with Bob was the same as with the General—great admiration and much liking for the person. Since the latter part of 1930 I have been continuously active in pulling together the talents and treasures of many fine sportsmen on behalf of Bob's club, the Augusta National. I am now in the process of transferring these responsibilities to others, but, here again, I doubt that I would be happy if I should be lucky enough to transfer all responsibilities.

My final introductory comment is that I have no regret about lost business opportunities. In all truthfulness, my life has been so enriched by the working association and the joyous companionship of Bob Jones and Ike Eisenhower, and many other Augusta National members, that I consider myself to be far richer today than could have been possible by any other measure of success. Briefly stated, I've been overpaid.

Augusta
National
Golf Club

PART ONE

Bob Jones and the author in the early thirties.

Bob and I Become Acquainted

Like all golfers—or, as one might more correctly say, like all Americans—I was an admirer of Bobby Jones. I saw him play a few times in tournaments and met him during the mid-twenties through mutual friends on a number of occasions.

One contact was Walton H. Marshall, who ran the Vanderbilt Hotel in New York and a chain that included the Bon Air Vanderbilt Hotel in Augusta, Georgia. Bob and his dad, Colonel Bob, always stayed at Walton's hotels because they liked him very much. I knew Walt by reason of our being fellow members of the Two-Cent Bridge Club in New York and the Knollwood Country Club in Westchester County, New York. Also, I was an occasional patron of Walt's hotel in Augusta, which was then a first-rate winter resort establishment. The Bon Air Vanderbilt importantly helped the Augusta Country Club, which at that time had two eighteen-hole golf courses.

Augusta is in a valley and at its low point is only 137 feet above sea level, compared to an elevation of 1,000 feet for Atlanta, Bob's home. The warmer temperatures resulting from this differential partially explain why Bob occasionally drove nearly across the state to play golf in Augusta during the winter season. In the 1920s Augusta had two courses that compared favorably with anything Atlanta offered, especially in the winter season. They were the Augusta Country Club No. 1 course and the Forest Hills Ricker Hotel course. I might add that the entire Forest Hills Ricker establishment was a casualty of World War II and is now part of a military hospital.

Each time I saw Bob or read his public comments, I respected and liked him more. I watched part of the final of the 1926 USGA Amateur Championship at Baltusrol, in New Jersey, in which George Von Elm defeated Jones two and one. Shortly afterwards, I was one of some half-dozen who were having a drink with the loser and trying to think of something comforting to say to him. My effort was to advance the argument that the par fives at Baltusrol were so designed that Bob could not take advantage of his superior length. But Bob would have none of it. He informed me that a good player should be able to compete on any type of course. Further, he said that Von

7

Augusta National Golf Club

Elm had won for the very simple reason that he had played better and therefore deserved to win.

The popularity of Bob Jones was probably the most incredible thing that ever occurred in American sports. His skill as a golfing competitor directed attention his way, but it was his innate modesty, plus his many great qualities of mind and heart, that developed widespread interest and adulation from people in all walks of life. Bob always seemed to do and say the things that were in good taste and pleasing to all, quite naturally and without any apparent effort.

It is difficult, I know, for today's young people to appreciate the extent of the deep and affectionate esteem in which Bob Jones was held. I will, nevertheless, make a brief explanatory effort along these lines. First, I would like to offer the reader one brief extract from the book *Farewell to Sport*, by Paul Gallico, which contains a chapter concerning Bob Jones:

I am, by nature, a hero-worshipper, as, I guess, most of us are, but in all the years of contact with the famous ones of sport I have found only one that would stand up in every way as a gentleman as well as a celebrity, a fine, decent, human being as well as a newsprint personage, and who never once, since I have known him, has let me down in my estimate of him. That one is Robert Tyre Jones, Jr., the golf-player from Atlanta, Georgia. And Jones in his day was considered the champion of champions.

Paul Gallico was one of the leading sports writers during the early days of the Masters, who gave up sports writing to become a successful novelist. I doubt that he ever wrote anything that has been so often quoted as his reference to Bob Jones in *Farewell to Sport*. Many regard it as the finest single tribute ever paid to Bob. Some think it to be the most remarkable compliment ever paid to anyone.

Next, I shall repeat a comment that was made to me, and to several others, by an eighteen-year-old golfer who was practicing very hard with the hope of qualifying for the National Amateur. This occurred at the Maidstone Golf Club at East Hampton, Long Island, in the late twenties. The young hopeful stated that his one golfing ambition was to be drawn to play against Bobby Jones so that he could have the honor and pleasure of being defeated by his idol, hopefully by just 4 and 3—but first he must improve through practice in order to qualify.

Finally, I'll repeat a story by a British golf writer during one of the Open Championships in Great Britain during the twenties. A contestant's drive had come to rest near where a dear little old lady was standing. She inquired as to the ownership of the ball, and was informed that it belonged to Bobby

Jones. "My!" she said. "Do you think it would do any harm if I just touched it?"

When Bob announced his retirement from tournament golf after completing the Grand Slam, the news was headlined in bold type by almost every newspaper in the United States. Many of the leading papers used banner headlines across their front pages. The treatment of the announcement by the press in Great Britain, and in many other countries, was likewise most remarkable. No act by any other golfer has ever come close to commanding so much attention as the simple statement by Bob that he was retiring from competitive golf. "Emperor Jones" was a name almost as widely used by the press, and understood by the public, as Bobby Jones.

I would describe Bob in his twenties as a quite handsome young athlete who seemed at the same time to be very manly. He had an engaging smile, but this did not prevent his looking squarely at the person to whom he was being introduced. His handshake was firm and his attitude quite friendly. He somehow managed to give everyone the impression that he was genuinely pleased about the introduction. Not once did I ever hear a person classify Bob as a bored celebrity.

Bob was five feet eight inches in height, and his average weight from 1920 to 1930 was about 165 pounds, although he regularly lost from five to eight pounds during each tournament. He was broad-shouldered but not heavily muscled. His hands were smaller than those of most great golfers. His long-hitting ability was generated by fluid timing rather than great strength. He liked to overclub and swing in an effortless and lazy fashion. Much has been said about Bob's long-driving ability. I would like to comment on his wise policy of keeping a part of this capacity in reserve. Whenever he chose to apply a maximum effort for distance, he could usually drive the ball an extra twenty-five to thirty-five yards. I am sure I would be correct in saying that no golfer in Bob's time, or since, has ever hit the ball as far with so little apparent effort.

Quite remarkably, Bob made a hole-in-one only twice in his life. I saw him make his second on the fourteenth hole at the Augusta Country Club on January 13, 1932. The hole measured about 145 yards. I reached the green with a six-iron, but Bob used a four-iron. I should explain that if Bob wanted to hit a six-iron shot quite hard he could have outdistanced my maximum effort with the same club by at least twenty-five yards. The wonder is that he was able to hit a controlled shot with too much club and not only hit it the proper distance but make it sit down when it arrived on the surface of the green. In order to appreciate the skill that such a shot requires, the reader might try stopping a four-iron shot on a small, mildly elevated green from a distance of 145 yards. He will do so only if he has the capability to "feather" the ball.

9

*Augusta
National
Golf Club*

While on this subject, I'll mention that Bob was also able to hit a full brassie shot and make it sit down when it reached the green. It was a type of shot that he could hit farther with more accuracy than any other player of his day. He once told me that he executed the shot by hitting down on the ball, and that a clean lie made it easy to do. I have more than once seen fine professional players watch Bob execute this shot, then shake their heads in wonder and indicate despair of ever being able to duplicate the performance. Bob could also lob a ball for a short distance with a niblick over a hazard and let it drop to the ground with little or no roll. The shot was executed without imparting spin of any kind to the ball.

As a putter, Bob Jones was outstanding. He stroked rather than noticeably "hit" his putts. He always tried to let the putt die at the hole. In other words, he did not believe it was to his advantage, as so many do, always to impart enough speed to permit the ball to overrun the cup. In answer to my question regarding this, he explained that, mathematically, the odds favored the putt that was struck just hard enough to die at the cup; that it will then often tumble in from any side of the hole, whereas a putt with enough speed to go past the hole will often roll around the rim and stay out.

Bob had the advantage of an exceptionally good and trained mind, and he made the most of this advantage in his approach to such golfing subtleties. I do not believe that any of the professionals during that period, except possibly Tommy Armour, was a college graduate. Whenever participating in a stroke-play tournament, it was always Bob's plan to play against the course, not against the other contestants. He first decided what score it would take to win and then played in a fashion designed to produce that score.

Bob never went into severe training in order to be at his best at any particular time. He felt that gymnastics were all very well in connection with many sports, but that golf required a different kind of muscular strength. He did no calisthenics, and did not even care to walk as a method of exercise. Possibly one reason for this was varicose vein troubles which required surgery several times. He was a moderately heavy cigarette smoker who always liked one before breakfast. He took a drink, preferably bourbon, whenever he felt like it, and, while I've seen him on special occasions indulge fairly liberally, he never lost control of his faculties.

Possibly it should be emphasized that Bob was never a slave to the practice tee. He had learned to play golf by imitating Stewart Maiden, the Scottish professional at the Atlanta Athletic Club, who is said to have had a flawless swing. Because of this, Bob developed a swing of his own that responded quickly to a few rounds of play. During a number of his years of competition he participated in only two tournaments. For example, following the National Amateur in the year 1922 he entered Harvard University and did not touch a club until early the following summer. Only his intention of participating in the Open then caused him to resume golf. During his eight most successful years in competition, 1923–30, he entered twenty-eight tournaments, an average of only 3.6 per annum.

Bob Jones was invariably considerate of his companions on the golf course, in the locker room, and elsewhere. He was a lot more interested in playing with people he liked than with the experts. His dad was invited to be a member of Bob's foursome more than anyone else. Bob was a good listener at the dinner table. Rarely did he interfere with the trend of the conversation, except if someone should tell a story that was just altogether too coarse and without any real humor. Whenever he undertook to contribute something, it was worthy of attention in that he was both a splendid raconteur and always able to provide fresh viewpoints on current topics. He had a wonderful sense of humor, and was simply incapable of being other than a gentleman at all times. In short, his character was the epitome of honor and integrity.

Bob never played golf for money. As an amateur he, of course, stepped aside in favor of a professional when it came time for the cash prizes to be awarded at the conclusion of tournaments. Bob's usual limit in friendly matches was a five-dollar Nassau, and I am certain he played many more rounds of nontournament golf when the stakes were lower rather than higher than that sum. I also think he played some of the best golf of his career both before and after his retirement in those friendly matches. As an example, Tommy Armour, when he was at his best, played a number of friendly matches one summer with Bob. And there are many who thought that, at his best, no professional golfer could be rated higher than Armour. Tommy told me in some detail about those friendly rounds with Jones, explaining that they settled down to a steady arrangement involving modest stakes with Bob starting Armour one up a side. "And that," said Tommy, "ought to give you some idea of Bob's ability as a player, especially when I tell you I lost money."

Over a period of many years, when my handicap ranged from six to nine, I had a standing bet with Bob wherein he started me nine up on eighteen holes. No matter who else was in the foursome, or what other bets were involved, I either took five dollars from Bob or paid him that sum on our individual contest. Finally, at a special party one evening at Augusta, Bob was asked how he made out with his bet with Roberts. "Well," says Bob jokingly, "if Cliff plays what he thinks is his game, he will win by as much as five and four. But if he plays what I consider his game to be, I'll bring him in one or two down." The fact is that, despite what appeared to be a lopsided handicap in my favor, I was obliged to pay more often than I collected.

There is no way of estimating how much better player Bob might have been if the competition had produced lower scores. Likewise, he might have played better if he had turned professional and devoted full time to golf. Most assuredly, lower scores by Bob could have occurred, almost automatically, if he had been playing on better-conditioned golf courses, with today's improved golf balls and clubs, and under the present rules which make putting easier. As it was, the betting odds by bookmakers were even money, Bob against the field, something that has not happened before or since.

Bob Jones was generally recognized as a good student—in fact "Deac" was his nickname. He was going to school until just three years before the time he retired from competition. He took special courses in engineering and English, as well as law, and sometimes did not touch a golf club for weeks or even months at a time. Then, too, his family and his entry into the practice of law mainly occupied his thoughts during the years that brought him so much golfing fame.

A New Golf Club Is Born

Bob Jones had planned for some years to build a golf course to his own liking. It was a creative instinct on his part.

In playing various courses, Bob had become a student of golf course architecture and was eager to try his hand at it. His idea was to utilize the natural advantages of the property that might be selected, rather than to impose any particular type of golf hole which might result in artificiality rather than the nature-made layout he had in mind. He wanted particularly to avoid

precipitous slopes, which are artificial in appearance and expensive to maintain. He planned to use mounds rather than too many bunkers, on the theory that they are more pleasing in appearance, require less upkeep, and can be quite effective as hazards. He hoped to find a mildly rolling piece of ground with a creek or two that could provide some water hazards. His chief objective was an interesting course that would be popular with the dues-paying members. Man-made hazards which penalize only the poor player were to be omitted. Punishing rough was also to be done away with, on the theory that golf is a game to be enjoyed, and that there is no fun in looking for lost balls, or in risking physical injury trying to recover from deep rough. He had no particular place in mind, so long as it was in the South and not too far from his home. He visualized a simple place devoted strictly to golf, rather than a country club with social activities. The club was to be open for play during the winter season only. By introducing a new concept of golf course architecture, he hoped to make a contribution to the popularity of the game, as well as pleasing his friends.

Just after the completion of what O. B. Keeler called "The Impregnable Quadrilateral," and the retirement announcement had been made, it was decided that Bob's course would be built near Augusta, provided a suitable piece of ground might be available in that neighborhood. The decision was made as the result of a ten-minute conversation between Bob and myself. I was one of a few who knew of Bob's idea about a new type of golf course. Without providing any money-making angle either for him or for me, I suggested to Bob that Augusta was the logical place. His immediate reaction was to embrace the proposal enthusiastically, but with a stipulation that I agree to look after the financing. This I agreed to do.

I might mention that, during the fall of 1930, numbers of corporations were making commercial propositions to Bob, a few of which he accepted. The principal one was a series of instructional movies done in an entertaining fashion, which were filmed by Warner Brothers. There are believed to be only three complete sets of these movies in existence, and the Augusta National, I am happy to say, owns one of them.

Although I was not surprised at Bob's willingness to locate his golf course in Augusta, several others were greatly disappointed, including some of his closest friends in Atlanta, who thought that his home city deserved first consideration. Some even went so far as to predict failure if an Augusta site should be chosen. But Bob knew Augusta was the better choice for winter golf, and he became impatient to get started so as to have a really private place to play the game he so greatly enjoyed. Whenever he played a round on one of the Augusta courses, or at any place outside Atlanta, he found himself playing what amounted to an exhibition match, with galleries that often numbered in the hundreds or even thousands.

A mutual friend, Thomas Barrett, Jr., of Augusta, was consulted, and, although Tom was not a golfer, he at once recommended a 365-acre property, called Fruitlands Nurseries, which was for sale. Once an indigo plantation, it was purchased in 1857 by a titled Belgian, Baron Louis Mathieu Edouard Berckmans, who was a horticulturist by hobby. His son, Prosper Julius Alphonse, was an agronomist and horticulturist by profession, and the two of them organized on a partnership basis in 1858 P. J. A. Berckmans Company, which, operating under the trade name of Fruitlands Nurseries, is said to have been the first commercial nursery in the South. Trees and plants of many kinds were imported from a number of countries, and the nursery made great contributions directly and indirectly to the landscaping of homes throughout the South.

The Baron died in 1883, and, when P. J. A. Berckmans died in 1910, the nursery ceased operations and the trade name was sold. But there remained

Thomas Barrett, Jr.

Louis Alphonse Berckmans, grandson of Baron Berckmans, and a member of the Augusta National.

Prosper Julius Berckmans, son of the Baron and active head of Fruitlands Nurseries.

on the property a great variety of flowering plants and a number of trees that did not exist anywhere else in this country. Moreover, a long double row of magnolia trees set out before the Civil War was intact. Said to be the finest thing of its kind, this double row of magnolias serves today as a most impressive entrance to the old manor house which is now our main clubhouse building.

When our friend Tom Barrett first showed us the Berckmans' nurseries property, he conducted us to a spot on elevated ground that is now the club's mammoth practice putting green. This afforded an excellent view over the central part of the land, which had been cleared for the growing of nursery plants. We could readily see out over the mildly rolling terrain for a distance equal to about two-thirds of the way across the entire property. It is quite true, as has so often been repeated, that Bob took one look and remarked, "Perfect! And to think this ground has been lying here all these years waiting for someone to come along and lay a golf course on it."

An option was obtained on the property at a price of $70,000, and an organization committee of five was formed, consisting of Alfred S. Bourne, of New York, who had a winter home in Augusta; William C. Watt, of New York, who made occasional visits to Augusta; Grantland Rice, of New York, the well-known sports writer; Bob Jones, and myself. Bob insisted that I was the logical one to be named chairman.

Before any committee meeting was held, Bob and I had lengthy discussions. Neither of us thought we would have too much trouble raising the necessary financing, but we deemed it prudent to get an underwriting group together, with each underwriter making a firm commitment for a minimum of $5,000. We agreed that we would try to build a national membership, knowing that only a few individuals in Augusta could be expected to help support a golf club in addition to the Augusta Country Club. Bob proposed that Augusta National would be an appropriate name, and that our new club operate only during the winter season. We planned to stay, as usual, at the Bon Air Vanderbilt Hotel. The club operation was to be kept as simple as possible, on the order of golf clubs in England and Scotland, with no living quarters. Men only were to be members, and no ladies' tees were to be built.

It was beginning to become the custom at new courses to sell off any excess acreage as building lots, and we planned to do the same, limiting the sale to about a dozen quite large homesites, to be constructed in locations well back from any fairway. Fortunately, only one lot was sold—to W. Montgomery Harison, an Augusta member—before we had a change of heart and called off any further sale of lots. We suddenly realized that, with even only a dozen family homes around the course, we would lose the very basis of our desire to organize a club primarily for men which would refrain from any kind of social activities not related to golf.

Bob decided quite early in the planning discussions that he would like to have Dr. Alister Mackenzie, of Scotland, a onetime practicing physician and later a renowned golf course designer, act as our architect. Bob knew that Mackenzie held views similar to his own, and was confident they could work together in harmony to produce a course that would take full advantage of the opportunities afforded by such an excellent piece of ground.

I asked Bob who he wanted as the club's golf professional. After some days of reflection he handed me a piece of paper on which he had written: "First choice, Ed Dudley; second choice, Macdonald Smith; and third choice, Willie MacFarlane." I was curious and therefore asked Bob how he had arrived at his preferences. He said, "First of all I want a gentleman. Next, I feel we should select a pro who likes to teach. And, finally, I believe we want someone who is a good player. You should understand that I do not support the idea that a good teacher can be someone who is not a good striker of the ball. These three professionals qualify on all counts." In the end we offered the place to Ed Dudley, who promptly accepted.

Ed Dudley, a native of Brunswick, Georgia, justified on all counts his selection by Bob Jones. He was an unusually patient and capable instructor, and found favor with all of our members who made use of his skill as a teacher. General Eisenhower was always trying to improve his game and sought lessons at various places from golf professionals. I am quite certain, however, that he accepted more tutoring from Ed Dudley than all others combined. And I am doubly certain he was especially attached to Ed and was benefited more by him than any other professional.

Ed Dudley remained at the Augusta National for twenty-seven years. During that time he was elected president of the Professional Golfers' Association of America seven years in a row.

After becoming the Augusta National professional Ed played in a relatively small number of tournaments. Bob Jones had a reason, however, to be happy with Ed's record in the Masters Tournament. In the first eight years, he finished in the first ten seven times.

Financing

The Depression was little more than a year old. We hoped that it might soon be over. Had we known that it was to become a lot worse, and not end until a world war came along, I am very certain that we would have called off the project.

Edward B. Dudley, Jr., Bob Jones's first choice for our club professional. Ed was the pro at Augusta National for 27 years.

Alfred Severin Bourne.

The first person I approached on the underwriting was Alfred Bourne, a sportsman who devoted a very large part of his life to playing golf. Once in a while quail shooting, for example, might interfere, but not often. Bourne's father was the head of the Singer Sewing Machine Company and, upon his death, a trust fund of approximately $25 million was established for each of his children. Alfred was a very shy person who tried hard to avoid personal encounter with anyone who was a salesman or a solicitor of donations. Nevertheless, he loved the game of golf so much, and admired Bob Jones so greatly, that he welcomed me and my proposal with open arms.

At this point, I'll digress briefly to relate one of the humorous incidents that will help our present-day members to understand better some of the remarkable and lovable characters who were prominently identified with the Augusta National.

Alfred was a middle-aged man at this time, and was no doubt the wealthiest person in Augusta—and the most generous as well. He regularly made a sizable cash gift to the Augusta Country Club, and the club, in turn, set aside a small room connected with the pro shop where he could change his shoes or eat a sandwich in private. And everyone understood that Alfred's privacy was not to be invaded. Then one year along came an ambitious local plan to raise $50,000 for a worthy charity in Augusta. As might be surmised, $50,000 was quite a considerable sum of money for Augusta to raise in those days for any project. A special committee was appointed to promptly solicit a contribution from Mr. Bourne, in the hope that he would start things off with a $5,000 gift. A letter was written for an appointment, but Alfred's secretary was slow in replying, so the committee barged in on Alfred in his secluded room at the Augusta Country Club. Alfred, of course, was annoyed, and, as the committee chairman was trying to explain their mission, he cut in with a demand that he be told at once how much they wanted. The chairman was confused and stuttered out something about $50,000, whereupon Alfred said, "All right, if you will now excuse me, I'll have a check for that amount sent to you the first thing tomorrow morning." It was not altogether surprising that, when Alfred's check arrived, the whole campaign organization held a victory celebration and called it a day.

When Alfred heard my story in 1930 about the proposed Augusta National, he at once said that he wished he could alone furnish all the money needed, and that, had we come to him a year or two earlier, he would gladly have done just that. He went on to tell me that he had no cash, but an income large enough for him to readily save $25,000 within a year, which he was prepared to pledge. Alfred went on to explain that $1 million was willed to him outright by his father, and this he used in a margin account to speculate in stocks. When the crash came in 1929 his equity in the account was about $10 million, but in a matter of months it was completely wiped out.

Five of the gang at the Bon Air Vanderbilt Hotel in Augusta during the formative years of the club. Left to right, Thomas Barrett, Jr., Charles McGee, Bob Jones, the author, and William H. Wallace, Jr.

"How I wish I had one of those millions to offer you today," Alfred said.

We had one other $25,000 underwriter in our friend Walton Marshall, not on behalf of his hotel corporation but as an individual subscriber. Quite a considerable number came along for $5,000 or $10,000, but I do not recall that any were quite as easily persuaded as Bourne and Marshall. Only one person from Atlanta, Harry Atkinson, the founder of the Georgia Power Company, was willing to become an underwriter. Atkinson was an elderly man, and he admired Bob immensely. I was one of several hundred guests of his when he chartered a vessel and went out in the harbor in New York to greet Bob upon his return after winning the first half of the Grand Slam in 1930. It was on this occasion that Bob and his wife, Mary, were honored with a ticker-tape parade up Broadway. This is the only occasion when a reception of this magnitude was arranged for a golfer and, so far as I know, for any type of sportsman. As my office was in the financial district, I witnessed a number of ticker-tape parades, including those for Lindbergh, General Eisenhower, and others. It is not possible to make comparisons, but it seemed to me that the turnout for Bob Jones was comparable to anything of its kind.

Bob Jones took the position that he would not ask anyone in Atlanta to help finance his project in Augusta, and urged me not to do anything other than take what was offered by Atlanta. While he never complained about it, I know he was keenly disappointed that only one of his Atlanta friends became an underwriter, which may have been one of the reasons why he volunteered on several later occasions to contribute $5,000 or more to the club. But everyone agreed that Bob was the one person who should never have been asked to become an underwriter. He was contributing far more than anyone else by lending his name and efforts. Moreover, he had no money. The first time he ever made anything worthwhile was after the Augusta National was launched. It came from the Warner Brothers movies, about a half million dollars. After that, however, when the going got really rough, and he saw his friends making sacrifices for the club, he insisted on chipping in, and was permitted to do so.

Publicity

When the announcement was made about the plan for a new course in Augusta which was to be sponsored by Bobby Jones, it resulted in a huge amount of newspaper and magazine coverage. Bob was the principal author of the releases, in which he tried to stress the plan of developing as many original type golf holes as the terrain and surroundings might make possible. Some of the holes might resemble to some extent a few of the famous existing holes or have some similar features. However, it was emphasized that there was no intention of attempting to create copies of famous golf holes on Scottish courses, something that had previously been tried in our country. Both Mackenzie and Bob knew well the folly of making copies of golf holes; they knew that in so many instances the charm or greatness of a golf hole depended to a very considerable extent on its background. Despite all the interviews and written explanations, one or two newswriters prepared stories based on rumors that Bob had selected eighteen holes in "the old country" and intended to duplicate them in Augusta. Many years elapsed before this story was to expire, but I am happy to say that I have not recently seen it in print.

One of the results of the enormous amount of publicity was a problem for us at the front gate. On average, more than two hundred cars per day stopped and wanted to drive in to see the site of Bobby's dream course. This required posting a guard to politely explain that no visitors could be allowed to enter. Surprisingly enough, there are still about the same number of would-be visitors who would like to look in on us. Some of these are, of course, interested in seeing the Eisenhower Cabin, or Ike's Pond, but we are in a position to state that the Jones course is to this day the main attraction.

I cannot recall any publicity that was not intended to be complimentary. Many letters arrived wishing us well. A number of people wanted to know how they could become members.

Memberships

One of the early policy decisions was to take in as members only those who were acquainted with one or more members of our Organization Committee. In practice, this meant that Bob and I were the ones who were active in the membership effort, nearly everyone who came in being a friend of Bob's or mine, a circumstance which remained substantially true for the next twenty-five years. Fortunately, both Bob and I had rather large acquaintanceships for young men, Bob then being twenty-eight and I thirty-six years of age. Our contacts were located in a number of states. Bob's friendships were quite largely based on golfing associations, including the USGA, on whose Executive Committee he served for three years. The majority of these committee-men occupied leadership positions in their home communities. My friends were largely business and banking people, many of whom liked to play golf. As the Augusta National grew in stature, Bob's and my acquaintanceship with golfers of desirable membership types continued to expand. That is why it is probably accurate to say that, during the first twenty-five years of the club's existence, practically all new members were already on a first-name basis with one or both of us.

At the start, the mechanics of taking in a new member involved the usual proposal by a member, plus endorsements by other members. It soon became apparent, however, that this procedure was not the right one for our club. Numbers of individuals asked members to sponsor applications for membership and, if they were not accepted, were unhappy to a degree that made things unpleasant for all concerned. Every golfer in the country liked Bob Jones to an extent of almost considering themselves to be personal friends of "The Emperor." If such an admirer were turned down for membership in Bob's club, it was a tragedy, not just a disappointment. Accordingly, the club was obliged to adopt an "invitation only" policy with respect to new members.

In the beginning, the club followed the usual custom of permitting its members to issue guest cards. As a result, the members were deluged with requests for playing privileges. Consequently, we were obliged to apply a strict rule which forbids a guest to play the course except in the company of a member.

The main thrust of my own efforts during the early organization of the club centered around prospective underwriters, each of whom was required to make a firm commitment for a minimum of $5,000. We also charged each one a nominal membership initiation fee of $350. There were, however, a few young men we wanted as members who could not possibly become underwriters. Not having a golf course for our members to use, and not knowing how much it would cost to operate the course when it became ready for play, we also decided to ask the members to pay only nominal dues of sixty dollars per annum.

Distinguished Officers

Melvin A. Traylor, who was head of the First National Bank of Chicago, and a former president of the USGA, was invited to be an officer of the club. The same was true of Charles H. Sabin, the chief executive officer of the Guaranty Trust Company of New York, who had also been active in golf association work. They were both anxious to be part of the new club, one being needed as vice president and the other as treasurer. But it developed that both harbored a desire to be Bob's vice-president. An argument ensued, each one contending that he was already the treasurer of too many things. Traylor finally convinced Sabin that, on this basis, he was entitled to the vice-presidency of Bob's club, and Sabin good-naturedly yielded.

In the Traylor-Sabin argument I was in Traylor's corner, for a very good reason. He warned me in the early part of 1929 to prepare for a storm. Mel is the only person I knew personally in a leadership position in banking circles who openly warned of the impending disaster.

Melvin A. Traylor.

Charles H. Sabin.

Important Policy Decisions

Two members who were quite prominent, one from Ohio and the other from Boston, proposed to us that, with the club's approval, they would like to build a monument on the club grounds to honor Bob. They had in mind raising the funds through a national campaign soliciting small sums from donors in every state in the Union. They also thought that a huge likeness of Bob in statue form, at the entrance to the club, might be appropriate.

However, at the outset Bob Jones had stated emphatically that he did not want any statue, or other type of monument, built for him on the club grounds, as the golf course itself was quite adequate in that respect. Thus this proposal was never seriously considered.

At a later date, we also decided against accepting gifts in the form of golfing memorabilia. This came about as the result of several generous offers made to the club, one of which was an extensive library of golfing literature. Fortunately, it was realized that the Augusta National could not operate as a private club if it accepted collectors' items from nonmembers. Then, too, the cost of maintaining suitable space and facilities might become burdensome. We therefore decided to suggest to donors of artifacts pertaining to golf that they contact the director of the museum of the United States Golf Association.

Dr. Alister Mackenzie

I think this is the proper time to furnish some information about Dr. Alister Mackenzie as a person, or rather as a most remarkable and likable character. I knew him for only the brief period of one and a half years—he died before the Augusta National was ready for play. The last time he saw the course the construction work was finished, but it was not fully covered with grass. He was quite ready, however, to declare the course to be his best, and he did so a number of times. What a pity Mackenzie did not come to this country earlier or did not live for another ten years! We surely would have had many more really interesting and pleasurable courses.

Dr. Alister Mackenzie, the golf course architect.

Several people who had known Mackenzie over a period of years told me quite a bit about his background. Best of all, he was an open-book type who came forth voluntarily with stories about incidents which provided the answers to questions one might wish to ask. I saw quite a bit of the good doctor and, in fact, went out of my way more than once in order to be with him. He was invariably entertaining, partly as the result of a calculated effort on his part to reminisce a bit or to tell a Scottish story. Then too, as often as not, he was hilariously amusing quite unintentionally. He spoke with a rich Scottish burr and punctuated his remarks with typical Scots exclamations. Let something occur that was just mildly unusual and the Doc would instantly come forth with a comment that was to him altogether normal, but that made the incident an unforgettable occasion for the rest of us.

The Mackenzie life story which relates to golf, as I know it, starts in South Africa during the Boer War, where the doctor served in the British Army. The Boers were clever in the art of camouflage. The British would heavily shell what appeared to be the enemy trenches some 1,500 yards away. When they were satisfied that the Boers had been adequately softened up, the British would leave their own trenches and start an advance. Whereupon the Boers would open up on them from a camouflaged trench only 500 yards away. This made a big impression on the Doc, and when he returned to Scotland from the war he decided to apply the art to golf course designing. His theory was that courses should be less artificial in appearance, more nature-made, and thus more pleasurable to play and less costly to maintain. He proceeded to ask his own golf club for permission to rebuild a few holes to illustrate the improvements he had in mind. The club declined, but later another club accepted his proposal and was made happy with the results. In a few years he found himself doing more golf course work than doctoring. Accordingly, he decided to take down his name plate as a medical man and to put up another listing himself as a professional golf course architect. In time, he became well and favorably known as an architect in a number of countries.

Before coming to Augusta, Mackenzie designed two courses in California, Pasatiempo and Cypress Point. I have never seen Pasatiempo, but I have played Cypress Point many times. It is a good example of Mackenzie's ability to recognize nature's beauty and to retain it. I doubt that he thought of himself as such, but he was truly an artist. And he had seemingly unlimited ability to create original types of golf holes, especially the greens. One of the greatest features of the Augusta National is that each hole bears no resemblance whatever to any other on the course. The same is true of Cypress Point, a short course partly because of ground scarcity, but a very interesting, beautiful, and enjoyable course for both the experts and the rest of us.

Dr. Mackenzie designed two eighteen-hole courses for Ohio State University at Columbus, Ohio, which were constructed after his death, neither of which I have seen. He also designed a course in Buenos Aires and one in Montevideo, both of which I have played several times, and both of which reflect Mackenzie's superior architectural talents. The one in Montevideo was especially interesting to me because it had mildly rolling terrain plus many beautiful trees and a view overlooking the harbor.

One of Mackenzie's policies I admired was that long walks from each green to the next tee should be avoided. Another was his uncanny ability of knowing where to cut a vista through woods so as to expose an unusually beautiful view. Still another was his pride in the fact that he had never spent more than $100,000 on a golf course. If he were asked to design a course on acreage that he felt was unsuitable, he would simply decline.

The Augusta National was mildly rolling and, except for a part of the thirteenth fairway, there were no rock problems. One sizable creek and several small streams made it easy to provide water hazards. With low labor costs, and the bargain-counter supplies that were available, it would seem that we should have been able to stay within the Doc's $100,000 limit. I'd like to be able to say we did, but I can honestly report that we did not miss it too badly. Ours was really quite an elaborate affair, with eighty acres of fairway area, which compared with thirty or thirty-five acres on the average course. The square footage of the eighteen greens added up to approximately 101,000, which was far more than the average of those days. Excluded from this figure were the thirty-six-inch collars that encircled each putting surface, which accounted for an additional 16,000 square feet of carefully mowed space. An immense amount of soil-conditioning work was done at Augusta, in addition to the special drainage installations. Quite a bit of extra money was spent in order to protect a number of fine specimens of longleaf pine trees which were strategically located on the golf course. One of the very disappointing occurrences to Bob and me was the loss of three huge pines that formed a triangle exactly where the twelfth tee was to be built. Elaborate precautions were taken not to disturb the root system of those three giant pines. But, to our great regret, all three trees died within a few years.

Shortly after I had first met him, I drove the Doc from New York City to a new course in Westchester County named Whipporwill. Situated on the highest ground in the area, it was extremely hilly. A friend of mine named William A. Willingham had bought the property just because he admired the place, the splendid scenery, and the numerous deer. Someone suggested that it would be a nice location for a golf course, and Willie, as we called him, had a course built and a club formed. I was invited to join and did so, partly because I was impressed with the exceptional views and one hole in particular that cost $100,000 to construct because part of it had to be cut through solid granite. Several members were on hand to greet the doctor and, after he had looked around for an hour or two, they pressed him at lunch-time for his opinion. He responded by saying, "It's most remarkable," and that was all they could get from him. On our way back to the city I asked what he meant by the answer he gave my friends. "I meant," said the Doc, "that it's most remarkable that anyone could be damn fool enough to try to build a course on ground that is so obviously unsuitable for golf."

I had taken Mackenzie to see Whipporwill expecting him to admire it. Needless to say, I felt considerably deflated, especially since it suddenly dawned on me after hearing his brief summation that the doctor was completely right.

Golf Course Construction

Bob and Dr. Mackenzie completed the plans for the course in time for construction work to begin in the first half of 1931. The engineer in charge was Wendell P. Miller, of New York. Once the design plans had been completed, no effort was spared not only to complete the course as quickly as possible, but to open it in first-rate playing condition, and, to ensure this, both Bob and Doc Mackenzie made several trips to Augusta while the construction work was going on.

I made only one visit during this time, as a guest of Tom Barrett. I had heard about how hot it could be in Augusta during the summer, sometimes 110 degrees to 112, but on Tom's front porch that first morning it did not seem unduly warm.

When we drove over to the club, I asked Tom to show me the thirteenth hole first, as it was my choice of the several nature-made holes that needed only be "discovered," as Mackenzie expressed it. The thirteenth's fairway soil was loaded with stones and, as it had rained the day before, hundreds of these stones made their appearance on the surface. We found about twenty-five men in a line, on their knees, picking up the stones and placing them in sacks. I was puzzled about all of them wearing gloves, or having burlap wrapped around their pickup hands, and I got out of the car to investigate. Before Tom could stop me, I picked up the largest nearby stone with my bare hand. Despite my speed in dropping it, my hand was seared to the point of needing a little doctoring.

I was informed of a quite unusual occurrence when the twelfth green, just beyond Rae's Creek, was being constructed—the discovery by the workmen of an Indian burial ground. Over the years this par-three hole has become famous because of treacherous, swirling winds that will often on breezy days catch a well-struck shot and drop it in the creek when it seemed certain to safely reach the middle of the green. This has happened so many times that some of the players are wondering if the spiritual displeasures of an Indian chieftain are causing the trouble.

Another incident was the discovery of what appeared to be veins of gold. Samples were sent to a laboratory for testing. Sure enough, it proved to be gold all right, but not rich enough to be classified as a commercial ore. Accordingly, everyone ceased to be a prospector and returned to the mundane job of building a golf course.

The only noteworthy thing I accomplished on this particular trip was to induce the construction engineer to smooth out a level space on the downhill ninth fairway. After calculating the approximate length of my drive on this hole, I realized that I would be playing my second shot to the green from a downhill, sidehill lie, a shot that I have always disliked even to make a try at playing. The engineer was not at all enthusiastic about accommodating me, but finally agreed to bring back a tractor and do the job. I have many times had occasion to congratulate myself on winning this particular argument.

Day laborers were readily available to us at fifty cents per day. In fact, many men on the farms were paid only twenty-five cents per day. There was no such thing as an eight-hour day, the custom then being to work from "can to can't," meaning from the time one could see until one couldn't see. Our construction engineer was told to pay a dollar per day for untrained laborers. I must report, however, that one job was let out on contract to the lowest bidder, and I was afterwards informed that the successful bidder paid his workers only fifty cents per day. This contract covered the clearing of certain heavily wooded areas which were needed as fairway space, as for example on holes ten and eleven.

An unusual amount of effort was expended on drainage, because our property had too little sand and much too much clay. The clay soil holds water, which is good for growing pine trees. The trouble begins when pockets of water suddenly start leaking into a fairway. The problem then becomes the equivalent of a spring, and the only way to eliminate it is to do a tiling job. When the Augusta National was being constructed, about twenty-five separate areas were tiled. Since the course was opened, no less than 350 additional tiling jobs have been done, and the end to this work is not in sight.

However, the construction of the course was importantly simplified in one respect, that being the necessity to build only twenty-nine bunkers. A golf course architectural plan that called for so few was a revolutionary development that resulted in much discussion. Almost all the courses in our country at that time had around a hundred bunkers, and large numbers had many more, a considerable percentage of them often being located within from

Bob Jones oversees the construction of the course.

seventy-five to a hundred fifty yards of the tee. Bob felt very strongly that such close-at-hand bunkers were entirely wrong, and Mackenzie heartily agreed. It was their contention that the high-handicap players, the ones who have difficulty making a carry of a hundred fifty yards, were adequately penalized by their lack of skill; they were the ones who pay well over 75 per cent of the dues at the average club; and to build hazards that penalize only these poorer players seemed entirely out of order. Probably more was written about the proposed lack of bunkers at the Augusta National than any other feature of the announced plans. Many officers of clubs, and some golf course architects as well, decided at once to begin doing away with some of the excess bunkers on their golf courses, and within three years hundreds of courses had followed suit. One prominent championship layout did away with two hundred bunkers and still had about two hundred left.

Plateau-type greens which invite the run-up type of shot were another new feature that was introduced at Augusta; examples are holes five and fourteen and, when the pin is on the left side of the green, seventeen.

Just about everyone who ever played the old eighth hole agreed that the green, a masterful use of mounds rather than bunkers as hazards, was the most original on the course. Our members were very happy with this green. The putting surface had a width of only some twenty feet, which extended straight back for about forty feet and then made a forty-five-degree turn to the left for another twenty-five feet. There were four mounds along the right of the green ranging in height from five to twelve feet. Four mounds of similar height served as hazards on the left. Number eight was a par-five which required an accurate approach shot of the precise length. If the pin should be placed in the rear, "around the corner" so to speak, the player had almost no chance to get down in two putts if his approach landed on the front part of the green. If the player missed the green on either the left or right side, he faced the difficult problem of trying to loft the ball over a high mound to a narrow green. By comparison, a bunker shot was a very simple affair. Unfortunately, this unique green had to be sacrificed in later years in favor of the Masters Tournament; we could not allow the patrons to occupy the eight mounds, as they would both interfere with play and too often be hurt by offline approach shots. And, if they were kept off the mounds, they could not see what was happening. But I have no hesitancy in saying that, if the Masters should ever be discontinued, the first order of business would be to restore the eighth green to its original form.

Possibly I should explain that quite a number of undertakings had to go forward simultaneously in order to open the course for play in 1932. I refer to the forming of a club corporation, establishing club policies, purchasing property, designing the golf course, obtaining underwriting commitments, and selecting desirable types of members and inducing them to join.

Bob and I both found it difficult to give all these matters the attention they required. Economic conditions steadily worsened. Many of our friends, who normally would have been delighted to come in, found themselves financially unable to do so. It was most difficult to keep money coming in as fast as it was going out. One thing in our favor was the opportunity to make each dollar do double duty as the result of so many business people wanting to be identified with "Bobby's course." The loan or a gift of equipment was many times offered. We accepted only some minor items, but were not adverse to buying things as cheaply as possible. For example, only a very few of the existing golf courses had fairway watering systems, but we were determined to have one, and were able to purchase pipe at a price that was below manufactured cost. (And I should mention that when this old cast-iron pipe system was replaced forty years later, it was still in serviceable condition, al-

Augusta
National
Golf Club

Bob Jones hits some experimental drives during the construction of the course in an effort to determine the best location for the eighth tee.

though corrosion had reduced the water-carrying capacity by one half.) A lot of humus to lighten the clay soil was needed. The largest company in the East, located in Florida, was, surprisingly enough, owned by the president of the New York Stock Exchange. He offered me all the humus the club needed at no cost, provided we pay the freight, as shipping charges were the main part of the total cost. I accepted to the extent of a number of freight-car loads of humus.

Good Neighbor Effort

In 1931 golf was still being played on sand greens at the Palmetto Golf Club in Aiken, South Carolina. The club officers were anxious to convert to grass greens, and sought our assistance at a time when our construction work was nearing completion. We were especially eager to help because some half-dozen of our members were also members of Palmetto. The difficulty of the times can be illustrated by the Palmetto Club's aggressive solicitation among its members which produced a total of only $25,000. This sum appeared to be inadequate, and it seemed impossible to proceed with the project at that point.

Dr. Mackenzie then volunteered to make his services available without charge, and this included the designing of several completely new greens. I am not certain about it, but our engineer probably donated his services and everyone was happy with his work.

The fortunate circumstance was that the equipment which had been assembled at Augusta needed to be moved only fifteen miles to reach the Palmetto Club in Aiken. Also, the Augusta National was able to order certain extra supplies at special low prices and make them available to Palmetto. In short, our construction organization, with a little help from us, accomplished the almost unbelievable task of modernizing the Palmetto Golf Course at a total cost of $25,000.

Two Young Nurserymen

P. J. A. Berckmans, whose father was the Baron, had three sons, two of whom helped to operate Fruitlands Nurseries. When their father died in 1910 they expected to inherit the property, but it was willed to a young second wife. The two sons, who were experts in their field, promptly left Augusta but continued elsewhere quite successfully in the same line of work. The elder was named Louis Alphonse and the younger was a junior, Prosper Julius Alphonse. Louis was the man chosen by the Rockefellers to select and set out all the trees and plants in Radio City.

P. J. A. Berckmans with his three sons.

We wanted both of them to help rehabilitate the trees and plants on the Fruitlands property. Fortunately, we experienced little difficulty in locating the two brothers, or in bringing them back to the place where they were born. The prospect of living out the rest of their lives on their home grounds, and having a hand in making it more beautiful than ever, was about all the inducement that was needed.

Louis was seventy-four years of age at the time and lived to be eighty-two. He had a little money and declined to be placed on our payroll, although he was willing to serve the club in an advisory capacity. Much to our surprise, Louis wanted to be a member, although he did not play the game. We lost no time, of course, in placing his name on the membership roster. Having his talents available is the reason we decided to give each hole the name of a flowering plant or tree. Louis was the one who decided where to locate the eighteen varieties. Some were already in their proper location, but plants or trees for the majority of the holes had to be brought in.

The younger brother, who was called "Allie," was sixty-five years of age when he returned to his place of birth, and he too remained there until he died seven years later. Although he had no knowledge of golf or of greenkeeping, we hired him as our general manager with over-all club responsibility. I am glad to say that he did surprisingly well in quickly acquiring the knowledge needed in caring for a golf club. He possessed at the start more experience and understanding about how to make things grow than most greenskeepers ever learn. Our first golf course superintendent, who served under Allie Berckmans beginning in 1933, was Simk Hammack.

Course Opening

The course was completed, and a limited number of members began using it, in the month of December 1932. The formal opening took place in January 1933. Grantland Rice and I organized a private train party which made the trip from New York to Augusta, the group including many of the eighty people who had become members.

As club president, Bob Jones was anxious to take advantage of the opportunity to make a report on the club's funds, received and disbursed, and invited the members to attend a special dinner meeting for this purpose. After the dinner, Bob assembled his papers and called the meeting to order. But, before he could proceed, Grantland Rice was on his feet demanding to be heard. Grant explained that he had several times previously become a member of new clubs, all of which had gone broke. In looking back for a reason, he realized that all these promising new clubs, born of much enthusiasm, had made the mistake of holding a meeting, and he didn't want to see the Augusta National make this same mistake. Therefore, he proposed a resolution to the effect that Bob and Cliff be asked to run the club as they saw fit without the hindrance of meetings, and all who favored should stand and say, "Aye." Whereupon everyone stood and yelled, "Aye," and Bob could do nothing but join in the laughter and capitulate, despite his previously expressed determination, born of legal training, to conduct the club's business in a proper fashion. The spirit of Grant Rice's resolution is still in effect, as the club's business has always been conducted with a minimum of formality.

One very remarkable occurrence was that Grant and I, when committing for the private train, wanted to have in the party a total of approximately a hundred people. When we pulled out of Pennsylvania Station, we had exactly a hundred on board. Business was so bad that the railroad promised not only a special low rate, but all new Pullman equipment with two club cars for card players and two dining cars. It was a "dutch treat" party, with each of us paying a hundred dollars, which covered everything: round-trip transportation, three days' stay at the Bon Air Vanderbilt Hotel on the American plan, and local transportation. Believe it or not, we had a modest sum left over for train crew gratuities out of the $10,000 raised.

The weather was miserably bad, both wet and cold, but most of the party went ahead and played golf despite the conditions. One thing that stimulated their determination was tents at the first and tenth tees, each with a keg of corn whiskey. Two of our local members provided some corn that had a little age. This being during prohibition, good corn was better and safer to drink than scotch or bourbon whiskey available through bootleggers in Georgia. However, some of those present had never drunk corn before, and did not know how strong it was until, let us say, it was too late.

The Clubhouse

The building that was to become the clubhouse was constructed in 1854 by the owner of the indigo plantation, Mr. Dennis Redmond. This is not at all an old house for Augusta. It became well known because it is supposed to be the first cement house constructed in the South. The concrete was made of lime from a nearby source and gravel and sand that came from the property.

An early photograph of the plantation mansion that became the clubhouse. It was constructed in 1854 and is recognized as the first cement house to be constructed in the South.

In an article prepared by Mr. Redmond, he refers to his country house as being made of concrete or "artificial rock."

The house had three floors, including an eleven-by-eleven-foot cupola with windows on all sides so that the master supposedly could overlook the fields and observe the slaves at work. The ground floor and the second floor each had seven rooms of about the same size, with a ten-foot-wide hallway running down the center. There was no kitchen, the cooking being done in a separate small building at the southeast corner, presumably to keep the old manor house cool in the summer. Winter heat was provided by numerous fireplaces. Porches nine and a half feet wide completely encircled the first and second floors of the building. The walls of the house were eighteen inches thick, and they were cracked in a few places by the Charleston earthquake in 1886.

Some consideration was given to the thought of erecting a new structure for a clubhouse, but the old manor house was so attractive and distinctive that we decided to keep it and use it as our principal club building. We were further persuaded by the knowledge that the local people would not like it at all if we scrapped this famous old concrete building. A new and larger clubhouse could possibly have been built for less than it cost to make the old one usable, but I am sure we have never had a member who did not agree that we made the right decision.

At the start, we used the house that was Baron Berckmans' home as our clubhouse, and continued to do so for several years with only a modest amount of repairs. One of the seven rooms on the ground floor was used as a kitchen and another as a dining room for lunches. The remaining five rooms became offices and related service space. The upstairs seven rooms provided space for a bar, locker rooms, and service facilities. The cupola room on the third floor was first used by the club as storage space. Later it became a dormitory divided into six sections.

Bartlett Arkell

It is difficult to talk about the clubhouse without recalling Bartlett Arkell, one of the most lovable and remarkable early members of the club, whom we called Bart. He was founder and for fifty years the president of the Beech-Nut Packing Company. He was an art patron whose home on Ninth Street in New York was literally filled with paintings by old Dutch masters, and he also bought many paintings of uncertain quality to assist young artists in the neighborhood of his summer home at Manchester, Vermont.

Bart played golf occasionally and was a very great admirer of Bob Jones. He carried over 250 pounds of weight, despite his height of only five feet five. In appearance, he resembled the cartoon of Foxy Grandpa. Anyone who ever met him never forgot him, principally because of his good-natured disposition and beaming countenance. He was recognized as a great connoisseur of good food and drink, and it is said that he could consume more food and beverage at one sitting than the famous Diamond Jim Brady. I cannot vouch for the accuracy of this story, but I can testify to his generosity and his almost unfailingly sweet disposition. I say "almost" because of two incidents which I shall try to describe.

To Bob Jones and Cliff Roberts
with Best Wishes
for the Augusta national
Bart. Arkell

Bartlett Arkell.

Bart had one very great dislike—our country's president at the time. One evening at Bart's New York home, when our host was close to eighty years of age, we listened to the Amos and Andy radio show before dinner, which left all of us in a good humor. Before anyone could turn off the radio, F.D.R. began speaking, whereupon Bart suddenly exclaimed, "I'm going to outlive that son-of-a-bitch if it kills me!" And he did, too, I might mention, by a year. Bart died in 1946 at the age of eighty-four. What a great heart he must have possessed to carry so much weight for so many years.

On one of my last visits with Bart, when I was again a dinner guest, I was ushered into the living room, where I was introduced to a Mr. Smith, the only person present besides my host. Mr. Smith sat down a little apart from Bart and myself and did not join us in taking a toddy, Bart's favorite appetizer. Neither did Smith take part in a lively conversation between the two of us. Finally, I felt a bit embarrassed about Mr. Smith being neglected, and, in an effort to include him in the conversation, asked if we might not have met previously. Smith replied by asking me if I had ever known Mr. Wilson, and then went on to explain that he had been with Mr. Wilson for two years until he passed away. Smith then made the same inquiry about a Mr. Williams, and proceeded to tell me that he looked after Mr. Williams for a year and a half until he died. By this time Bart had had enough, and, after clearing his throat for attention, he directed Mr. Smith to go in search of two more toddies. After Smith was out of hearing range, Bart said to me, "Cheerful damn fellow, isn't he!" Only then did it dawn on me that Bart had reached the point that age and weight had finally forced him to submit to the assistance of a male nurse.

Several times at Augusta, Bart remarked to me that something must be done about rebuilding the old manor house in order to make it more usable as our clubhouse. I agreed with him, but there were so many pressing financial problems that I was in no hurry to tackle the job. Finally, in 1938, Bart's wife, Louise, came to me and suggested that I call a meeting of those members who might be in Augusta at the time. She explained that Bart wanted to make a contribution to help rebuild the clubhouse, and was worried that the project might be delayed beyond the time he would be available to assist. A meeting was called at once and about ten members were present. I explained the need for prompt action to convert the old manor house into an attractive clubhouse, with a quite large assembly room on each of the two lower floors, on the side facing the golf course. Also needed were a new roof, new stairways, floors, steam heat, plumbing, and steel beams to strengthen the building. The estimated total cost was $50,000. By a show of hands everyone indicated that they favored the proposal as important, and as a necessity for the future of the club. Bart then spoke up and said he was prepared, as a starter, to make a gift to the club of $20,000. Others who might ordinarily have been expected to chip in with $500 or $1,000 came forth with pledges of $5,000. Everyone present agreed to contribute, and the entire $50,000 was subscribed.

Let me say that Bart's generosity represented a turning point in the club's affairs. Rebuilding the clubhouse was a difficult hurdle that had to be cleared in order for the club to undertake various other improvements at later dates. I should also add that $20,000 represented a sum of money then much more difficult to obtain than during later years, and that it would buy a lot more then than at this time. If the rebuilding of the clubhouse had not been done prior to World War II, there is no way of telling when it might ever have been accomplished.

I doubt if the contractors made any money out of the several jobs. Many difficult situations emerged. At one point, only the exceptionally thick walls were left standing. However, the old manor house was completely done over at a total cost of only a little more than the $50,000 raised at the Arkell meeting. The same job today would probably run to $200,000 or more. An entirely new building might have been less difficult, but, as I have said, we would never have been forgiven for destroying a historical structure. It was indeed fortunate that we could preserve the original style of architecture. All of the buildings that are a part of the present complex follow the style dictated by the clubhouse, and our members seem to think the general pattern is quite pleasing to the eye.

Bowman

The first clubhouse employee to be hired was Bowman Milligan, and we named him our steward. He was twenty-eight years of age when he called on me seeking a job, large and strong and a fine-looking black man who had several years of previous golf club service experience. I was impressed by the fact that Bowman's father had worked for many years on our property. In fact, I was so impressed with what he said to me, and what I saw in him, that I hired Bowman on the spot.

Bowman is now in his forty-third year of faithfully serving the club, although in recent years he has accepted mandatory semiretired status. In fact, he was faithful to such a degree that his record might possibly excel all others doing similar kind of work. Bowman Milligan never missed doing a full day's work, every day the club was open, over a period of forty years. After living quarters had been constructed at the club, and the midnight closing rule had

Bowman Milligan (right) with another early staff member called "Cadillac."

been established, Bowman regularly opened the club at 6 A.M. and closed it at 12 P.M., seven days a week for more than twenty years. If there are endurance records to equal this one, I've never heard of them, especially since no one ever caught Bowman sleeping on the job.

I must digress to recite a story about one of Bowman's working experiences in the North, during the summer seasons. His first such job was at a golf club in Michigan. Prohibition being in effect at the time, Bowman had been hired with the understanding that he would see to it that liquor would be discreetly made available to the members and their guests. For a few months the club gained in popularity and Bowman was very much liked. Then one evening a raiding party entered the front door. Bowman politely inquired if there might be something he could do for them. The reply from the leader stated that they were looking for a man named Bowman Milligan. "Yes, sir!" said Bowman. "I know right where he is and I'll go get him for you." With that, Bowman left by the back door, and has never been seen since in the State of Michigan.

The first time Albert Bradley, board chairman of General Motors, came to the Augusta National, he did so as my guest. When he entered the clubhouse, he immediately spotted Bowman and greeted him with much enthusiasm, explaining to me what had happened in Michigan. He and numbers of others in Michigan had long wanted an opportunity to congratulate Bowman on his resourcefulness and to wish him well. Albert never tired of repeating this story at Augusta, but I am sure none of us would ever have learned of the incident if we had been obliged to wait until Bowman told us about it.

Claude

Another very noteworthy employee during the early days of the club was Claude Tillman. He came to us shortly after the death of our member Tom Barrett, of Augusta. I saw a lot of Tom from the planning stages of the club until he died in 1934. During that period I developed a very strong liking for Claude, Tom's faithful helper. But, while I liked Claude, Tom loved him. The little black fellow couldn't read or write, but he was able to drive a car, mind the children, keep the yard clean, mix drinks, relieve the cook when necessary, shave and dress Tom in the morning, and give him a rubdown if Tom had a morning-after feeling. I recall one occasion when Tom got into a heated argument with a friend from Macon as to who had the better servant.

Claude Tillman at work.

After another drink of corn, the question of who loved his man the most nearly precipitated a fist fight.

Tom Barrett's war injuries were credited with bringing on a fatal illness, and during that time he told me that he wanted me to have Claude. He apparently made a stipulation to that effect, because Tom's widow, Louise, placed a Christmas wreath around Claude's neck, tied a card to it bearing my name, and sent Claude to me. After conferring with Bowman, I passed along my gift to the club by placing Claude in charge of the kitchen. After my arrival in Augusta from New York some six weeks later, the following conversation took place between Claude and me:

"Claude, how are you doing in the kitchen?"

"We is doin' jus' fine."

"Are we doing a good volume of business?"

"We is doin' lots of business."

"But are we making any money?"

"Yes, suh!"

"But how do you know? Give me an example."

After scratching his head for a bit, Claude said, "You takes my milk. I measures it out very careful and I serves five glasses from a bottle at fifteen cents a glass, and a bottle only costs us fifteen cents. And on that basis, Mr. Cliff, we is 'bliged to show a profit."

Ty Cobb and Grantland Rice

Ty Cobb was a native of Augusta. When he retired from baseball he moved back to Augusta and golf became his hobby. Ty played at the Augusta Country Club, and quickly developed considerable skill. I am told he liked to enter all the club tournaments, but he created some problems for a time. It seems he adopted a very aggressive attitude toward his opponent, the same as he did in baseball. Doing and saying things to upset the man he was paired against in a golfing contest seemed quite all right to the former baseball star.

If I recall correctly, Ty Cobb moved to the West Coast before the Masters Tournament began, but he returned to Augusta several times to see it played. On one such occasion, at a dinner party with Grant Rice present, Ty told for the first time how he managed to use Grant's position as the sports writer for the Atlanta *Journal* to further his own ambitious plans. Ty was just starting his baseball career as a player on one of the teams that composed the South Atlantic League. Being anxious to have his talents recognized, and publicized, he mailed a series of letters to Grant from the various towns in the league, signing fictitious names to the letters. They told about the wonderful talent of a new player named Ty Cobb and urged Grant to see him in action. Some of the letters he wrote right-handed and some with his left hand to help hide the fact that all were written by the same person. At the end of Ty's confession, Grant cheerfully acknowledged his clear recollection of having provided Ty with the publicity he was seeking, and happily forgave Ty for having tricked him into doing it.

Augusta National Golf Club

Left to right, Johnny Farrell, Grantland Rice, Bob Jones, and Ty Cobb at Augusta in the early thirties.

Grantland Rice, the Hero

In the early thirties a golfing social organization named Artists and Writers existed in New York. The members had a winter outing each year in Florida which included a medal-play tournament. Granny Rice was the best player, scoring most always in the 70s, and therefore often winning the event.

When he won for the fourth time, the Augusta National was just beginning to function and Bob Jones and I were both in Augusta. When we received word from Granny that he was headed our way, we decided to herald his fourth Artists and Writers triumph as being equally important as the Grand Slam. Accordingly, we enlisted the assistance of our friend Tom Barrett, the newly elected mayor of Augusta, who provided a band to greet the champion when he arrived at the railroad station. Tom also assigned all of the motorcycle policemen in the town to escort a motorcade, with sirens blowing, to the home of the mayor.

Tom, Bob, and I were, of course, at the station and in the motorcade. When we arrived at our destination, with much noise and commotion, Tom's faithful helper Claude was busy as per instructions preparing the mint juleps for "Mr. Rice and his friends." But, after looking out the window and seeing a number of policemen, and forgetting for the moment that his boss was the mayor, he promptly disposed of the chief ingredient for the mint juleps. As soon as Tom came into the house, Claude went straight to him and said, "Mr. Tom, do you know what I just did? When I saw all those uniforms, I thought they were prohibition raiders, and I poured five gallons of your oldest corn right down the sink. Ain't I the most no 'count little kinky head in the whole world?"

A New Golf Tournament Is Born

During late 1932, and early in 1933, some discussions occurred about holding the U. S. Open on Bob's course. The Open had never been played in the South, and Augusta seemed to be the logical place. Bob was intrigued with the idea, but, after much thought and a number of meetings, it was decided that our club could render a more important service to the game of golf by holding regularly a tournament of its own. We had a fairly accurate idea of the work involved in hosting the Open, and it was believed that it might not be much more of a problem to operate a tournament annually than to do so occasionally. Moreover, by staging a golfing competition of our own design each year, we would be in a better position to decline various other tournament proposals involving our golf course which we foresaw in the offing.

The final decision was made at a meeting in New York in the office of our member W. Alton Jones. The first year of the new event was fixed as 1934. I proposed that it be named the Masters Tournament, but Bob vetoed such a designation on the grounds that it was too presumptuous. The name

Augusta National Invitational Tournament was adopted, and the club officially used that title for four years.

Our friend Tom Barrett was disappointed that the name Masters was not approved, so much so that he confided his feelings to a small-town newspaper friend, who promptly wrote the story. During the 1934 tournament a few press writers began referring to our event as the "Masters Tournament." By 1935 most of the news media did so, and in 1936 no one except the club called the tournament by any name other than the Masters. However, it was not until 1938 that Bob Jones relented and the name Masters was officially adopted.

Augusta then had a population of only a little more than sixty thousand and a very small percentage of its permanent residents had any interest either in playing golf or watching the game played. Neither the large percentage of black citizens nor the millworkers could be expected to do very much about supporting a golf tournament. This meant that we were undertaking to establish our event in a town that could not provide more than a fraction of the needed number of ticket buyers. I feel sure that, had we fully realized at the time the number of disadvantages with which we were faced, the Masters might never have been born. I am even more certain that, had we foreseen the degree of success to be attained and the resultant responsibilities, the plans for the Masters might have been dropped. When I refer to "resultant responsibilities," I include the ever-increasing contributions and sacrifices that must be made by our members, whether or not they are active in the tournament organization.

Another initial problem was Bob's participation in the tournament. Should he act as an official or become one of the contestants? He could not do both, for obvious reasons. Bob greatly preferred not to play, and he pointed out the advantages in his acting the part of an official. But some of those who took part in the discussions were afraid that the best players might not all respond to an invitation without Bob being a participant. I particularly was concerned about gate receipts without the enormous drawing power of Bob as a contestant. In 1930 the U. S. Open, with Bob in the field, established a record of $23,382 in gate receipts. In 1931, without Bob, the sale of tickets dropped to $12,700. It was therefore plain to see that our gate receipts might easily be twice as large if Bob played than if he did not. This was in part due to the Southern people never having seen Bob play in an important tournament. The final argument that persuaded Bob to agree to play, or so he said, was one I advanced, to the effect that he simply could not invite his golfing friends to play on his course and then decline to play with them.

Augusta
National
Golf Club

Tournament Policies

Once the die was cast, we were obliged to make prompt decisions with respect to a number of problems. For example, we at once determined that ours was to be an invitational tournament—but who should be invited? The responsibility of selecting the most talented players was placed on Bob's shoulders, with the following guidelines established in advance:

Present and past U. S. Open champions
Present and past U. S. Amateur champions
Present and past British Amateur champions
Present and past British Open champions
Present and past U. S. PGA champions
Present members of the Ryder Cup team
Present members of the Walker Cup team

These guidelines, I might mention, were the basis of a formal set of Qualification Regulations, which were established in 1935. I agreed to act as tournament chairman, with a commitment in hand from Jay R. Monroe, a member from Orange, New Jersey, that he would actively assist me. Jay had had previous tournament experience at the Baltusrol Club, and his business was well enough organized that he could set aside six weeks or more for Augusta each spring.

I might mention that we were the first to use Pinkerton's at a sporting event. The club then had no fence around its property and, because of this, a considerable number of people saw no reason to buy a ticket to see our tournament. This is where Pinkerton's came in handy. The deputies and police had too many personal friends, whereas the Pinkerton men played no favorites. Although they were not able to cope very effectively during the first several years with those who preferred not to pay, they have long since done a splendid job. Such sporting assignments now account for over 75 per cent of the total Pinkerton's income, we are informed by the company.

Because of the announcement of Bob's intention to participate as a contestant, it was an easy matter to get a lot of advance publicity. We tried to intensify this coverage within driving range of Augusta in places such as Atlanta, Macon, Charlotte, Savannah, Charleston, and Columbia. There were no air services in those days and Augusta was not on the main line of any

Jay R. Monroe.

railroad. But we were agreeably surprised when golfing fans drove from cities as far away as Birmingham and Nashville.

We realized that, in order to build a tournament of stature that could survive Bob's eventual separation from the event, it needed to be operated in a better fashion and made more enjoyable than any other. As a beginning step, we made it a four-day stroke-play competition of eighteen holes each day, instead of the established custom of playing thirty-six holes on the third day. Free parking space on the club grounds was made available to purchasers of admission credentials. Complimentary one-page pairing sheets that carried all essential information for the patrons were also provided. A Spectator Suggestion Booklet, prepared by the club's president, was later to be supplied to the patrons.

One of the first things Jay Monroe and I agreed upon was that every person working in the tournament organization who would accept pay should be paid. This was partly for the reason that our club had no chance to recruit a large number of member volunteers. Only a few on our roster were local members, the large majority living in various other states, almost none of whom could be expected to make a long train trip to Augusta just to do a week's work. The main thought Jay had in mind was that we could obtain better control over both young and older volunteer workers if we could put them on the payroll. This was done with respect to high school and college students, soldier volunteers, gallery guards, deputized peace officers, Pinkerton men, and others.

We determined at the outset not to permit anyone inside the ropes other than the players and their caddies. This was to provide the patrons with an uninterrupted view of the tournament action. It was most fortunate that this practice was established in the early days of the Masters, when golf writers and news photographers were not very numerous.

Entry fees by the contestants were not required, and the player invitational basis of the tournament eliminated qualificational rounds. Another very important policy decision was to undertake to forbid the commercialization of the tournament in any form. Still another early decision was to rule out the use of the tournament to promote anything other than the game of golf. We found it difficult to give a negative answer to some very worthy charities, but so much money was needed for tournament improvements that the event could not have succeeded had we not concentrated all income and all our efforts on just one objective.

A difficult problem that developed was the classification of Bob as a contestant. Should he be listed as an amateur or as a professional? This question was decided without consulting the president of the club. As tournament chairman, I ruled that, as everyone in the field was a master golfer, no player would be given a rating or classification any different from that of the others.

The 1935 Masters field.

Rather to my surprise, the press did not find any particular fault with this explanation.

When Bob retired from competition, he made two important commitments to engage in golfing activities that were definitely professional in character. A few people then began asking if Bob were still an amateur, or if he should be classified as a professional. The United States Golf Association took the position that it would be improper to make a ruling unless Bob undertook to enter a golfing competition as an amateur. Some of the Royal and Ancient officials of St. Andrews gave voice to their emotional feeling that Bob should always be regarded as an amateur, no matter what he might do.

I am certain that, had it become necessary to classify Bob, and had I sought his guidance, he would have told me to go ahead and mark him down as a professional. I say this despite the fact that he greatly cherished his position as an amateur, and had, up until his retirement, scrupulously observed the terms of amateur status. I never had occasion at the time or in later years to discuss this subject with Bob. More than once, however, I've wondered if Bob's consent to participate in the tournament as a contestant would have been so willingly given if he had realized he might be classified as a professional.

In the literature that was issued describing the field, each player's major titles were listed after his name. After Bob's name came merely the words, "President, Augusta National Golf Club." This action pleased Bob to the extent that he remarked to one of the tournament committeemen that he thought the listing was in good taste. I suspect that he also liked it because he thought of himself as club president rather than as a tournament contestant.

Bob never made any real effort to prepare himself as a Masters contestant, either through intensive practice or by playing in tune-up tournaments. He saw himself in the role of a host, not as a competitor anxious to defeat his guests. I know he sometimes became annoyed at himself because of a flubbed shot, but he never failed to appear among his player friends after the day's round as a congenial companion who was genuinely concerned about their comfort and their enjoyment of the event. I am sure that, if the outcome of each tournament could have been decided by ballot by the contestants, Bob would regularly have been declared the winner. The golfing public pulled for Bob, and most of the players predicted again and again that he would once more reassert his superiority as a player. But it was not to be. Of the nine prewar tournaments, in all of which Bob participated, his best showing was thirteenth place in 1934.

Tournament Financing

Our biggest initial problem was to find the extra money to finance the first tournament. Some special work was needed to get the course into the best possible condition. Tournament equipment of many kinds had to be purchased. It was necessary to erect several types of small buildings, and to rent several tents. Printing and sign making were other expenses.

To accurately describe the state of our club's finances at that point, one would have to use the old saying about being only one jump ahead of the sheriff. Accordingly, we tapped a number of sources for funds. One was to publish an official program, something that has been done, I would guess, since sporting events began. The business people in Augusta were canvassed to buy advertising space, but, as there were no large companies in the town, the total from this source was not very substantial. A few full-page spaces were sold to club members and friends who were officers of companies in other parts of the country. The total program profit was enough to be helpful, but so much effort was required that I doubted if it would be possible to regularly repeat the operation in the future. One experience caused me to conclude definitely that there was no future for a golf tournament program in Augusta.

A club member, the head of a tobacco company, when asked by me to buy a page of advertising space, handed me the cash from his pocket, and then stipulated that the name of the company was not to appear in the pro-

The cover of the first tournament program.

gram. He then went on to explain that he considered program advertising to be of such limited value that, if the name of his company were to appear in our program, it would be a reflection on the management, and he therefore might lose his job.

We enlisted the aid of local members, hotels, and the Augusta banks in the sale of tournament tickets, but total sales to Augustans were considerably below out-of-town buying. The admission charge was one dollar daily during the practice rounds, and two dollars daily during the four days of play. Series tickets covering all eight days were five dollars.

Augusta was a cotton town, but both it and the neighboring town of Aiken were well established as winter resort centers—Augusta mainly for golf, and Aiken chiefly for horse breeding and polo. Florida then was just too far away by train, thus the mid-South enjoyed a considerable volume of tourist business. Augusta had two large winter resort hotels of good quality and several smaller ones. The leading establishment, the Bon Air Vanderbilt, managed by our friend Walton H. Marshall, came forward with an offer to take any part or all of our field of contestants at a special rate of five dollars per day American plan (room plus three meals a day). This represented an important plus in our project planning. In comparison with today's housing problems during the week of the Masters, it seems like a blessing that was too good to be true.

Our one really great asset—beyond, of course, Bob Jones—was the Augusta National course. Its location on a generous number of acres of outstanding beauty gave us an immediate advantage. Then, too, we had plenty of room and unlimited opportunities to make golf course improvements. Moreover, we were in an independent position, which permitted the introduction of new tournament procedures.

I would like to emphasize at this point that Bob Jones was the one who prepared our publicly announced policy to invite and to consider carefully all suggestions to improve the course and to keep it in step with the development of the game. The same policy applied to spectator conveniences and tournament procedures. The club received large numbers of suggestions from players, golf course architects, the news media, tournament patrons, and others, and a considerable number of these suggestions were adopted.

The Early Years

Despite all of the disadvantages, the attendance of our first tournament in 1934 was fairly good. The number who bought tickets was a respectable total as compared to the U. S. Open of the same year, and, in fact, based on the available information, I am inclined to believe we had a larger attendance than any tournament in this country other than the U. S. Open. If time factors are considered, the golf course can be said to have been in remarkably good shape.

I must confess that the financial results were a bit disastrous. The start-up costs exceeded the amounts raised to cover such outlays. Our ideas of how a golf tournament should be conducted required expenditures that resulted in a deficit even before provisions for the prize fund. This cash prize fund of $5,000 was to be divided among the twelve leading professionals, ranging from $1,500 down to $100. I passed the hat among some of our mem-

The first five Masters champions photographed in 1939. Left to right, Horton Smith, Byron Nelson, Gene Sarazen, Henry Picard, and Ralph Guldahl.

bers, and the prize fund was thereby fully covered. However, the tournament continued to lose money each year, and the prize fund was regularly made available by member gifts until World War II forced discontinuance of the tournament. The prize fund never varied during the nine prewar years, and the list of donors of the prizes was substantially the same. I recall that Bartlett Arkell usually donated a sum equal to the first prize, and that Jay Monroe did the same with respect to the second prize.

The club experienced operating deficits as well as tournament losses during its early years, and these also were financed principally through gifts by members. There were some twenty individuals who could be counted on annually to help make up the deficit.

Bad weather was another big problem during the nine prewar tournament years. On five occasions a day's play had to be postponed. In 1936 two days of play had to be postponed, with a tournament conclusion of thirty-six holes coming on Monday. In 1938 play could not commence until Saturday, which resulted in another Monday ending. On one occasion Rae's Creek resembled a young Mississippi River, with both the eleventh and twelfth greens under water. Moreover, both bridges which spanned Rae's Creek were washed away.

There were other days when rain or hail forced a temporary postponement of an hour or more. In 1939, when a considerable part of the field had finished, a serious hailstorm occurred. The players and their caddies who were caught out in the open were quick to discover that a golf bag, or a spread-out raincoat, held aloft, afforded good protection against a crack on the head. A special ruling was made that gave the contestants the option of continuing play or marking their balls and waiting for the hailstones to melt. Predictions of bad weather, and the bad weather itself, both hurt the gate receipts. On more than one occasion Augusta was threatened with a tornado during the tournament. Other towns in Georgia suffered much actual damage, but Augusta was fortunate enough to escape. The tournament receipts, however, suffered because of these storm warnings.

The starting date of the first tournament in 1934 was March 22. So few tournaments were being played at that time that we could take most any date we liked without adversely affecting anyone; thus our event was held on varying dates without any fixed pattern during the first six years. Beginning in 1940, the Masters adopted a fixed arrangement calling for the tournament to be scheduled each year during the first full week in April.

Despite tournament deficits and club operating losses, we somehow managed to make some improvements each year for the following year's Masters. This policy was based on the assumption that no public event ever stands still, but gets either better or worse. We were determined that our tournament must constantly improve. In this regard, we had the advantage of the club's being closed during the summer months, which meant, for example, that a spectator mound could be made, a bunker moved, or a green rebuilt, during the growing season. By the time the course was opened for play in the fall, the wounds would be healed by new Bermuda turf, and quite often the members were unaware that changes had been made.

Tournament attendance fell off a bit after 1934, and continued to be lower for five consecutive years thereafter, because the public was disappointed that Bob had not reasserted his position as the number one tournament player. Bob still, however, drew by far the largest individual gallery. During that period the press gave more space to Bob's poor scores than to the doings of all the other players combined. Finally, I decided to have a visit

Jock Hutchison and Freddie McLeod the first time they played together in the Masters, in 1935.

with Alan Gould, golf writer for the Associated Press, who in later years became the executive editor of AP. I asked why he didn't devote himself more to the good golf that was being played by a number of our contestants, and less to bad golf by Jones. The reply I received was direct and emphatic. Alan said to me that I should run the tournament and allow him to write about it. He then stated that, "There is more news value in a putt missed by Jones than brassie shots being holed out by any other player in the field." I had meant to explain to Alan that Bob's main interest was to establish a golf tournament, and that he deserved the co-operation of his friends in the news media. But Alan's blunt remarks knocked the wind out of me for the moment, and I left it until another time to try to enlist his understanding and support.

Jock Hutchison and Freddie McLeod at the first tee in 1971, the last time they paired as honorary Masters starters. Their player numbers indicate their ages.

Finally, in the years 1940, 1941, and 1942, the Masters gate receipts exceeded those of 1934. This was a clear signal that golfing fans were beginning to attend the tournament to see the talented field compete rather than to hope that one man might pull off a miracle. In other words, the Masters as an event had developed drawing power of its own. I am sure the reader will appreciate the sense of gratification that came at this time to all of those who were actively engaged in the tournament organization. Everyone had labored hard with just one thought in mind: they wanted to establish a golfing fixture that would be in keeping with the stature of Bob Jones in the world of golf. And the gate improvements of the 1940s indicated that they were succeeding.

PART TWO

Lieutenant Colonel Robert T. Jones, Jr., during his war service as an Air Corps intelligence officer.

World War II

When our country began preparing to enter World War II, the Augusta National began to face even more serious problems than it had experienced previously. In addition to the five existing military establishments in Augusta, a number of others soon sprang up within a seventy-five-mile radius. Civilian transportation to Augusta was to become most difficult, which forced the closing of our golf course, as well as the cancellation of the Masters Tournament in 1943, 1944, and 1945. Many of our members joined one of the branches of military service or accepted war jobs in Washington, D.C. Bob Jones put on the uniform of an Air Corps intelligence officer and departed for England. Before leaving, Bob agreed that, as our members could no longer use the course, we could not ask them to pay dues. He suggested that the club help the war effort by buying cattle and allowing them to gain weight by grazing on our fairways and greens. The outlook was so dismal that one of our members who was quite familiar with our past difficulties expressed his sorrow about the approaching demise of the club. He also expressed surprise when told that an effort was going to be made to save it.

The first order of business was to make an estimate of the annual cost of looking after the club's property on a caretaker basis, i.e., taxes, the salary of the superintendent, and various other essential requirements. The 128 members were then notified that they would not be billed for dues but would be asked to make a gift to the club of $100 annually. It was believed that the cattle would eliminate the need for any grass mowing, and that the golf course crew could therefore be dispensed with, as could the clubhouse personnel. On this basis, if all or nearly all members sent in $100 annually, the club could retain ownership of the golf course.

Two hundred head of young steers were bought and everything worked out according to plan, except that the cattle were not satisfied with just eating the grass. They also ate a large number of valuable azalea and camellia plants, together with the bark from the trunks of some young trees. Then, too, during the winter seasons there was no green grass for the cattle, as the club discontinued the planting each fall of winter grass and the Bermuda grass became dormant and therefore offered no nourishment. Accordingly, the club was obliged to purchase expensive feed during five to six months each year. When the steers were finally sold, they brought, instead of an antici-pated substantial profit, a loss of about $5,000, which figure does not include the considerable damage caused by the voracious appetite of the cattle.

The club also raised turkeys, an undertaking that we were told was quite hazardous. It was done because Simk Hammack, our superintendent, was an experienced turkey man, and he convinced us he could raise them success-fully. There may be some who are familiar with turkey raising who will doubt the club's success story, but, with the use of very little capital, a profit sufficient to offset the $5,000 cattle loss was realized.

As a further small war effort, in 1942 the club undertook to finance and supervise the construction of a driving range and a mammoth-size putting green for the soldiers in training at Camp Gordon, which has since been renamed Fort Gordon. The cash outlay was $2,669. Additionally, our members and the pro shop made gifts of golfing equipment and balls. This golfing center at Camp Gordon later had a nine-hole golf course added to it, built by the soldiers under our direction.

During the latter part of 1944, after the cattle had been sold, the big job of rehabilitating the golf course was begun. The club hired forty-two German soldiers, prisoners of war from Camp Gordon, for a period of about six months. They worked mostly on the golf course, but some were skilled crafts-men who built bridges and did other special jobs.

Beau Jack

During the early years of the club, with no quarters on the grounds suitable for card playing or other diversions, Bowman Milligan, our club steward, did his best to produce local talent capable of providing evening entertainment. In addition to dancing teams and spiritual singers, he would occasionally ar-range boxing contests, which were staged in a large room at the Bon Air Van-derbilt Hotel. The closing feature would be a battle royal. This meant plac-ing some half-dozen young boys in a ring, each one wearing full-size boxing gloves. Everyone would start swinging, with the last boy on his feet being de-clared the winner.

One of these battle royal contestants was called "Bo," and he usually won, even when the others ganged up on him and tried to knock him out. The boy was a waif, could not read or write, and was in doubt about the identity of his parents. However, Bowman took a liking to Bo, gave him a job as a shoe shiner at the Augusta National, and renamed him Beau Jack. Bowman also promised to help him become a fighter.

Beau Jack was happy with his shoe-shining job, but he wanted to fight at every opportunity, and to become as soon as possible a big-time fighter. Fortunately for the boy, he was built to be a boxer—overbuilt, if anything, because his arms and chest were disproportionately larger than his legs. Additionally, Beau Jack was exceptionally strong and possessed a seemingly inexhaustible supply of stamina. His weight automatically placed him in the lightweight division, and he had already beaten, without any compensation, every similarly sized boy in the Augusta area who was willing to get into the ring with him. The only thing lacking was professional training. In fact, he had never received boxing instruction of any sort.

In 1941, after two years of shining shoes, eating regularly, fighting in both Massachusetts and Georgia, and doing whatever else he was told to do by his guiding mentor, Bowman, Beau Jack went to New York.

His bouts in Massachusetts came about because Bowman had a summer job at the Longmeadow Country Club, near Springfield, Massachusetts. Boxing contests were held at a nearby place called Holyoke, and here Beau Jack gained experience by reason of a number of fights, most of which he won by knockouts, the same as in Georgia against local talent.

Beau Jack made it to the big league in New York, not because any of us at the club thought he was a qualified fighter, but rather because Bowman had faith in him. Bowman calculated that, if he had but an extra $500, he could take Beau Jack to New York and give him his chance. Accordingly, I passed the hat and twenty individuals put in twenty-five dollars. We did this with lots of good wishes for Beau Jack, but more particularly because we liked Bowman and were happy to back him so that he could back Beau Jack.

A lawyer was brought in by Slats Slater, one of the backers, to draw up a formal contract. Bowman and Beau Jack were to be equal partners. Since Beau Jack was not of age, Bowman was also made his legal guardian. Upon arrival in New York, Bowman discovered he could not act as manager, it being necessary to employ someone who had a license to act in that role. Such a man was available, at a reasonable percentage cost, who turned out to have a flair for publicity. Much to our surprise, we began reading a lot of newspaper releases concerning ourselves as backers of a prize fighter from Georgia. We were still more surprised when Bowman paid back, later on, the twenty-five-dollar loan made by each backer.

Events occurred rapidly. Beau Jack was booked to fight an experienced lightweight professional in a preliminary bout, and promptly knocked him out. Several of us saw the fight, which took place in Brooklyn. Beau Jack made up for lack of boxing skill by throwing so many hard punches at such

Beau Jack with Augusta National member Gene Tunney.

speed that his opponent was completely overwhelmed. I shall never forget the look of bewilderment on that experienced fighter's face just before he went down for the count.

A second fight was relatively easy to arrange just nine days later, but this was not as soon as Beau Jack wished. He would have been happy to fight twice a week, or more, and displayed no interest in whether or not he was to receive some of the gate receipts. Bowman arranged to be excused from his summer job in order to be in New York to look after Beau Jack. He gave the Beau only enough spending money to go to a movie, or to take a taxi to the gymnasium where he skipped rope and punched the bag just like the regular fighters. There was no trainer, however, since Bowman could not afford one, and didn't think Beau Jack needed one, anyway.

Beau Jack was a crowd pleaser because there was never a dull moment with him in the ring. He never seemed to tire, and no one could back away fast enough to stay out of his reach. Lightweights do not ordinarily knock each other out, but Beau knew nothing about the customary practice and often put his opponent out of business. Accordingly, he became quite popular with the boxing fans. Likewise, he was especially popular with his twenty backers, the majority of whom made a practice of having dinner together, going in a body to see Beau Jack fight, and then celebrating together in a pri-

Beau Jack and his backers, as seen by Billy DeBeck.

BILLY DeBECK

Dear Pug =

I chipped in a right smart piece of foldin' money — $25⁰⁰ to be exack — to "fetch a leetle darkey whose callin' name is "Beau Jack" up to New York.

I din't realize I wuz stickin' my neck out as th' sayin' goes an' gittin' mixed up wif a litter of bodacious idjits who don't know their arse from a gopher hole an' onless they cut out all their do-less motions an' git down to business I shall hotly demand the return of my hard-earnt 25 dullers wif intrist 6%

Howsomeuer =

If them two no account varmints Vidmer and Roberts will gorrontee to interduce me to Mistofer Beau Jack an' Mistofer Bowman, his overseer, an' Chick Wergeles his manager an' Sammy his trainer Pee Wee an' Lawson · I'll recornsider my complaint an' knuckle down wif malice towards nobody an' charidy fer all

NOW YO' TALKIN' BOSS

So = I take it fer granite th' next shindig at th' Park Lane Ho-tel I'll meet them ristercratic s'uthin' gem'mem an' ever'thing will be peaches down in Georgy

Yours fer Victory

Billy DeBeck

PARK LANE

vate room at the Park Lane Hotel. On several occasions Bowman was asked to bring the Beau and join us, so that we could congratulate them and brag on Beau Jack a bit.

The backers came in handy when several persons wanted to share in the prospective prosperity. The manager was authorized to show a list of Beau Jack's well-wishers to any such person, and the list was always headed by Grantland Rice and R. T. Jones, Jr., who were the best known. The manager also explained that he had to account to the backers for every penny Beau Jack earned. Invariably, the request for a piece of the action was withdrawn.

The year 1942 was the big one for Beau Jack, as he won the lightweight championship in December of that year. Except for a period of time when Uncle Sam tried to make a soldier out of him, Beau continued fighting until early in 1947, when he split a kneecap. Bowman then told his boy he was through, and that it was now time for him to forget about the ring and go home to Augusta. Beau Jack tried again at a later date, against Bowman's wishes, to do some more fighting. But, with a stiff leg, he was no longer a star attraction who could be matched against the top talent. Consequently, his earnings during his comeback effort were meager.

Fortunately for Beau Jack, his so-called "backers" performed two rather important financial services for him. First, they saw to it that a reserve from his earnings was set aside to pay the high wartime income taxes, making him one successful fighter of his race who during that period did not wind up hopelessly in debt to Uncle Sam. Secondly, they set up an investment account for the Beau in which his net earnings were deposited.

The unfortunate part of the finance section of Beau Jack's career story is that, while he never smoked or drank, he found other entertaining ways of spending money. Partly as the result of paternity suits, Beau began drawing money out of his investment account faster than he was putting it in. When Madison Square Garden's biggest drawing card broke a kneecap, less than $10,000 of what he had earned remained. However, there was on hand another $20,000 plus resulting from profitable transactions in stocks before his capital had been depleted. It was deemed advisable to close Beau Jack's New York account and to send the funds to Augusta for the purpose of establishing an irrevocable trust. Added to this was a pig farm which Beau Jack had wanted, and which had been bought for him. The Beau never raised any pigs on it but the land increased in value, and on top of this the managers of his trust made some wise investments in his behalf.

Some fanciful stories were at one time circulated about huge earnings by Beau Jack. Actually, he had only a very few years as a main-event fighter, and during those years his net earnings after taxes averaged only about $25,000. The same was true, of course, with respect to Bowman. The only difference was that Bowman received no financial guidance. Beau Jack and Bowman each made his own choice about the best way to convert prosperity into extra pleasures. Bowman's idea was to put a bet down at the fifty-dollar window instead of the two-dollar window. Although his love of the track cost him the major part of his ring profits, he had the fun of seeing his fighter become a champion. And his job at the Augusta National was never in jeopardy.

During the Beau's active ring years he sometimes returned to Augusta for short periods. He would at once start shining shoes, working as a caddie, or giving massages. The only difficulty about his massages was his very strong hands, which might leave his customer with muscles that hurt more than when he began. Gene Tunney, a member of the Augusta National during those years, became very much interested in Beau Jack, and after considerable research effort wrote a detailed account of Beau's career that was published in the September issue of *Sports* magazine in 1955.

Finally, Beau Jack decided he liked living in Florida, where he returned to his old trade as a shoe shiner. One difference, I believe, is that he owns the shoe-shining concession at a hotel. Another is a very large family. Then, too, he has memories of doing what he most wanted to do—fight. In fact, the record book says he fought well over a hundred professional fights.

Beau Jack still likes to come to Augusta occasionally, sometimes just to see Bowman, but more often than not to talk the trust officer out of a check. It is the same thing he has been doing for more than thirty years, and his good-luck well has yet to run dry.

The Club Reopening

The club was reopened in 1945 for play by members and their guests during the spring and fall seasons. Just before the beginning of 1945 it had been determined that, since the war was going our way, it was advisable to return to the operating of a golf course. We were convinced by then that we had no future in feeding cattle or raising turkeys.

Transportation in and out of Augusta had improved considerably. Some of our members would soon begin drifting back from war service, and likely would be hoping to find the Augusta National open, even if only in a limited way. For example, once our troops were firmly established in France, there was soon no need for the type of Air Corps intelligence work Lieutenant Colonel R. T. Jones, Jr., had been doing, and he was excused from further duty. This was fortunate, because the club was running true to form in that it was faced with additional problems. The big one this time was a lot larger than anything previously encountered.

The Bon Air, operated as a year-round commercial establishment during the war, had ceased to be a quality-type resort hotel. Its ownership or management had changed several times, and those of our members who tried to continue to use it were not happy. The Forest Hills Ricker Hotel had been taken over for use as a military hospital. Some of our members tried the smaller Augusta establishments, and a few of us rented a house in Augusta for the winter season. None of these arrangements, however, could take the place of the pleasurable club atmosphere of the Bon Air Hotel when it was operated by our member Walton Marshall. He saw to it that the food and service were first-rate, and this attracted a clientele of an interesting leadership type, including men of letters. None of those who had planned the Augusta National had had any thought other than to use the Bon Air as our living headquarters, with the club serving nothing more than simple luncheons.

During 1945, however, it was realized that the Augusta National was doomed unless the club provide living quarters on the grounds. This was something we did not at all want to do, but we were forced by unforeseen circumstances to undertake such a program. The first step was a very modest one: the third-floor cupola room of the clubhouse was transformed into a dormitory, with six sections to accommodate six stags and one bathroom sufficing for the six occupants. Next, the house bordering Washington Road, which was originally built for one of the sons of P. J. A. Berckmans, was put to use as a place where members could sleep. These two steps represented only minor and temporary measures, but they did prove that the members very much liked staying at the club rather than going back and forth to a hotel.

Burton F. Peek

Burt Peek is our candidate for top honors as the man who hit the most golf balls in one lifetime. He began playing in his teens, and never stopped until he died in 1960 at the age of eighty-eight. Every day whenever possible he would hit two buckets of balls, then play eighteen or thirty-six holes. Burt went to work for Deere and Company at the age of sixteen and continued there all his life, except for a brief time-out to acquire a law degree, eventually becoming chief counsel and later company chairman.

In 1934, Burt became a member of the Augusta National and lost no

Burton F. Peek.

time in making himself both useful and popular. He knew the Rules of Golf and readily agreed to serve as a rules official. I am sure no one ever admired Bob Jones more than he, and for an illustration I'll cite an incident that took place next to the practice putting green during an early tournament. Burt was watching a contestant practicing when a nearsighted lady peered into his weather-beaten old face and asked if the man with the putter might be Bobby Jones. Burt was so disgusted that anyone did not know exactly what Bob looked like that he replied, "No, madam, that man is Sarazen. I am Bobby Jones." The good woman decided Burt was demented as she took one more look at Burt—a frightened look—then scurried away in great haste.

Burt's intense devotion to golf was widely known. One of his friends addressed a letter to him at the Bon Air Vanderbilt Hotel with the following notation typed on the envelope: "If not found at the hotel, please look in the first bunker of the first hole at the Augusta National Golf Club."

One of the many traits that made Burt so likable was his optimism. When he was about eighty-two years of age his bootmaker in Chicago told him that he was going to retire, and, as there was no other bootmaker left in the city, he wanted to know if Mr. Peek wished to order a reserve supply of shoes. At this point in the story I asked Burt to stop and let me guess the number of pairs he ordered. "OK," said Burt. "Twenty pairs," I ventured. "No," said Burt with a grin. "But I did order ten pairs." He knew just as well as I that it is hard to wear out one pair of fine, handmade leather shoes in less than two years.

Our Building Programs

Our problem was how to finance, when building materials became available, the construction of a large, three-section east-wing structure. The wing we planned would contain a modern kitchen, a large dining room, and some comfortable sleeping rooms. Separate units to provide living quarters were also in mind. Then, too, a pro shop to the west of the clubhouse was needed. We wanted to move a step at a time over a period of years. But the large east-wing structure had to be done first, and all at one time, as a basic necessity to support the other improvements that were to follow. This was a financing hurdle which appeared to be insurmountable.

At this juncture my long-time friend Edward J. Barber, of the Barber Steamship Lines of New York, stepped into the breach with a most remarkable proposal. Eddie stated quite simply that he appreciated the wisdom, under normal circumstances, of moving deliberately, one step at a time. Nevertheless, he did not have too many years left to enjoy golf on this his favorite course, and he therefore wanted to provide funds to enable us to shift into high gear. Specifically, he offered to arrange a long-term $100,000 credit for the club through his bank in New York, at whatever rate of interest I might stipulate based on the club's unsecured note. Eddie also offered to give the club $25,000 in cash for whatever living quarters might be designated for his preferential use. Additionally, Eddie stated he would provide in his will a gift to the club sufficient to liquidate the $100,000 note. I suggested an interest rate of three and a half per cent, which was agreeable. Eddie was a very popular member of the club, but everyone, including myself, was a bit overwhelmed by this extremely generous offer.

Hoping to be able to start construction in 1946, the club at once engaged an architect to draw up plans for the east-wing extension, which would include the kitchen, a sizable dining facility to be named the Trophy Room, and a section with five suites to be known as the Suites Building. The latter was to have sufficient upstairs space to permit conversion into six modest-sized bedrooms. Plans were also drawn for two small cottages, which were to be called cabins, each one to consist of two bedrooms and a living room. The name of cabin was borrowed from the old plantation custom of calling everything other than the master's house a cabin.

Eddie Barber's idea of paying for a place where he would be entitled to do his sleeping gave us what proved to be a novel and practical method of financing the three proposed types of living quarters: rooms, suites, and cabins.

The club authorized an issue of building certificates which bore no interest, had no due date, and were not transferable. They were usable as script in payment of 50 per cent of room rentals or greens fees contracted by the member or his guests. A member could purchase an amount of certificates to cover the estimated cost of whatever type of living quarters he might desire, the member thereby becoming the "owner" of a room, a suite, or a cabin. Actually, the club retained title, but the "owner" had preferential lifetime rights with respect to the use of his unit. Upon the death or resignation of an "owner," the club was to be free to assign his unit to another member. Also, the club could rent any unit to others when not in use by the "owner," and the club in return assumed all maintenance responsibilities.

The whole arrangement proved completely viable with regard to our own particular situation. Over the years it provided the principal means of financing living quarters with a total of ninety-four beds, together with attendant facilities. One other source of funds for improvements was an issue of three and a half per cent Sinking Fund Mortgage Bonds in the amount of $200,000, which were sold to the members in 1948.

E. J. Barber.

The Jones Cabin.

In 1946 the club let contracts to build the three-section east wing and two cabins. Eddie Barber was given his choice of the five suites. Although Eddie died in 1953, his name plate is still on the door, where it is expected to remain permanently. In his will Eddie provided for a gift to the club of $200,000, which might be classified as about the nicest thing that ever happened to a golf club.

For my own use, I asked for the suite that is the farthest from the Trophy Room. The reason for my choice is that it is the only suite that could have a fireplace. I am happy to say that I am still the "owner" of the same living quarters.

The first cabin, which faces the tenth tee, was allotted to Bob Jones. His name plate is on the front and is expected always to remain there. Bob stipulated that certain memorabilia were to remain in the cabin, such as cartoons done in the 1920s by Tom Webster, old Scottish golfing prints, several awards and trophies, and also a map drawn to scale in 1924 by Alister Mackenzie of the Old Course at St. Andrews. The principal item is a large oil painting of Bob by President Eisenhower.

The cabin next to Bob's was assigned to Burton F. Peek. It was the second in what was later to become a circle of cabins. Upon Burt's death in 1960, this cabin was reassigned to J. H. Whitney and Walter N. Thayer. They declined to change the name plate on the door out of respect to the original "owner," believing that Burt's early support of the club had merited permanent recognition.

The pro shop used by Ed Dudley at the beginning was a house to the east of the clubhouse, built originally for one of the sons of P. J. A. Berckmans. It had to be torn down in 1946 to make way for the large, modern kitchen, and at that time a new, modest-sized pro shop was built to the west of the clubhouse.

Also in 1946 construction began on a bachelor wing with six bedrooms, located to the west of the clubhouse. The following year our third cabin was built, the "owner" being J. S. Kerwin, after whose death the cabin was reassigned to Dwight J. Thomson. In 1949 twelve members chipped in to cover the cost of a fourth cabin, which was named the Duplex, as it had two bedrooms on the ground floor and two above. A further seven single rooms were added over the Suites Building that same year. In 1953 a cabin was built to accommodate one of our members who was to become President of the United States. This cabin is fully described in a later chapter. The Firestone-McCollum Cabin was completed in 1956, its sponsors being L. K. Firestone, R. S. Firestone, and L. F. McCollum. In 1959, the Tennessee Cabin was made available by S. M. Fleming, O. H. Ingram, and Eldon Stevenson, Jr. The Butler Cabin, named for Thomas B. Butler of Baltimore, was built in 1964, the basement floor containing a TV studio that was used for the first time during the 1965 Masters. The ninth and last cabin to be constructed, the Jackson T. Stephens Cabin, as built in 1969. All our accommodations can be serviced by cart from the main club kitchen.

The Jamboree Party

I do not know if Burt Peek ever realized it, but he was responsible for the Augusta National Jamboree Party, an annual stag gathering of members that Bob Jones and I long ago agreed did more to establish the club on a sound footing than any other event. It has always been the most popular of the member gatherings.

In the late spring of 1936, when Burt was preparing to leave Augusta, he said to several of us, "It's a long time until the club opens next fall. Why can't we get together somewhere this summer?" Accordingly, a golfing expedition was organized in Burt's honor for a five-day weekend the following July. The eighteen who attended went by boat from New York City, played two rounds at the National Golf Links of America at South Hampton, Long Island, one round at the Maidstone Club, East Hampton, and two rounds at the Fishers Island Club near the Connecticut coast.

I devised for the occasion a new method of betting among ourselves. Each member of the party was assigned a starting handicap, and each day he lost or gained one stroke depending on whether he won or lost money. Also, each day every player put a small amount of money into a pot which was divided among the three who turned in the three lowest net scores. Additionally, an auction pool was held with respect to each day's play, every player being put up for auction during the previous evening. The total money derived from all the sales was allotted to the three lowest net scores, and the money went, of course, to those who had purchased the players who made the three best scores.

The theory behind the betting scheme was that every man, mathe-

The auction pool at the club's first Jamboree Party.

matically, should win one of the three prizes on one of the five days. At any rate, everyone liked the format, because the losers always looked forward with renewed anticipation and confidence to the next day's play because their handicaps had been raised again, while the winners were penalized a stroke. Moreover, those who were not fortunate to win through their own skill always had a chance to prosper by selecting and bidding in, at the auction pool, one or more prospective winners.

In saying that "everyone liked the format," I must confess that this was definitely not the case after the first day of play. The reason for the initial displeasure was because the author of the new betting plan turned in the low net score. However, I had one remaining friend that evening. His name was Ellis Dwinnell Slater, an early club member, better known as Slats. He had bought me in the auction pool.

The following year, 1937, the Jamboree Party was launched at Augusta, and it was an instant success. Aside from making it a four-day party instead of five, there was no basic change made in the format established the previous summer. The competition did, however, become a team event, in order to accommodate more players. The teams were drawn out of a hat for three days, and on the fourth day each player selected his partner.

It was soon discovered that the club had some good auctioneering talent. One fine auctioneer was W. D. Wilson of New York, another was John Murray of Augusta, and the third John O. Chiles from Atlanta. The last-named was never called anything other than "Johno," and he was the star performer. Johno employed quickie stories, antics, fast talk and double-talk, a limitless volume of original and highly humorous comments, and, in fact, every trick in the trade known to professional auctioneers and a lot more besides. Over the years Johno caused a bidder, on more than one occasion, to raise his own bid as many as three times in a row. On several occasions he sold a team to an individual who had merely scratched his nose or rubbed his head. No Jamboree participant dared to doze off during the auction. Anyone doing so would likely awaken to find himself the owner of a team he had no intention of buying. On the rare occasions when a hapless buyer objected, Johno simply sold the team to himself at a still higher figure. This action, of course, got everyone in the room in a still better mood, and more reckless as well. Indeed, the participants in the Jamboree had so much fun, and became with the help of Johno so enthusiastic, that the pools at times got a bit too big. Accordingly, Bob Jones or I would arbitrarily cut them in half.

Beginning in 1934, auction pools were held in connection with the Masters Tournament. They were public affairs and were held at the Bon Air Vanderbilt Hotel. Our club did not sponsor those public pools, but we tried to see to it that they were run by responsible people. For those who are not familiar with the history of golf auction pools, I will say that it was quite

John O. Chiles, our inspired auctioneer (right), seen here with Hollis Lanier.

usual over a period of many years to operate such pools at professional, amateur and pro-am tournaments. However, in 1949 the USGA strongly urged all golf clubs to discourage auction pools, and the PGA officially supported this action. As our officers had for many years recognized the USGA as the ruling body of golf in this country, our compliance was automatic.

The club at once asked its members not to participate in the public pool held at the Bon Air, and, shortly thereafter, the private pool held at the club was discontinued. Additionally, we asked our Pinkertons to discourage professional bookmakers from entering the club grounds during the Masters, and a long period of time has now elapsed since the Pinkertons found the last bookmaker on the club grounds.

Our club's Jamboree Party is as well or better attended than ever, but it occurs now without the excitement of an auction pool, betting being limited to Nassau bets made by participants among themselves for nominal stakes. The main attraction is the contest for silver trophies that are awarded to the winning team. I might add that, when the Jamboree auction pool was eliminated, several of us were fearful that the club's most popular gathering might not survive, but happily its attendance continued to grow.

The USGA deserves high praise for the initial action taken to eliminate golf auction pools. It represented a giant step toward disassociating the game of golf from organized big-money gambling. Since that time, the Internal Revenue Service has adopted regulations that come close to eliminating all inducement for anyone to try to hold a golf auction pool.

Returning to the original Jamboree Party, held in the summer of 1936, I want to repeat that each contestant was on his own. The following year in Augusta we had a two-man team contest, and the popularity of playing each day with a new partner and a new handicap brought about a four-man team contest which proved to be the most popular of all.

I say this because the club soon began holding four "members only" gatherings each winter season on the basis of each foursome competing against every other foursome. The Jamboree is still played on the basis of twosomes, but the foursome arrangement is played throughout the season at most any time when several foursomes might wish to compete in this fashion. During the four special foursome parties it is not uncommon for fifteen to twenty foursomes to compete, and the reason why the foursome-against-foursome concept is so enduringly popular is because it creates a team spirit. Usually in golf each person has an individual bet against the three other members, or two will play against the other two. But in the best-ball foursome contest against other foursomes, on full handicap basis, an altogether new and wholesome atmosphere prevails. Every time a shot is fired there are four players hoping it will be a good one. In the usual type of competition,

Augusta
National
Golf Club

the opposite kind of hope will creep in at times, no matter how well we may appear to succeed in behaving like good sportsmen.

There are still other advantages in foursome competition, such as the speeding up of play. Assuming that all are willing to forego individual side bets, either within or outside the foursome, any player who is hopelessly out of it on any particular hole can simply pick up his ball. There is, in our case, no need to be concerned about handicaps, because the member handicaps at Augusta are determined by the number of birdies and pars that are made, and the medal score is not taken into consideration.

In making up the teams for foursome competition, we find it best to try to arrange things so that each team includes one good player, two medium players, and one high handicapper. One way to arrange such an event is to let the club professional use this formula to make up the teams. Another is to appoint the best players to serve as captains and have them choose the players, taking turns—in other words, "choose up sides." If the number who wish to compete cannot be divided equally by four, the teams can be made up as threesomes. If the total cannot be divided by four or by three, it becomes necessary to make up teams of both four and three players. In that event, the foursomes start the threesomes one up a side, assuming the stakes are based on Nassau bets. The sums of money to be wagered should be kept low, so that this form of competition will attract the largest possible number of participants.

The most important angle of all is that the formula provides an opportunity for each member to broaden his acquaintanceship within the club roster. The Augusta National membership is drawn from thirty-odd states and several foreign countries. Despite this geographic dispersal, our average member probably enjoys more friendships at the Augusta National than at any other club. Most assuredly, one of the chief reasons for this are the "members only" club parties that cause the participants to abandon any idea of playing golf continuously with the same people.

Hard-Luck Tony

No book about the Augusta National could be complete without a chapter devoted to Tony Sheehan, who named himself our official photographer; no one disputed this title because he was liked by all the members. If he saw fit, he would intrude when a group might be talking privately, but the intrusion would not be resented.

"Hard-Luck" Tony Sheehan.

Tony was an oddball in appearance and dress, and he made comments at times that were just as unusual and unexpected. Neither he nor his battered old camera looked to be qualified to make even a passport photo, but he was a remarkably capable photographer. Tony took some of the pictures that appear in this book; in fact, some of the most treasured likenesses of early club members. His specialty was to sneak up unawares on his subject and photograph the man as he normally appeared, not as he tried to appear when he posed for his picture.

Many of us experience accidents as we go through life, but I doubt that any man endured bad luck so often and so continuously for so many years as Tony Sheehan. Every time an epidemic of any kind came to town, Tony was the first to catch it.

Tony tripped over something and broke one or more bones so often that it almost appeared to be a habit. On one occasion, while he was waving to friends, his car plowed into a large stone marker on Walton Way in Augusta, which cost him a number of teeth but gave him some distinctive battle scars on his face.

In another instance, just after leaving the hospital on crutches, Tony undertook to cross Augusta's Broad Street (which, it should be mentioned, is within one foot of being as wide as the famous Canal Street in New Orleans). As he left the curb his crutches skidded and he fell to the pavement in the gutter. A passer-by said to him, "Let me help you up." Tony is reported to have replied, "No, I think I'll be safer down here."

Tony survived a half-dozen major operations, plus numerous patching-up jobs. His one lucky day was when he was married to the nurse, Eva Smith, who had looked after him in the hospital so many times that she felt lonesome between his visits.

Tony finally got himself into really serious trouble—his car was hit by a train. Over a year's period the hospital lost track of the number of jobs that had to be done on Tony. Finally, the great day arrived when he could leave. His wife picked him up in her car and headed for home. When they arrived at the railroad track, the same one where Tony was wrecked, he asked her to stop the car. He then walked ahead and looked in both directions to make sure no train was approaching. As he was about to signal her that all was clear, her foot slipped off the clutch and she knocked Tony down. Whereupon she picked him up and took him back to the hospital for another stay.

Believe it or not, our friend Tony Sheehan lived to be eighty years of age, and died in 1974 of natural causes.

Golf Course Changes and Improvements Over the Years

1930s

During the first three years the course was open, the nines were reversed from their present order, the original first tee now being the tenth tee and vice versa. The change was made because we learned through experience that play could begin earlier after a frost on what is now the first nine, due to its being on higher ground. The first Masters Tournament, held in March 1934, was played under the original arrangement. The switch was made in time for the fall season club opening of the same year.

The first major change made on the golf course came in 1937, and it was done with the enthusiastic approval of Bob Jones. The tenth green was originally in a hollow to the right of its present location. It was moved to high ground to the far left of the fairway, primarily because this downhill hole, with the green in its original location, played too short for proper tournament standards, and also because the green's location in a low area did not drain readily. Our tenth hole is now generally regarded as a great test of golfing skill and an exceptionally beautiful golf hole. The credit for this important improvement belongs to golf course architect Perry Maxwell, who was a disciple of Alister Mackenzie. Maxwell proposed the change and supervised the building of the new green.

The second major course change was on the seventh hole in 1938. The green was originally located a little to the left of its present position, more toward the third tee, and the hole played too short and too easy. Horton Smith proposed a "postage stamp" green surrounded by bunkers, to be located directly in the line of the fairway with about twenty additional yards of length. Horton's idea was adopted by Bob Jones, and architect Perry Maxwell supervised the construction of the new green. It is the only heavily bunkered green on the course. Pines were already established on the right side of the seventh fairway, and a considerable number of pines were added on the left side. As these are now quite sizable, the fairway today can be classified as narrow. In consequence of both changes, what was once a weak hole from a tournament viewpoint is now considered to be a splendid test of precision golf.

1940s

Originally, the par-three sixteenth tee was located back of and a little to the right of the fifteenth green, at which time the length of sixteen was not much more than 110 yards, the green being located in the general direction of the sixth tee and just beyond a small stream. The members enjoyed the hole, but it was too weak for tournament play and its tee area was needed for use by tournament spectators. Consequently, in 1947, Bob Jones designed a new arrangement that placed the tee well to the left of the fifteenth green, and brought the play of the hole in the direction of the sixth green. The stream was transformed into a pond, with water extending from the front of the tee to the edge of the new green and along its left side. This green sloped to the left, with the area nearest the water substantially flat. With nothing but water for a fairway this is now a beautiful hole that is well suited for tournament play, and the members are happy with it. The golf course architect, Robert Trent Jones, implemented on a volunteer basis the plan conceived by Bob Jones. Trent also directed, at Bob's request, the building of a bunker on the left front of the first green. This was Trent's final contribution to the golf course as it is today.

A few years later it became apparent that our eleventh hole was too short to meet tournament requirements. Because the hole was a dog-leg to the right, with woods on both sides, the longer hitter was obliged to use an iron off the tee, or to execute a slice with a wooden club in order to keep the ball in the fairway. This was fine, except that a strong player with a correct degree of fade could drive the green. The tee was then located beyond and a bit to the right of the tenth green, at which location there was no room to lengthen the hole by extending it to the rear. I suggested to Bob that we build a separate championship tee short of the tenth green but well to the left, which could lengthen the hole by about seventy-five yards; also that a pond be created on the left of the eleventh green. Rather to my surprise, Bob enthusiastically embraced the idea. The work was done in 1950 by our own organization, and, from a tournament viewpoint, the change was at once recognized as an important improvement. Likewise, the pond at the green made the hole more sporting and much more attractive to the members, the Masters field, and our tournament patrons.

Another feature of the eleventh hole is the championship tee, which is bordered on three sides by twelve stately longleaf pines that are a hundred feet in height and close to a hundred years of age. Anyone stationing himself in the fairway about 150 yards out and looking back at the tee will see those magnificent pines forming a half-circle around the tee. The cathedral-like picture can be described as nothing less than unforgettable.

It was in 1952 that a fairway bunker on the fourteenth hole was eliminated, making it the only hole on the course without a single bunker.

In 1953, two large mounds for tournament spectator use were built, one at the right rear of the first green, and the other just beyond the fourth green. The second green was revised and extended to the left to provide a more exacting pin area. The third tee was shifted a bit to the right in order to cause the one fairway bunker to become more of a hazard. Also in 1953 a second large parking lot was made ready for use, extending the parking capacity on the club grounds to a total of 10,000 cars.

In 1956, our eighth green was rebuilt as previously described. Spectator mounds beyond the fourteenth green were enlarged, and a quite large mound was built on the left of the fifth green.

In 1957, the fairway bunker on the eighth hole was enlarged and moved to the right, in order to provide a bigger premium for the player who makes a long carry and reaches the preferred position from which to get home in two shots. Also in 1957, at the suggestion of Ben Hogan, a bunker was added on the right of the fifteenth green.

The small pond in front of the sixth green was eliminated in 1959. It could not be seen from the championship section of the tee, and the location of the pond made almost impossible the task of maintaining clear water.

1960s

Flood control measures unquestionably must be listed as the principal accomplishments during this ten-year period. I question if any golf club ever faced such large-scale difficulties of this sort as we encountered. Four separate major flooding problems had to be dealt with. Two resulted principally from a fast runoff of water from a new six-lane highway bordering our property. One was caused by nearby home building developments, which created much water overflow on our property. The fourth drainage emergency was our own doing, and I will describe it first.

Our forty-seven-acre number one parking lot had had gravel added to it each year since the first Masters Tournament in 1934. This was done, of course, to make all of it usable in wet weather. The result was a hardened surface that caused a rapid runoff of water such as might have been expected from a paved parking lot. We began experiencing floods across the first, ninth, tenth, and eighteenth fairways, and one of our practice areas. To remedy the situation, the club was obliged to lay 2,812 feet of forty-eight-inch drainage tile.

Rae's Creek was a very small stream when the course was built in 1931. After a period of time it occasionally flooded the relatively low area where are located the eleventh and twelfth greens, as well as the twelfth and a part of the thirteenth fairways. In the end, the club had no choice other than to raise the level of approximately two and a half acres by a minimum of one and a half feet to as much as two feet. Close to four hundred truckloads of fill were required to reduce this flooding hazard.

The next major drainage project involved approximately 1,355 feet of thirty-six-inch pipe at the northeast part of the club's property, where the nine-hole par-three course is located.

The last of the big problems of this nature was an overflow near the fourth green which involved five fairways. About 1,060 feet of thirty-six-inch drain tile and 755 feet of forty-eight-inch tile were required to solve the problem.

In 1960, nine greens were converted to the new hybrid Bermuda grass called Tifton 328. During the following year the other nine greens were likewise converted. Also in 1960, the Japanese custom of having the caddies fill the divot holes with a mixture of soil and seed was adopted.

In 1964, additional mounds were constructed at the right front of the fifth green. Two sizable mounds bordering the rear of the fifteenth green were eliminated. They had served as a backstop for too strong approach shots.

THIS IS THE GOLF BALL USED BY GENE SARAZEN IN SCORING A 2 ON THE PAR 5 FIFTEENTH HOLE IN THE 1935 MASTERS TOURNAMENT.

Their removal gave a clear view of the water hazard provided by the sixteenth-hole pond, which improved the appearance of the fifteenth green and also introduced a mental hazard for the player who might be debating whether or not to go for the green on his second shot. Also in 1964, the championship tee was relocated to the right rear at the fourth hole, and a large spectator mound was added at the left of the second green.

In 1965, a new split-level tee was built at number twelve.

In 1966, at the suggestion of Gene Sarazen, a fairway bunker on the short left of the second hole was moved to the right side of the tee-shot landing area. It was designed to require an accurate drive down the left center of the fairway. In the same year, a two-section bunker was built on the left side of the eighteenth fairway in the tee-shot landing area. This was designed to create a fairway width of not more than thirty yards between the two-section bunker and the woods on the right.

Between 1961 and 1968, all the fairways were converted from the old common Bermuda grass to Tifton 328 hybrid Bermuda. The mounds behind the sixteenth green and the one to the left of the fifth green were substantially enlarged in 1968.

In 1969, the fairway bunker on the first hole was moved twenty-seven feet farther toward the green. This was done to make it more difficult for the contestant to place his tee shot in the favored position on the right side of the fairway.

Augusta National Golf Club

Bob Jones congratulates Gene Sarazen at the ceremony dedicating Sarazen's Bridge at the fifteenth hole on April 6, 1955. The plaque reads: "Erected to commemorate the twentieth anniversary of the famous 'double-eagle' scored by Gene Sarazen on this hole, April 7, 1935, which gained him a tie for first place with Craig Wood and in the play-off won the second Masters Tournament."

That same year the championship tee at the fifteenth hole was moved to the right. Also, several small mounds and a quite large one, which is readily visible from the new tee, were built on the right side of the fifteenth fairway. This arrangement was designed to require either a straight tee shot or one with a fade. The player who wishes to reach the green in two must now place his tee shot between the mounds on the right and some trees on the left. The ground in this preferred area slopes slightly to the left, and the strip of open fairway which provides a clear shot at the green is only about thirty yards wide.

These changes were made because a too large percentage of the field had become able to reach the green in two, often using a medium-iron on the second shot. This was due, first, to the condition of the fairway having improved over the years; second, to the inordinate amount of distance a player could obtain by hitting a hooked ball onto the slightly leftward-sloping fairway; and, third, simply to the capacity of the field to hit the ball a bit farther. The ground behind the tee had a sharp downward grade, which made it impractical to lengthen the hole by moving the tee to the rear. Accordingly, it was moved to the right, which brought into play the pine trees along the right side of the fairway. As a result, the player can no longer start his tee shot out to the right and bring it in with a trajectory corresponding with the ground slope at the tee-shot landing area.

Scoring records indicate that our objective, the retention of number fifteen's par-five classification and the preservation of the authenticity of Gene Sarazen's famous double-eagle, has been attained. Unless a strong wind is against them, a substantial number of players still try to reach the green in two. This means that the hole continues to provide many thrills for the spectators, as well as for the contestants. However, those who reach the green in two usually do so with a wooden club or a big iron, which is as it should be.

1970s

In 1970 the Augusta National acquired from the Augusta Country Club a strip of ground, approximately one and three-quarters acres in size, that runs along and beyond Rae's Creek to the left of and behind our twelfth green, and behind and to the left of our thirteenth tee. This was a small but important acquisition, as it permitted the growing of more trees on land separating the two golf courses; additional weeping willows should be especially noticeable within a very few years. Also, we were able to move back the storm fence, which discourages tournament spectators who do not possess admission credentials. More importantly, we could eliminate a number of trees directly back of the twelfth green which had deprived the green of adequate sunshine and air circulation. The final item on the list of advantages was an opportunity to enlarge the thirteenth tee and move it to the rear.

In 1971 the club installed a new and completely automatic watering system (to be precise, the main part of the job was done in 1971 with the unfinished sections left for the following year). The complete system now includes the par-three course and the three practice fields. The total area that can be watered is approximately 120 acres. The number of sprinkler heads is 1,021, while the number of feet of polyvinyl chloride pipe is about 95,000.

The original watering system, made of galvanized pipe, was installed when the course was built in 1931. After a period of forty years we thought it had done its full duty. The pipes had become corroded to a point that, in some sections of the system, water could be supplied at not more than 40 per cent of the original capacity. As all the sprinkler heads had to be turned on at night by hand, it was impossible to accurately provide each area with the proper amount of moisture. This meant a wastage of water, in some instances accompanied by damage; also, excessively dry and hard ground in other areas because of insufficient water. We have found, after several years of experience, that our club possesses one of the best new watering systems in the country. However, our golf course supervisors have also discovered that much study and care, plus good operating judgment, are just as essential to keeping the course in fine condition as the updated watering equipment.

In 1972, it was deemed advisable to comply with the demands of the Masters Tournament for enlarged spectator space in areas near the clubhouse. This involved several rather large earth-moving jobs. First, the mammoth-size practice putting green was moved nearly twenty yards to the east, toward the Eisenhower Cabin. This gave our patrons much more room in which to walk between the practice green and the first tee, the ninth green, the eighteenth green and the tenth tee. The foot traffic being more widely dispersed, the turf in this area is no longer completely worn out during the week of the Masters. When extending the eastern part of the practice putting green, it was also made larger, and undulating surfaces simulating the most severe on the course were incorporated.

The second change was to move the championship tee of the first hole about five yards to the right, thus permitting enlargement of the spectator mound to its left, next to the ninth green. This change also made the placement of the tee shot on the first hole a bit more exacting.

Credit for all changes made near the clubhouse belongs to golf course architect George Fazio. He conceived the original plan and assisted in its implementation.

The third noteworthy change was to move the tenth tee about ten yards to the left, which provided the extra space needed for spectator traffic and also helped to provide room for an extension of the large mound on the right of the eighteenth green. This mound now accommodates an additional 1,500 patrons who may see the winning putt holed out.

Also in 1972, the championship tee and the members' tee at the fourteenth hole were moved a bit to the left. Here again the purpose was to provide added space for spectator traffic. The area between the thirteenth green and the fourteenth tee is actually a part of the thirteenth fairway, but, being too narrow, it could not be kept in good playing condition during the tournament. Then, too, more room was needed for a proper drop area next to the creek at the thirteenth green.

In 1973, the championship tee at the ninth hole was moved back. The hole had begun to play a little too short, especially on days with a following wind. The hole was originally designed to require a four- or five-iron second shot, but a number of players had become able, under favorable conditions, to drive all the way down to the bottom of a hollow, from where an eight- or nine-iron second shot might suffice. The new arrangement adds a minimum of fifteen yards to the length of the hole. Four- or five-iron second shots are now again customary.

Another change in 1973 was to move twelve fairly sizable pine trees into an area on the left side of the first fairway opposite the large bunker on the right of the fairway. This grove of pines is intended to serve as a hazard for tee shots that hook to the left.

A third 1973 improvement was a change to new types of winter grass on both the fairways and greens. Ever since the course was opened, the fairways have been overseeded with common rye, which keeps them looking green during the winter before the Bermuda has become dormant and turned brown. In 1973 the rye grass was replaced with a new type of fescue grass which permits closer-cut fairways that do not require such intensive mowing efforts in the spring season. The new grass also makes possible cleaner lies and longer life through the closing period of the winter season. In the past, our greens were overseeded with a combination of several conventional winter grasses. This practice was discarded in favor of a new type of perennial rye which provides putting surfaces that are a bit more true while reducing mowing problems in the spring. Both the new grasses are also less susceptible to disease. The only problem is the relatively high cost of the seed, but we are in hopes that this can in time adjust itself.

The most important undertaking in 1974 with respect to the golf course was the introduction of a new policy concerning the tees. All of them, including the practice tees, began receiving substantially the same treatment as the greens, including the use of the new type of winter grass. A considerable number of tees were rebuilt during 1974 to provide better drainage and more uniform surfaces.

All bunkers were filled with new sand before the course was opened in the fall of 1974. The new sand comes to us from the northwest section of North Carolina and is a by-product of the mining process that produces feldspar. Its consistently sized grindings represent, in our opinion, a near-perfect sand for golf course bunkers, due to the absence of foreign matter, the uniformity of particles, the stability of placement, and the lack of compaction without being fluffy. Then, too, this sand is self-draining without retaining excess moisture, and it resists out-of-sight penetration by a golf ball. We regard the introduction of this new sand in our bunkers as a major improvement in the playing conditions of the golf course.

There is a grove of large pine trees on the left side of the eighteenth fairway, but there is a gap of about seventy-five yards between this grove and the two-section fairway bunker. During the month of March 1975, this opening was filled with new pine trees to provide a potential penalty for a duck-hooked tee shot. This fashion of tightening up the eighteenth fairway is almost identical to the tree hazards introduced on the left of the first fairway in 1973.

During the summer of 1975, both the championship and member tees at the second hole were completely rebuilt to provide better drainage and more uniform surfaces. The same was true of the sixth, seventh, and thirteenth tees. On holes four and eleven, the championship tees only were treated in the same fashion.

In rebuilding the thirteenth championship tee, it was moved back ten yards. Such additional yardage would not ordinarily make any appreciable difference on a par-five hole. In this instance, however, the extra distance could be a factor to the player who is trying to get home in two, the hole being a sharp dog-leg with a creek on the left presenting a dangerous hazard. The thirteenth green was also rebuilt, something that has been done several times in the past because of sour soil resulting from too much shade. The green had lost some of its original two-level definition, and this feature was fully restored and extended in 1975. The combination of a slightly more demanding tee shot and a slightly more difficult putting surface could be noticeable in the 1976 Masters scores. This famous nature-made hole has many times importantly influenced the outcome of the Masters, and it will likely continue to do so.

Also in 1975, herringbone type of French drainage was installed in a number of bunkers in order to more quickly eliminate pools of water after heavy rains.

Special recognition and thanks are due to golf course architect George W. Cobb, who has helped to supervise many refinements on our golf course as well as on the par-three facility. Over a period of eighteen years, he has continuously made himself available as a consultant on maintenance problems, in addition to undertaking improvements.

Experimentation by others, and our own tests of the improved strains of winter grasses, caused us to adopt new policies for 1975. Our fairways were planted in the fall season with a fifty-fifty mixture of Yorktown perennial rye and the Jamestown type of red fescue. The greens and tees were planted with a fifty-fifty mixture of Pennfine perennial rye and the Jamestown type of red fescue. Rutgers and Penn State universities are credited with the development of both the rye grasses our club is using.

Tournament Developments

As I have noted, during all the prewar tournaments daily admission tickets were sold at one dollar each during the four days of practice rounds and two dollars each during the four days of play, while a series badge covering all eight days could be had for five dollars. During 1946–52 inclusive, tickets for the practice rounds were raised to two dollars; for the first two tournament days the price of daily tickets was increased to three dollars, and for the last two days to five dollars; while series badges were doubled in price to ten dollars. It is our understanding that the Masters was the first golf tournament ever to charge as much as five dollars for a daily ticket.

The first postwar tournament, in 1946, was most encouraging, because the attendance increased although admission charges had been doubled. The club also raised the cash prize fund for the professionals from $5,000 to $10,000. Thereafter, the admission receipts steadily increased, and the same was true of the prize fund.

The Masters was favored from the beginning with unusually spectacular play and exciting finishes. The highlight was, of course, Gene Sarazen's double-eagle in 1935, "the shot heard round the world," an incident that is discussed today almost as much as in the 1930s. All such happenings helped to draw more spectators. There were, however, two unheralded but carefully

Horton Smith directs the golf clinic regularly held during the early days of the Masters.

developed programs that did their full share to eventually cause the Masters to be classified as something special. One was a series of news releases each year, which were prepared and sent out by the club to every golf writer and commentator in the United States, with smaller coverage to other golfing countries. The second important factor was the building over a period of years of a patrons' list. At the beginning, as we wished to circularize all the golfers in Georgia and bordering states, all golf clubs within 225 miles of Augusta were asked for a list of their members. The clubs that declined were then asked to forward a letter from us to their members, and the great majority of them responded favorably. By various other means the patrons' list was expanded to cover golfers from distant states, largely those who wintered in Florida and would be driving north about Masters time.

The ownership of 365 acres gave the club the important advantage of making available, as needed, a total of 107 acres of land that was suitable for parking. Accordingly, every patron who made an advance purchase of tickets was always accommodated with "preferential" or "guaranteed" parking space at no extra cost. This inducement was an immeasurable stimulant to the sale of tickets. Our form letter, which was signed by myself in the first instance and thereafter by Elbert P. Peabody as tournament finance chairman, offered one preferential parking sticker to each purchaser of four series badges; or one guaranteed parking sticker to each purchaser of two series badges, these patrons being assured of parking space on the club grounds but not as near to the golf course as the owners of preferential stickers.

Following are some of the more notable developments relating to the Masters over the years:

• Radio coverage was first provided by CBS in 1934, at which time one tower was provided for the network's use. In 1947 a switch was made to NBC, and this arrangement continued until 1956, when CBS once more did the radio broadcasting.

• The first platforms and small towers for cameramen were provded prior to the war, but the exact date cannot be verified. The same applies to the first tower for the press.

• Also prior to the war, the club constructed wooden comfort stations around the course. They were called "Chick Sales" rather than privies, in recognition of the author of the book about these important facilities. It was in 1948 that the first permanent rest rooms, made of cement blocks and equipped with modern plumbing, were made available for the tournament patrons. The same year check-stand service was provided on a no-charge, no-tip basis.

• In 1938 a limited number of pine tree log benches were made available for the comfort of our tournament patrons. They were placed at popular viewing locations and seemed to be much appreciated. In later years, large numbers of lighter-weight benches were placed in selected locations.

• In 1949 our eleventh fairway was roped, and it was at once recognized as a better arrangement for both the spectators and the players. Greens and tees had been roped at tournaments for many years, but our fairway roping is recognized as a first. Later the U. S. Open followed suit, and now roping of all playing areas is common practice.

• The Augusta National green member's coat came into existence in 1937. A supply of jackets was purchased from the Brooks Uniform Company, of New York City, and our members were urged to buy and wear one during the Masters Tournament with the thought that patrons would thereby be able to identify a reliable source of information. The members were not enthusiastic at first about wearing a conspicuous Kelly-green garment. Besides, the original coats were made of material that was too heavy, so that the wearer became uncomfortably warm. Within a few years, however, lighter-weight made-to-measure green coats were available at the club's pro shop, and all members regularly wore them whenever they were at the club. In 1949 one of the club's green jackets was awarded to the winner of the Masters. At this late date we are unable to determine who proposed the idea, but it proved to be a very worthy one. There is nothing quite as widely understood about the Masters as the putting of the green coat on the new champion by the previous year's champion.

• In 1953 a press, radio, and TV building was constructed, of sufficient size to accommodate nearly all segments of the news media, including newspaper and magazine writers, TV and radio commentators, and photographers, together with special rooms for picture development and transmittal equipment.

• In 1954 a new and main concession building was constructed, where about 150,000 sandwiches are now prepared annually for the eight smaller concession stands on the course.

• The Masters was first televised in 1956. It was an ambitious effort to report a golf tournament in a manner designed to attract a large viewing audience. CBS did the telecasts, with a half-hour show on Friday, April 6, one hour on Saturday, and one hour on Sunday. Holes fifteen, sixteen, seventeen, and eighteen were covered by seven cameras beginning on Friday, with three more in use on Sunday.

• In 1957 the field was cut after two rounds to 40 plus ties.

• In 1959 a permanent first-aid building was made available for the medical unit which serves over four hundred tournament patrons annually. In the same year a quite sizable tournament headquarters building was constructed, and this was substantially enlarged in 1966. It is a two-story unit, plus a large basement vault where the tournament records are stored. All of the top officials make their headquarters in this structure, including the rules, finance, pairings, scoring control, gallery, pin-setting, and executive commit-

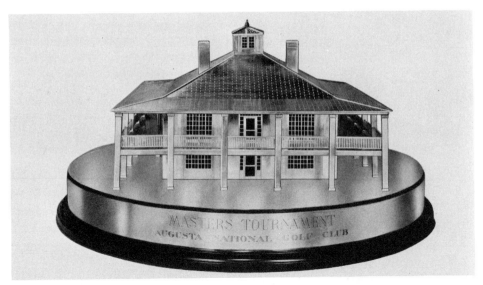

A drawing of the permanent Masters Trophy, which resembles the clubhouse and is made of eight hundred individual pieces of silver.

	WINNER	SCORE	SECOND	SCORE
1934	HORTON SMITH	284	CRAIG WOOD	285
1935	GENE SARAZEN	282	CRAIG WOOD	282
		SARAZEN WON PLAY-OFF 144 TO 149		
1936	HORTON SMITH	285	HARRY COOPER	286
1937	BYRON NELSON	283	RALPH GULDAHL	285
1938	HENRY PICARD	285	RALPH GULDAHL HARRY COOPER	287

The first section of the engraved band that embraces the Masters Trophy.

teemen. On Wednesday, the day preceding the start of each tournament, the ground-floor main room is used by the Golf Writers Association of America to hold its annual meeting.

• An altogether new type of score-reporting facility was introduced in 1960. We call it a "Scoring Standard." One or more of these standards are provided at each hole, the operators furnishing up-to-the-minute scores of each team of players for the patrons as the teams reach each of the holes.

• It was in 1960 that the unique over-and-under method of reporting scores was introduced at the Masters. Under this system, all scores are shown on a cumulative basis by indicating how each player stands in respect to par. On both the scoreboards and standards, under-par scores are shown in red numerals; over-par scores in green numerals; and even-par scores are indicated by a green zero.

• A central scoring control room was devised and placed in use for the first time in 1960. Since then, all scores are reported by telephone to scoring control, which then relays the information that is to be posted at the official scoreboard and in the press building. Scoring control also determines the scores to be recorded on the various leader boards.

• The first time the champion was interviewed for TV, the ceremony took place in my living quarters in 1960.

• Two picnic areas were provided in 1960. One is located near the main parking lot, and the other is near the second largest parking section, which borders the fifth fairway. Each picnic area is equipped with outdoor-type tables and seats. Patrons can purchase refreshments from nearby concession stands, or they may bring their own picnic provisions. Approximately one and a half acres of wooded land was set aside for each one of the picnic areas. They are popular but not overcrowded.

• The present permanent trophy, which resembles our clubhouse, was introduced in 1961. It was made in England and consists of eight hundred separate pieces of silver. The trophy rests on a pedestal, and a band of silver provides space on which can be engraved the names of the winners and runners-up for a fifty-four-year period. A bas-relief replica is presented each year to the Masters champion.

• The first observation stand for spectators was erected on the golf course in 1962. It is our understanding that the Royal and Ancient Golf Club had previously erected stands at the eighteenth green for the Open Championship in Great Britain. The first ones to be located around a golf course were at Augusta. It is our policy to locate such conveniences only where they can have a background of foliage. All are painted green.

• The Bill Inglish Book of Masters Tournament Statistics was supplied to the news media for the first time in 1964. In the same year, closed-circuit television coverage of player interviews was furnished to the radio and TV section of the press building. Also, taping blocks were provided for direct tape recording of the player interviews.

• In order to accommodate all of the working press, a balcony was constructed in 1965 at the rear of the main room of the press building. It provides space for an extra fifty-three reporters, who are furnished with binoculars as well as typewriters. In the same year, a special section in each observation stand was set aside for the news photographers.

• Masters Tournament series badges in counterfeit form made their appearance in growing numbers in the 1960s—not just a few made by amateurs, but a considerable quantity of professionally made badges. A new type of molded badge was therefore developed, and first placed on sale in 1966. It would require such a sizable investment to produce a passable counterfeit of the new badge that no one has so far undertaken to do so.

WATER COLOR PAINTINGS
OF THE GOLF HOLE
FLOWERS

1. Tea olive

2. Pink dogwood

3. Flowering peach

4. Flowering crab apple

5. Magnolia

6. Juniper

7. Pampas grass

8. Yellow jasmine

9. Carolina cherry

10. Camellia

11. White dogwood

12. Golden bell

13. Azalea

14. Chinese fir

15. Firethorn

16. Redbud

17. Nandina

18. Holly

• In 1966 the attendance was cut back and thereafter limited. In the same year, darkrooms for photo development were provided in the press building for Associated Press and United Press International. These organizations were thereby able for the first time to furnish wirephoto service directly from the site of a golf tournament.

• In 1967 the BBC, of Great Britain, carried a live telecast of the Masters via satellite. It was the first live overseas showing of an American golf tournament.

• In 1968 a portrait of Charles Bartlett was hung in the working press lounge in the press building. The room was named the Charles Bartlett Lounge. Bartlett had served as the secretary of the Golf Writers Association of America since its inception in 1946 until his death in 1967.

• Pedestal-type towers were designed and used for the first time at the Masters in 1969. They are especially useful in critical areas, as they do not interfere with the spectators' viewing of tournament action as much as towers with four legs. The only disadvantage is the cost of construction, plus setting them in six feet of concrete.

• When the Masters was first televised in 1956, all CBS broadcasting stations within a radius of approximately two hundred miles were blacked out. This was done, of course, to help the sale of admission credentials. When such sales were sufficient to provide adequate receipts, the club gradually lifted the blackout. In 1969 the last of the eleven broadcasting stations that had been blacked out were privileged to carry the Masters telecast.

Our Beautification Program

Ever since the beginning of the Augusta National there has been a continuous beautification effort, along with the golf course improvements. Our nurseryman and a trained crew of ten devote year-round attention to the plant life on the club's 365-acre property.

Among the legacies the Augusta National inherited from the Berckmans family was the original importation into America of privet, which serves today as a hedge and remains in good condition. There are literally thousands of miles of privet hedge throughout the South which were propagated from this mother hedge. Another legacy is the wisteria vine (*Wisteria sinensis*) next to the clubhouse, which is recognized as the first wisteria to be established in this country. It is also believed to be the largest vine of its kind in the United States. A third inheritance are two live oak trees (*Quercus virginiana*) near the clubhouse, the age of which is estimated to be 250 years. Probably our most important possession of this type is the double row of Southern magnolia trees (*Magnolia grandiflora*), which, as previously mentioned, line the 250-yard entrance driveway. A recent report furnished by an outstanding authority assures us that these sixty-five magnolia trees, if given the same care and attention they now receive, may be expected to live for another century and a half.

Pines have always been the most numerous trees at the Augusta National, and in some respects are the most important. On many of the golf holes they define the fairway areas. On others, large pines that are strategically located serve as hazards.

Our longleaf pine trees represent a priceless heritage. There are many hundred-year-old, hundred-foot-high, stately specimens that are in perfect condition. About half of the pines are longleaf, while the other half may be described as slash pines. The latter are a bushy type that do not grow as tall as the longleaf pines. Since our club was first organized, far more new pines have been set out than have been lost by lightning, disease, and old age.

The club operates a three-acre nursery where it grows a large percentage of its flowering plant requirements. As a part of the long-range beautification plan, additional live oak trees, which are very slow-growing, have been established. Some two hundred wisteria vines have likewise been planted in recent years, and these will soon be making a showing.

We display among the color illustrations in the book, in watercolor picture form with written descriptions by our nurseryman, the eighteen varieties of trees and plants which provide the names of our eighteen golf holes.

1. *400 yards. Par 4*

The first hole, Tea Olive, gets its name from *Osmanthus fragrans*, a native of Japan. This tree has gained popularity from its unusual period of bloom, from December to March, with intermittent displays of small white flowers which are extremely fragrant, as the botanical name *fragrans* implies. The plant will attain a height of sixteen to twenty feet, as some of the thirty-three tea olives on this hole indicate.

2. *555 yards. Par 5*

Hole No. 2 is flanked by nearly a hundred pink dogwood trees. The pink dogwood, *Cornus florida rubra*, is one of America's contributions to the world of horticulture. This tree is a chance mutation which is propagated by grafting onto a white dogwood seedling. Depending on the weather, this plant will usually come into bloom in the Augusta area during late March through

April. What appear to be four petals are technically called bracts, with these bracts surrounding the true flowers, which are clustered in the center. The pink dogwood is a light shade of pink when the blossoms open, and it slowly deepens in color until it attains its full intensity. Height will range from sixteen to twenty-four feet. In various areas on the property, over five hundred of these trees were successfully transplanted from a nursery in Tennessee. They are now eighteen years of age and extremely attractive, the flowers being such a deep shade of pink that they are almost red in color.

3. 355 yards. Par 4

The botanical name, *Prunus persica*, indicates that the flowering peach hails from Persia. Like the pink dogwood, this plant is also a mutation, being a chance development from the fruiting peach. By an accident of nature the stamens were converted to petals, making an extremely beautiful double flower about one and a half inches across which will only rarely bear fruit. The flowers may come in white, pink, red, or variegated colors, and they usually bloom in late March and early April. The plant makes a superb small tree with a spreading head, and eventually reaches a height of sixteen to eighteen feet. There are twenty-eight flowering peaches surrounding the third hole.

4. 220 yards. Par 3

At the flowering crab apple hole are planted fifty-eight of these colorful spring-flowering trees. These trees belong to the genus *Malus*. Since these varieties were produced from much hybridizing, a species name is usually not given, but instead a variety is listed after the genus. Although we have a native crab apple, our flowering crab apple plants are oriental crabs, which are more resistant to some diseases. The crab apple blooms in late March and early April, with numerous single and semidouble flowers which range from three-quarters to one inch in diameter. The light-pink-to-deep-rose flowers are followed in the fall by colorful one-inch apples, providing a popular food for many wild birds. These trees are propagated by grafting, since they will not come true from seed, and they will attain a height of sixteen to twenty-four feet at maturity.

5. 450 yards. Par 4

The magnolia is one of the most famous trees of the Augusta National. This aristocratic tree, though native to the Southeast, is extremely popular in European gardens, where it flourishes. The botanical name *Magnolia grandiflora* is somewhat descriptive of the large white flowers which bloom in May and June. These ten-inch flowers are followed in late summer by cone-shaped fruit which bear small red berries. The trees will reach a height of eighty feet in the wild, where they are in competition with other trees, but, under normal conditions, fifty feet is considered average. There are twenty-one excellent specimens on this fifth hole.

6. 190 yards. Par 3

This hole, Juniper, *Juniperus virginiana,* is a native small tree. The plant is commonly referred to as red cedar, although it is not really a true cedar. The wood from this tree has a fragrance which makes it popular for building cedar chests and other items of furniture. Botanically speaking, this plant is dioecious, meaning that the tree is found in male or female form. The male tree provides pollen for the fertilization of the female flowers, which produce numerous small blue berries in late summer. Juniper trees may attain a height of forty feet, but, as a smaller plant, it is popular as a Christmas tree, as it gives off a characteristic coniferous odor.

7. 365 yards. Par 4

The seventh hole, Pampas Grass, *Cortaderia selloana,* is a clump-growing grass native to Argentina and sends up its plumelike flowers in August. The plumes are usually a creamy white, as found on the eighty clumps around the seventh hole. They are unusual and most attractive throughout the winter season. The clumps may reach a height of ten feet when fully mature, and they slowly increase in diameter.

8. 530 yards. Par 5

The yellow jasmine, *Gelsemium sempervirens,* is a twining vine, native to the Southeast and is found in almost every lowland area. The one-and-a-half-inch trumpet flowers begin to show their bright yellow color during the first warm period in February, and will continue to exhibit their brilliant display into April. Yellow jasmine will climb small trees and shrubs to a height of twenty feet, but it rarely if ever inflicts any damage to its supporting plant.

9. 420 yards. Par 4

This hole derives its name from the Carolina cherry, *Prunus caroliniana,* a small native evergreen tree. The plant bears prolific clusters of small white flowers in late April, followed by black berries in later summer. The Carolina cherry will reach a mature height of twenty to twenty-four feet, and its small berries serve as an abundant source for bird food. Being native, many Carolina cherry trees are found over the course with several good specimens located at this hole.

10. 470 yards. Par 4

Camellia derives its name from the numerous varieties of *Camellia japonica* and *Camellia sasanqua*. The Berckmans imported these plants from Japan, France, England, Germany, and Belgium, and listed twenty-four named varieties in Mr. P. J. A. Berckmans' catalogue of 1861. Many of these first varieties are still alive today on the course. They have an extended blooming period from November through April, depending on the varieties, which range in color from white, pink, red, through variegated. Since a named variety cannot be grown from seed, many of these plants are grafted on *Camellia sasanqua* root stocks. The spectacular flowers, which range in size from two to six inches in diameter, adorn 190 Camellia plants which are concentrated around this hole. They may reach an ultimate height of thirty feet, but ten to twelve feet is more common under cultivation.

11. 445 yards. Par 4

The white dogwood, *Cornus florida*, is one of the most familiar flowering trees native to the Eastern United States. This small tree may attain a height of sixteen to twenty-four feet, with the branches arranged in a layered pattern. The dogwood tree has year-round interest, with the white flowers giving it the reputation of the king of native flowering trees. The four white petals are really bracts which surround the minute yellowish flowers clustered in the center. Each bract has a characteristic notch on the outer edge, which is the basis for the legend of this tree being that on which Jesus Christ was crucified, because the mark resembles a wound. The flowers, which bloom in late March and early April, are followed by shiny red berries in August. When the leaves turn brilliant red in the fall, the tree appears to be flowering a second time. Encompassing this hole are 155 dogwood trees, with many more interspersed throughout the club property.

12. 155 yards. Par 3

Golden bell, *Forsythia intermedia*, is native to China, but it has become one of the more popular spring-flowering shrubs in America. Few plants can match its brilliant display of yellow flowers in March. The three-quarter-inch yellow blossoms cover the pendulous branches of the shrub, which may attain a height of eight feet. The branches remain bare of leaves during the winter, but upon the first hint of spring blossoms will begin to pop open.

13. 485 yards. Par 5

The thirteenth hole bears the name of the plant for which the Augusta National is most noted, the azalea. This plant will be seen in many forms on the course, from the native "honeysuckle" types to the exotic Kurume, Kaempferi, and Indica types. Depending on type, the native species have pink or yellow flowers which are tubular in shape and usually quite fragrant. The more familiar evergreen varieties are those which give the greatest display of color. The azaleas belong to the genus *Rhododendron* and are the results of intricate hybridizing, as with the oriental crabs. The colors range from white, pink, orchid, rose, through red. The Kurume types are smaller-growing plants ranging in size from two to four feet, with flowers from three-fourths to one and a half inches in diameter. The larger-growing Indica types may reach a height of ten feet, with large delicate flowers up to four inches across. Many of the rare older varieties are to be found here, with newer ones being added each year. The bloom period will range from early March through mid-April. From tee to green, this hole is flanked on its south side by approximately 1,600 azaleas of all of the major horticultural types. An almost endless number are planted at various other locations where color is deemed to be desirable.

14. 420 yards. Par 4

The exotic Chinese fir, *Cunninghamia lanceolata*, is an unusual tree. It goes by many common names due to a unique appearance. This plant is native to China, but its botanical name indicates that it was discovered by a Western botanist, J. Cunningham, in 1702. The flowers are inconspicuous green catkins, but they are followed by a very ornamental cone one to two inches long. This tree has the very unusual characteristic of shedding some of its branches in the fall even though it is an evergreen tree. The tree may reach a height of eighty feet in its native China, but in America forty feet is considered mature.

15. 520 yards. Par 5

Firethorn, or pyracantha, *Pyracantha koidzumii*, is one of the most prolific bearers of orange berries known to horticulturists. It belongs to the rose family, as do many other common plants such as apple, dewberries, photinia, and loquat. In April this plant will cover itself in numerous small creamy white flowers, which in turn form the brilliant orange berries for which it is so well known in late summer. The fruit will usually persist until late winter and thus provide much bright color over a period of months when the bird population will take its toll. Since the pyracantha bears such a heavy crop of berries, it will usually alternate between a good year and a bad. The name firethorn comes from the multitude of thorns which cover the branches and serve to protect the fruit from many predators. Over fifty plants flank the fairway of this hole, and these specimens will mature at a height of eight to ten feet.

16. 190 yards. Par 3

Redbud is a small tree native to the entire Eastern United States. It is also commonly called the Judas tree, which might be a better name than redbud since the flowers are really not red but rather an orchid pink. The plant is in the legume family along with peas, beans, and mimosa, as indicated by its small pealike flowers and beanlike seed pods. This tree flowers from early March into April, with the heart-shaped leaves following the blossoms. The Judas tree, *Cercis canadensis*, will mature at a height of sixteen to twenty-four feet, and fifty of these native flowering trees flank the left side of the sixteenth hole.

17. 400 yards. Par 4

The nandina is an oriental shrub. Its botanical name, *Nandina domestica*, has reference to the plant being located near the doors of Japanese homes, since it is a good-luck symbol in that it will mediate family disputes. An unusual plant, the nandina grows in a clump form made up of many unbranched cones which bear large, fernlike, compound leaves near the top. In April and May, large clusters of small, creamy flowers flow from the terminal buds of each branch. These are followed by small green berries which turn brilliant red in the fall. Upon the first hint of frost the leaves will also turn various shades of pink, red, and purple. There are sixty-five of these unusual shrubs, which may attain a height of four to six feet, on the left of this hole.

18. 420 yards. Par 4

Holly, *Ilex opaca*, is a small evergreen tree and would have to be termed the queen of American trees if the magnolia is called the king. When holly is mentioned, this is usually the plant which immediately comes to mind. Like the juniper, the holly is dioecious, with male and female trees. Both bear small inconspicuous flowers, with the female tree being the only one to produce the berries. The fruit begins to turn red in the fall and sometimes may persist on the plant up to ten months. The tree is native to the Eastern United States and is found in many named varieties, which are propagated for their good berry-bearing qualities or unusual form. On occasion, one may also see such a tree with yellow berries. These trees have been known to reach a height of eighty feet, but under most cultural conditions thirty feet is considered exceptional.

The gold medal presented annually to the Masters champion.

The gold and silver Amateur's Bowl awarded annually to the low-scoring amateur in the Masters.

PART THREE

General Eisenhower's First Visit

General of the Army Dwight David Eisenhower arrived at the Augusta National Golf Club on April 13, 1948, for an eleven-day stay. It was his first vacation in ten years.

The General's arrival made an electrifying impact on the town, the club, and its members. In fact, he changed the lives of a number of us to a considerable degree. His intimate association with our club was such that he will automatically be thought of, along with Bob Jones, as a principal member of the Augusta National just as long as it endures. The General's interest, the time he spent here, and the things he did here, make it essential that an important part of this book be devoted to him.

I became closely associated with the General in several fields of activity, but, in recounting his doings as a member of our club, I shall confine myself largely to golf, bridge, and the like. I intend also to avoid, with a few notable exceptions, listing the personal friends who were entertained here by the General and Mrs. Eisenhower. Reference to the many government officials who came to the club to see the General will also be rather severely limited.

One of our members, William E. Robinson, general manager and later publisher of the New York *Herald Tribune*, had become acquainted with General Eisenhower during the war. Bill and I played a good deal of golf together in New York and at Augusta, and one day he mentioned to me that the General was planning a long-awaited vacation but could not decide where to go. It seems that he had never discovered a place liked equally by both him and his wife Mamie. They now had the additional problem of privacy.

Knowing the General liked to play golf, I suggested to Bill that he let them know they would be welcome at the Augusta National; that we could make them comfortable and see to it that the recreation and rest they sought were not disturbed. Partly because the General had already heard some favorable comment about the club, he promptly accepted. As for Mrs. Eisenhower, the idea of a golf club sounded better than a fishing camp or a hunting lodge.

Although we did not have very much advance notice, we were quickly

General Eisenhower during his first visit to Augusta National in 1948. The inscription reads: "For Clifford Roberts—who did so much to make our visit to the Augusta National the most delightful vacation of our lives—Ike Eisenhower and Mamie."

able to make the necessary preparations. The security problem was solved by asking the Pinkerton Agency to reassemble and bring back to the club as guards some of the people who were on duty during the last Masters Tournament. A few deputies patrolled the outskirts of the property. The General was so very popular that none of us felt concerned for his safety, but we knew he would need protection from the curious and the overly friendly. The news media were told that the General would be asked by the club to grant one interview, either during or at the end of his visit to Augusta. Arrangements were made so that all telephone calls were intercepted by the General's aide, Colonel Craig Cannon. The same was true of all mail or telegrams. Any of the club members coming to Augusta were asked not to bring guests during the General's visit.

The Eisenhowers were assigned to the Jones Cabin, with Bob's approval, and, although it was not very spacious, they were delighted with it. I have never met any two people quite so famous who were so easy to know. I began calling them Ike and Mamie before realizing I was doing so.

Ike fell in love with the place. He wanted to become a member—a full-fledged, dues-paying member. This was fortunate, because Bob and I had determined at the club's beginning not to have any honorary members. It was also most fortunate that Mamie liked the club just as much as Ike. This was difficult to understand, because she had no real interest in golf, and ours was essentially a man's club. Possibly the knowledge that Ike was happy and that she could be with him pleased her most of all. She thoroughly enjoyed the informal atmosphere. Also, Mamie liked the club staff, particularly Mrs. Helen Harris, who was in charge of the office, and Bowman Milligan, the club steward. Then, too, she appreciated the plants and flowers. Partly because of a rheumatic heart and no exercise, Mamie did not appear to be very strong, but her lovely clear complexion and her friendliness and sweetness made her a most attractive person.

Being a great admirer of the nation's most popular war hero, I expected to like the man. However, I do not think any of the members who were present expected to find him possessed of so much charm and happy companionship. Ike wanted to play golf, practice golf, or take golf lessons, all day long. He did not care what he did in the evening, so long as we got started playing bridge as early as possible. It was golf and bridge with almost no interruptions for eleven days in a row.

As a golfer, Ike was an average player, meaning a 90–95 shooter. He was very much out of practice, but it was plain to see that he never had been nor ever could be much better than an 85 player. This was mainly due to a football-injured left knee, which deprived him of anything to hit against. As a result, it might be proper to say that he was a congenital slicer. Then, too, he was usually a bad putter, partly because he did not have the natural talent to read the greens correctly, but also because he did not seem to have sensitive fingers on his big-boned hands. In other words, he had no instinctive "touch" for putting. Moreover, he was always impatient to take a crack at the hole, and, too often going far by, he would then miss coming back.

The irony of the situation was that Ike liked golf more than any other game, and very much wanted to play it well. He had been an expert or a near-expert in a considerable number of sports, such as baseball, fly-casting, football, pistol- and rifle-shooting, poker, bridge, and the hunting of duck, quail, and dove. He had no chance at all, however, to play his favorite game with a comparable degree of skill.

I doubt that Ike had ever played golf for more than a one-dollar Nassau, but he rather reluctantly agreed to our usual stakes of five-dollar Nassau, plus a birdie deal that was predicated on each player's handicap. The stakes at bridge were set at one cent a point, compared to our usual two cents. I explained our custom of conceding all bids of one that did not make game in order to speed up play. Ike argued against this, but finally agreed on the premise that a conceded bid of one no-trump would be scored as 30 rather than 40. This is, to this day, the regular practice of the bridge players at the Augusta National.

Before the end of his eleven-day visit, Ike had extracted from me a very great deal of information about the club, the tournament, and the policies of both. He learned the names of a number of those in the organization, and he also decided that our professional, Ed Dudley, was the best of all golf instructors. In selecting a green coat for the General to wear while being photographed, Bowman picked out one that fitted him perfectly. It happened to belong to W. Alton Jones, a member whom Ike liked very much when they were introduced some two years later.

When departure time arrived, I am sure that Mamie and Ike, and all the club members present, knew full well that the initial visit had brought about a deep feeling of kinship between the Eisenhowers and the Augusta National.

Bob's Health

On February 14, 1949, in my capacity as chairman of the Masters Tournament Committee, I issued a press release which contained the following passage:

Mr. Robert T. Jones, Jr., our President, will not participate this year as a contestant. I think it is proper to state frankly to Bob's friends that his operation was quite serious but that a complete recovery is expected. As the result of an injury to the upper part of the spine which is believed by his doctors to have occurred when he was quite young, Bob has occasionally suffered, for some years, from what he called a "crick" in his neck and a lame shoulder. The first noticeable discomfort occurred in Scotland in 1926, but the exact cause of the trouble was never accurately determined until 1948. (The condition never interrupted tournament play except on one occasion—the 1940 Masters Tournament.) The operation was to relieve pressure on the spinal cord which pressure had, during last year, seriously affected his central nervous system. He has not as yet regained the full use of his right leg but otherwise is in excellent health. He has already visited the Augusta National once this season and will be present during the Masters. Moreover, Bob plans to lend a hand in the directing of the tournament, something that his non-playing status leaves him free to do.

It is my intention here to add to the information contained in this statement by furnishing more details. I do this because there has been a never-ending discussion about Bob's illness, in medical circles as well as by the public. The fact that he became, after some years, a helpless cripple brought rumors that his operation was bungled. These stories were repeated so many times that they were known to Bob, and it is possible that they could have raised doubts in his own mind. Many other misunderstandings occurred about the nature of Bob's illness and the sequence of events pertaining to it. No single person ever knew the true story in its entirety, but, as I was regularly given information from well-informed sources, principally by Bob himself, I will furnish in layman's terms the facts as I know them. Bob is the central figure in this book, and, since his years of suffering served to bring out the greatness of the man's character, I deem it an obligation to recite briefly the knowledge I possess. The least I can hope to do is to dispel the notion that arthritis was the trouble, or that he died of the disease which afflicted Lou Gehrig.

Bob made a special trip to New York in 1948 to discuss his personal finances with me, but, more importantly, to let me know that he was soon to undergo an operation on the upper part of his spine, called the cervical area. He was so strong, and always seemed to be in such good health, that it was hard to believe him at first. Even when I realized he was dragging one foot a bit, I was unable to comprehend that my friend was physically in such deep trouble.

Bob told me about the number of times over a period of years that he had been bothered, and sometimes painfully, by a shoulder or neck soreness. Some half-dozen doctors had been consulted. One recommended whirlpool water treatments, which he tried. Another suggested osteopathic treatments, and these he took a number of times. One doctor decided the absorption of poison into his system from bad teeth might be causing the trouble, and a tooth or two was pulled before this theory was disproved. The remarkable thing is that no one suspected a nerve problem, and consequently X-ray pictures were never made. Finally, when Bob became lame, this was done, and an obstruction was at once discovered at the sixth vertebra.

I wanted Bob to go to one of the big-name places and suggested Lahey Clinic in Boston. He explained that only some twelve or fourteen operations had been done in the United States, up to that time, in the upper spinal area where his trouble was located. Two of them had been performed by the doctor he had chosen. Also, while the doctor practiced in Atlanta, he had been trained at Johns Hopkins in Baltimore.

After the operation it was reported that Bob had a bone growth on the front side of his spine, something that might have been caused by a fall in his youth. The growth, which had been pressing on a nerve, was successfully removed. It was hoped that the nerve had not been permanently damaged, in which case complete recovery was expected.

When Bob became more lame, he decided in 1950 to go to Lahey Clinic. I was not in the Boston hospital during the second operation, but I saw the head surgeon who performed it shortly afterwards. He informed me everything that could have been done had been accomplished in Atlanta; and that, aside from removing some proud flesh which might make Bob more comfortable, nothing more could be done. The surgeon went on to explain that, as the central nervous system had been permanently damaged, there would occur a gradual deterioration of his system of nerves below the level of the point of damage. He finished by asking me to help convince my friend that no mistake was made in the first instance. He felt it to be important that Bob not undergo unnecessary mental torture of this kind, because at best he faced lingering physical torture during the remainder of his life.

Bob made one more effort some two or three years after his trip to Boston. He had learned about an especially capable doctor at Presbyterian Hospital in New York. This doctor already knew something about the history of Bob's case and readily agreed to review it. After a thorough examination he gave Bob quite frankly the same kind of report which had been given to me at Lahey Clinic. We spent that evening together in my apartment. Both of us made an effort to bring up other subjects for discussion, but we were not very successful.

The General's Recuperative Visit

Ike arrived in Augusta on April 12, 1949, a sick man, and remained until May 11. Quite a bit of background information is needed to explain how this came about.

The General had resigned in the fall of 1948 as Chief of Staff of the Army, and moved to New York to become president of Columbia University. He was just in the process of becoming acquainted with his new post when President Truman began sending for him to perform urgent military tasks. Ike was asked to take an active part in the effort to unify the armed services. Likewise, he was called upon to help Secretary Forrestal, who was showing signs of cracking up. After several months of fourteen to fifteen hours a day, in large part in Washington, Ike's stomach began giving him trouble. The diagnosis was ileitis, and his doctor, Major General Howard McC. Snyder, informed Ike that he must take a rest.

Truman liked to go to Key West, and, assuming this locale would also be good for Ike, the President urged him to use the Presidential plane and go there. After about a week General Snyder phoned me that his boss was not doing well at all: too hot, nothing to do, and no golf course. I urged him to bring the General to Augusta, which was done the following day.

When I first saw Ike, I was shocked. He was weak to the point of almost trembling. What had happened in the short time since I last saw him in New York was alarming. But just to get a look at the club seemed to lift his spirits. The first day he could do no more than walk a few holes, the next day he was on the practice tee for an hour, and the third day he played nine holes of golf. His ability to recuperate was astonishing. In less than a week he was ready for bridge.

Doctors from a nearby military hospital made thorough examinations. General Snyder told me that the reports showed nothing organically wrong, but that Ike was subject to a complete stoppage of normal stomach functions whenever he built up too much tension. This was his third ileitis attack, the first one having occurred in the Philippines. Fortunately, Ike had not suffered an attack during the war.

Snyder asked Ike to cut down on cigarettes. For many years the General had smoked excessively, especially during the war—three to four packs every day. Ike said it would be easier to quit than to cut down, and he did quit, for

Ike's Pond.

good—no chewing gum, no sucking on a piece of candy, and no chewing on a cigar. He refused all offers of helpful aids, but I know it must have required a considerable amount of willpower. I say this based on personal experience but, more particularly, because of his answer to a question at a later date. In 1950 someone asked him how long it had been since he quit smoking. Without a moment's hesitation, Ike answered, "One year, two months, twenty-six days, and four hours."

It was during this second visit to Augusta that the General walked through the woods on the eastern part of the club's property. Upon his return he informed me of a perfect place to build a dam, should we ever wish to have a fishpond. A member named L. B. Maytag, whom we called Bud, was on hand at the time, and I at once named him the chairman of the Fish Pond Committee. Ike's Pond was promptly built and properly named, and the dam was located exactly where Ike said it should be placed, the construction engineer concurring in the location. The pond occupies three acres and is fed by a dependable spring just 150 yards above it.

The General as Bridge Player

Early in 1950, eight stags, including Ike and myself, engaged a private railroad car in New York and made a six-day trip to Augusta (January 20–26). Nothing unusual occurred, but it was a very enjoyable junket.

Ike and Mamie were next at the club beginning just after the Masters for thirteen days from April 10. Ike's older brother, Ed, an attorney from the State of Washington, was also with us for a few days and proved a surprisingly good golfer, with a handicap of five or six. General Vandenberg was

Left to right, Carl Wood, L. J. Kalmbach, Clifford Roberts, President Eisenhower, and, in the golf cart, General Gruenther.

present for a brief stay, and General Gruenther was on hand for a number of bridge games.

As a bridge player, Ike would have to be rated as a near expert—indeed, many in the armed services rated him second only to his friend, General Gruenther, whom I would nominate as a full-fledged expert.

Al Gruenther was known in the Army as "The Brain," because of his great memory and mental capacity. His consuming hobby was bridge. I happened to meet him in the thirties because, as a West Point instructor with the rank of lieutenant, he occasionally refereed a bridge tournament at the Knickerbocker Whist Club in New York City. Later he became a recognized world authority on the rules of bridge.

Ike wanted to include Al at the bridge table as often as possible in order to improve his own game. In turn, the General was always anxious to help the rest of us. He played bridge—and, in fact, every game—for all there was in it. He would sometimes lecture or scold any one of us, partner or opponent, for a bad bid or a careless play. He never seemed to lose patience or to become discouraged, although some of Ike's favorites in my gang at Augusta could never play well in a thousand years. There were several who liked the game but lacked natural card sense. Ike was a serious student of the game of bridge, but there were relatively few members of the Augusta National who could be so classified.

Sergeant Moaney

This might be an appropriate time to talk about Sergeant John Moaney, who answered to the name of Moaney when the General, or anyone else for that matter, called him. He had served throughout the war as the General's orderly. No one could have more faithfully pressed clothes, shined shoes, and performed countless small chores than Moaney did over such a long period. He could also cook or wait on table when necessary. Ike liked Moaney a very great deal.

When it came time, in 1948, for the Eisenhowers to move into the former home of Nicholas Murray Butler at Columbia University, it was discovered that the house was large in some respects but short on bedrooms. There was no place available for Moaney, except one tiny, shoe-box-size room. This would have been all right, except that Moaney had just recently acquired a bride, and two people could not possibly squeeze into the small bedroom. Ike explained the situation to Moaney and told him how disappointed he was

General Eisenhower, Sergeant Moaney, Bowman Milligan, and the author in 1952.

that there seemed to be no solution to the problem. Moaney urged the General not to worry about it, that he would as usual go right along with him and look after him as always. Ike wanted to know what he proposed doing about his wife, to which Moaney replied, "It looks to me like I got to choose between you and her, and I knowed you first."

Toward the Presidency

After a lapse of more than two and a half years, Ike arrived in Augusta as President-elect at around 4 P.M. on November 5, 1952.

The reason for his departure from New York City the morning after the election was because he and I had made a firm compact to do just that, win or lose. I had chartered a Constellation plane from Eastern Air Lines some weeks in advance, and no one knew anything about the plan until after Stevenson finally conceded defeat. The reason for chartering the largest plane available at the time was my hope that we would be obliged to take along a crew of Secret Service men.

Many things had happened to Ike since his last visit to the Augusta National. To highlight these events, I will first list President Truman's appointment of the General to organize and to become the Supreme Commander of NATO Military Forces. His task was to persuade our twelve impoverished allies to join, and then to finance their respective quotas of fighting men equipped with modern weapons, planes, and naval vessels and it was a near-to-impossible assignment. Ike made a quick plane trip to talk to all the heads of government, after which he made a report to the President and to a special session of Congress. He then left for a one-week vacation at a U. S. Air Force base at Puerto Rico which was supposed to have a good golf course, asking three of us from the Augusta National to go along for obvious reasons. Shortly after the vacation trip, Ike and Mamie left by boat for Paris, where they temporarily occupied a floor of the Trianon Palace Hotel in Versailles, the hotel Ike used as his French headquarters during the war.

During 1951 more and more American individuals and organizations had sent messages to Ike urging him to run for President. Numbers of people went to Paris to see him. I made several trips to see Ike, not to advise him to enter the political field, but, as per his request, to keep him informed on developments; and also to play golf and bridge, as did several other Augusta National members. Then, too, I managed Ike's investment portfolio under a power-of-attorney arrangement. When he realized approximately $500,000 net from his book *Crusade in Europe*, he turned it over to me to look after.

Mamie definitely did not want Ike to become President. I know, because she once took me to task in Paris in critical terms, thinking me to be one of those who were trying to involve Ike in politics. She felt that Ike had earned complete retirement after he finished his tour of duty at NATO. I am also definitely certain that Ike himself did not want to be a candidate. We discussed all sides of the political situation but, the more we talked, the less able we were to introduce some new and constructive plan for discussion that might let him off the hook. We were both a part of the growing number who doubted Taft's ability to win. Ike was shocked when Dewey failed to win. He felt the socialistic trend initiated by F.D.R. must be arrested. The General was easily the most patriotic American I have ever known. He never forgot having been educated at public expense. Duty to country came ahead of all other considerations in his life. That is why he could not take the easy way out by issuing one of those "If elected, I will not serve" statements.

In the fall of 1951 I called a meeting, in New York, of a carefully selected group to review the political situation and to give Ike the benefit of our collective thoughts. While I had kept in touch with each one of the group for some months, we had never previously tried to hold a meeting. The majority of the group were members of the Augusta National whose homes were in or near New York City. Ike had come to know them well by reason of his being made an honorary member of my three favorite golf clubs in the New York area, Blind Brook, Deepdale, and the National Links, at which clubs a number of members of the Augusta National also held memberships. Moreover, most of those who played bridge at Ike's home at Columbia University were Augusta members.

When Ike's friends finally held a formal meeting they did not urge him to run, since that was not their mission. No doubt everyone hoped he would become a candidate, but the only action taken by the meeting was to authorize two messages. Bill Robinson and I left at once to advise Ike on behalf of the group that, first, the time had come for him to declare himself unavailable if he intended ever to make such a statement. We felt that a number of splendid individuals were coming out for him, and that their political future would be jeopardized if Ike left them hanging on a limb by issuing a negative statement at a later date. Our second recommendation was that, if he did not wish to issue an "unavailable" statement, he should refer everyone who cared to talk politics to Lucius Clay. Lucius attended the meeting, and, because he was familiar with the serious confusion among the relatively few big-time politicians who had come out for Ike, readily agreed to meet with those who wanted to talk personally with Ike. (The confusion was the result of several individuals returning from Paris and reporting their own interpretation of

General Lucius D. Clay.

some chance remark made by Ike that turned the remark into an important decision or announcement.)

Ike's answer was "no statement" to our first suggestion, and "yes" to our second suggestion. We then discussed the New Hampshire primaries, which required a prompt decision because the state is first on the calendar and the state law required that each candidate be entered well in advance and his party affiliation declared.

I asked Major General "Jerry" Persons to look up the military regulations, and it was evident that Ike could not actively seek any political office even if he wished to do so, which of course he didn't. Ike finally agreed that he would not object if someone saw fit, of his own volition and without authorization, to file for him in New Hampshire.

Ike had never voted prior to 1948, at which time, so he told several of his intimates privately, he voted Republican. Accordingly, Lodge was the logical one to enter Ike's name, and to certify his party affiliation. Shortly thereafter, as per a suggestion delivered by Bill Robinson, Lodge held his famous press conference in Washington, D.C., and made his announcement.

A warm friend of mine, Frank Sulloway, was the Republican National Committeeman from New Hampshire. He had asked questions of me many times about Ike. Finally, he and his friend Sherman Adams, Governor of New Hampshire, neither of whom had ever met Ike, decided to come out for him. This was very timely, because they selected an outstanding slate of delegates pledged to support the General.

The steering committee trying to nominate Ike (Dewey, Duff, Lodge, and others, with Clay handling liaison) decided to concentrate principally on New Hampshire. They knew that, if Ike failed to make a good showing in that state, the ball game was over. Taft already had large numbers of firmly pledged delegates, particularly in the south. The Ike Committee was very happy about Sulloway and Adams, but Taft was campaigning in every town of 1,000 or more population in the state, while their candidate was in Paris with his lips sealed.

Just prior to the New Hampshire primaries the Ike pros had a poll made, which was not favorable. They then asked me to go to Paris to prepare the General for the possibility of Taft winning the majority of the delegates. The somber message I gave Ike did not seem to disturb him, and he went calmly about his business the next day, taking me along to Germany with him. But, when we returned to Paris that night, and were told by a large gathering of the news media the extent of his big New Hampshire victory, Ike was delighted. He commented to the effect that no one could help feeling proud that some of his fellow Americans should want to vote for him.

However, I feel here that I should reveal that Ike did not seem to realize the extent to which he was by then committed to a political role. I say this

126

Augusta National Golf Club

because he asked me if I could congratulate Adams and Sulloway on his behalf without anyone knowing about it. In the end, I convinced him that he should communicate directly with the Governor, whom I did not know, and, as per his authorization, I would then congratulate Frank Sulloway. The Governor released his congratulatory telegram from Ike, and the reaction was most favorable.

The Convention and the Campaign

When Ike resigned his army position as a five-star general, and came home to campaign for the Republican nomination, a number of the members of the Augusta National, including myself, became almost full-time campaign workers. Almost to a man, the whole membership provided or helped to raise funds for Eisenhower organizations. As the club membership was drawn from thirty-odd states, the influence geographically was rather potent. All of this represented a remarkable development for a golf club membership that had never been politically oriented. But, of course, few of us had ever had an opportunity previously to support a fellow club member for President. And a very popular one at that!

When Ike returned to the United States, he took up residence again at Columbia University. For a time he received at his home various state delegations that wished to meet the new candidate and to ask questions. Some of our Augusta members helped to bring delegates to New York. Others, who were a part of news organizations, or who could influence the various media, were also active in Ike's behalf. Some raised funds for the Citizens for Eisenhower organization, while several became officers of the organization. A number of members who knew delegates from their home states undertook to influence them. A few worked directly with the small group of professionals who were master-minding the effort to deprive Taft of the support of certain delegations where their legal status could be challenged. In short, there was almost no part of the effort to nominate Ike where some Augusta member could not be found lending a helping hand. Even Bob Jones made the trip to the convention and managed, with the aid of a cane, to call upon delegates he knew from two states. He also kept appointments I arranged for him to make TV appearances in behalf of Ike's candidacy.

I sometimes wonder if there are very many people who realize how close Taft came to being nominated. Ike was definitely the underdog, as was indicated by the betting odds. If our side had failed in just one of the several convention contests that were won, Ike could not have been nominated. Or, if there had been a single instance of serious defection in the ranks of the Eisenhower delegates, Taft would have been declared the winner. Two-thirds or more of the professional element of the Republican party were working day and night in Chicago for Taft. It therefore seems a miracle that Dewey, for example, could have withstood the effort that was made to take away from him some of the ninety-odd New York delegates that were pledged to vote for Ike.

This book is not a proper place to try to describe in a detailed fashion either the nominating or the election campaigns. However, I shall relate a few human-interest happenings of which I have direct knowledge.

• When Ike left Paris to embark on a political career, he was scheduled to make his first campaign speech in his home town in Kansas. Knowing the importance of the occasion, Ike had planned to write the speech before leaving France, but the pressure of his final NATO duties prevented his doing so. He then planned to do some work on the speech during the flight to the United States, but Ike could not see, and I was to blame for that. I had presented the General with the newest thing in shaving materials, a can of aerosol foam soap, which in his case caused such severe eye irritation that he was almost blinded for about forty-eight hours. Added to this problem was near cyclone weather at Abilene. The result of all this was a huge TV audience watching the few hairs on Ike's head being blown in all directions while his open-air audience deserted him with fear on their faces as he doggedly delivered, in his maiden effort, an uninspiring speech.

• It was proposed to the General that he debate with Stevenson on TV, and, without consulting with anyone, Ike promptly declined. I asked him why, and he explained that one of his very few advantages was being a bit better known than his opponent, as a result of which he thought it would be unwise to share his audience with Stevenson through any media.

• Much to the surprise of everyone, including Ike, Mamie became a real trooper. Because of her delicate health it was not thought she could do much traveling. Once Ike's hat was in the ring, however, she went along most of the time, especially on train trips. Mamie let Ike do all the talking, but she appeared with him on the rear platform as many as fifteen or more times a day, sometimes in a dressing gown before breakfast just to wave to a small group at an unscheduled stop. Her radiant smile got through to the people. The crowds began calling for her if she did not at first appear. Mamie became nationally popular without saying a word.

• One of the surprise campaign developments was the release by Stevenson of a list of his assets, something new for a Presidential candidate to do. We could only assume that the Stevenson managers hoped in some way to embarrass General Ike, and it was a foolish move if they expected to pin a big-money label on our candidate. As I was in possession of all needed data, we were able to release promptly for publication, with Ike's approval, a statement of his assets certified by the accounting firm of Haskins and Sells. The Eisenhower assets added up to less than the net worth of Stevenson.

• About thirty people were invited to gather in Ike's suite in the Blackstone Hotel in Chicago to watch the final balloting on TV. When our man attained the majority vote, he shot out of the room so fast he lost his one-man guard, a Chicago cop. Ike crossed the street and called on Taft, instead of waiting for Taft to come to him. I know for a certainty that this was Ike's own idea.

• Ike developed symptoms of another ileitis attack the night he was nominated. Fortunately, the condition yielded to treatment, which meant mainly determined willpower on the part of the patient. No one disclosed anything about this incident, but for a short period of time it was doubtful if the Republican nominee for President could appear at the convention to indicate acceptance. This incident was especially alarming to me, because I was with the General in Paris when he was stricken with a severe ileitis attack. It was sudden and very painful, but Ike made a quick recovery and was back at work in a few days.

• As soon as we felt certain that Ike was elected President, I was delegated to conduct him from his quarters in the Commodore Hotel to another room on the same floor where he was to meet with Joseph M. Dodge, the prospective Director of the Budget, who needed to be put to work immediately. On the return trip Ike complained of being very tired and said he would like to lie down for a few minutes, something he knew he could not do in his own suite, as it was full of people. Stevenson was refusing to concede defeat, and I happened to notice a small empty bedroom with a key in the door, which was ajar. At my suggestion, Ike climbed into bed, while I locked the door and stood guard outside. Several people stopped to ask me if I had seen General Eisenhower, and I gave negative responses. After about three-quarters of an hour, several bigwigs with worried looks told me that Stevenson had conceded, but they could not find the President-elect. With that I unlocked the door and we found Ike still sound asleep. Within a matter of two or three minutes he was making a talk on TV, and how he was able to do it as well as he did was just one more instance of his remarkable ability to rise to the occasion.

W. Alton Jones

I have forgotten why, but W. A. Jones was always called "Pete" by his friends, and, because he was a popular person, the name Pete Jones was widely known. After the crash in 1929, Pete was moved up to the top post in Cities Service Company. Once it was a certainty that Cities Service would be able to survive the chaotic financial conditions, Pete hired a private railroad car early in 1931 for a long-awaited vacation trip to Augusta. Grant Rice and I were in the party. After our arrival, Bob Jones came over from Atlanta to join us. Since the Augusta National course was not yet completed, we played golf at the Augusta Country Club.

Some four or five in the party were not members of the Augusta National. Pete promptly offered to buy a membership for each of them, and, as they were all readily eligible, Bob and I offered no objection. Pete was exceptionally capable as a money-maker, and extremely generous when he chose to be. Over the years, he several times assisted the club financially. Once he became interested in a project it became an intense interest. Indeed, on more than one occasion we felt obliged to slow him down a bit. In 1953, when the club undertook a number of improvements, costing close to a half million dollars, Pete offered to finance the whole program, but we limited his participation to $50,000. He greatly admired Bob Jones and, after he became acquainted with General Ike, his enthusiasm knew no limits.

In 1951, when there seemed to be a possibility of inducing Ike to become a candidate for the Republican nomination for President, Pete did a remarkable thing. He offered to make available through me as much money as could be used legitimately and legally—the limit to be one million dollars. Up to that time I doubt whether any one individual had ever considered using personal funds politically to that extent. Needless to say, I called on him for only a small part of the million.

Along with his hard-earned wealth Pete had acquired some unusual eccentricities. He invariably wanted to pick up the dinner or bar check, and was always so insistent that we decided it was better to let him have his way without an argument. However, it was a different story on the first tee! Pete was equally determined to get enough strokes to ensure his being a winner on the golf course, no matter how small the stakes. Also, he refused to ever buy a tee, and would tell his caddie to get busy and find some while the matter of

W. Alton Jones.

strokes was being negotiated. The most remarkable of all Pete's eccentricities was his great pride in getting twenty-five or more shaves out of a safety razor blade during the days when blades were relatively cheap and poor in quality. Whenever Pete traveled he would lug along in his suitcase a cumbersome metal razor sharpener of considerable weight. Moreover, he could not understand why anyone should be surprised upon learning that he spent from ten to fifteen minutes each morning cranking that old sharpener.

When the Republican convention was held in Chicago in 1952, I saw to it that a special invitation was extended to Pete. Bob Jones joined me there, but Pete declined. He asked me to keep him posted, but explained that he was so anxious to see Ike nominated he could not bear the strain if he were too close to the action. Also, he was afraid he could not resist the temptation to jump in and try to help. And such an effort, he knew, might be more harmful than helpful.

Pete stood ready with cash or talent to help the Augusta National or the Eisenhower administration at all times, although he never once tried to influence club policy at Augusta, nor to obtain a favor from President Eisenhower.

After Ike left the White House, Pete was still on call whenever Ike wanted him for golf, bridge, or a fishing expedition. It was such a call that resulted in Pete's death in 1962. Ike was in Palm Springs, California, and, instead of using his personal plane, Pete took an airline jet which was faster. The plane crashed almost immediately after takeoff.

This unusual wreck caused much publicity, some part of which was stimulated by the discovery that Pete had approximately $60,000 in currency in his pocket. There was much speculation, of course, as to what Pete intended doing with all that cash. The answer is a very simple one which I can supply. It was a habit of his to regularly carry a large sum of cash, just for the satisfaction of knowing he had plenty of money with him. I once undertook to persuade Pete not to carry so much cash (which always included one or more $10,000 bills) unless he had some good reason for doing so. He replied by telling me he was quite poor as a boy, and never had enough in silver pieces to make a jingle in his pocket. He therefore enjoyed the feeling of knowing that, if he saw something in a store window he wanted, he would have enough money in his pocket to pay for it—and he did not propose to allow anyone to deprive him of that very satisfactory feeling.

Exactly one year earlier, I had taken the same flight with Pete to Palm Springs to join Ike. I was delayed in returning from a trip to Barbados when Pete was killed, otherwise I might have been with him in the plane crash.

Bob Jones the last time he played golf.

Our Club President

Although Bob Jones was obliged to wear a brace on one leg, he tried occasionally for a few years to play golf after his operation in 1948. In one instance he joked about his big accomplishment of making a par on the eighteenth hole. It required three full wood shots, with no pivot and his weight largely on one leg. It also required a chip shot into the hole from off the green. This is a hole that he formerly played with a drive and a seven-iron.

Bob Jones in the special golf cart that gave him added mobility as his illness advanced
The Augusta National President in Perpetuity is here flanked by President Eisenhower,
the author, and Senator Taft.

President Eisenhower presents to Bob Jones the copy he made of a Thomas Stephens painting of Bob based on a photograph taken at the height of his golfing career. The presentation took place in 1954. The painting hangs permanently in the Jones Cabin.

Bob continued to come to Augusta, although not as often as in the past. He enjoyed the special stag parties, especially the Jamboree. He also liked very much seeing President Eisenhower, and it was very apparent that a warm friendship existed between the two.

About one hundred of the members chipped in and engaged Thomas E. Stephens to do a large painting of Bob. Stephens worked from a photograph supplied by Jerry Franklin, taken in 1930, which accurately portrayed Bob as he looked at the height of his golfing career. The painting was presented to the USGA, with all the donors listed on the back of the frame. It was so attractive that many prints were made which can be seen today in numbers of golf clubs. The President liked the painting so much that he made a copy of it and presented it to Bob. This Presidential copy has hung over the fireplace in Bob's cabin ever since, and, I trust, it will always remain there.

Partly, I suspect, because of the President's intense interest in the game of bridge, Bob decided to learn to play. He began by reading a number of the best books on the subject, and eventually he became more knowledgeable bookwise than any of us. The only trouble was that too many of the club members had too little respect for the conventions that had been developed by the experts and, in turn, absorbed by Bob. Nevertheless, Bob got a considerable amount of enjoyment out of the game, and continued to play it beyond the time when his hands were no longer strong enough to shuffle or deal the cards.

As Bob's physical condition gradually deprived him of outdoor excursions, he depended more and more on classical music. Always a lover of good music, he built up a considerable library of recordings, which he would play by the hour while the rest of us were on the golf course.

John W. Herbert

One of the very interesting personalities among the original group of underwriters and club members was Judge Herbert. He was a lawyer by profession from New Jersey, but it is my understanding that he was called Judge as a mark of respect and not because of his having served on the bench. As a young man he was a member of the 1869 Rutgers football team which played against Princeton in the first intercollegiate football game.

The Judge had a large winter home at Augusta, and he was a remarkably strong man both physically and mentally. In addition to playing golf nearly

John W. Herbert.

every day, he entertained considerably at his home. Although he was in his early eighties at the time I first met him, the Judge could play bridge without the aid of glasses. His cronies insisted that it was his regular practice to consume as many cocktails before dinner as anyone present, and then to take several highballs during the evening bridge session.

During July and August, Judge Herbert swam in the ocean, and also played golf at the Maidstone Golf Club at East Hampton, Long Island. I, too, was a member of the same club, and used to see the Judge there occasionally. One day I observed him swimming in the ocean, not just timidly but going on out beyond where the surf was breaking. Because of a strong undertow and a heavy surf that day no one but a young, strong swimmer should have ventured out where the Judge was displaying his aquatic talents. Finally, he timed his exit from the ocean perfectly, coming in on a big breaker to a firm footing. He then sat down on the beach with me to rest. Just then, along came Nicholas Murray Butler, president of Columbia University, who was also a regular winter visitor to Augusta. The conversation between the Judge and Dr. Butler was as follows:

"Doctor, I have never thanked you adequately for that wonderful speech you made at my home last winter in Augusta. With the small company that was present, I really had no right to call upon you, but you responded with just about the most interesting talk I've ever heard."

"Well, well, Judge, I had no idea I did as well as all that. Now, let me see, what did I discuss that made such an impression on you and your guests?"

Said Judge Herbert, after a considerable pause, "Damned if I can remember either, Doctor!"

Not long after this incident, the Judge was celebrating his birthday in his customary fashion, which meant playing thirty-six holes of golf in one day instead of eighteen. This was, of course, long before the day of golf carts. As a result, the Judge developed a blister on one foot. The locker-room attendant urged him to have it looked after by a doctor, but the Judge resented the idea that something as minor as a blister on his foot required medical attention. Blood poisoning resulted, and it finally became necessary to take off the leg. The shock proved to be too much, even for the powerful old judge. And the Augusta National lost one of its truly remarkable characters.

Augusta
National
Golf Club

The General's Augusta Reception

I do not know when the news media learned that President-elect Eisenhower was headed for Augusta. Our club manager knew nothing until I phoned him around 2 A.M. Arrangements were made immediately with the county sheriff and the city and the state police. Once more we called on the Pinkertons to help patrol the unfenced borders of the 365 acres of club property. The Secret Service assembled a considerable number of men at Augusta. But all these efforts produced results that were pitifully small as compared to crowd-control requirements. It seems that, through TV and radio, everyone in the Southeastern part of the country must have learned, hours before his arrival, that Ike was on his way to Augusta. Endless numbers must have jumped into cars with the idea of welcoming their new President.

The South turns out to greet a new President. The twenty-mile route from the airport to the club was similarly lined for President Eisenhower's arrival in Augusta on November 5, 1952, the day following his election.

I saw several huge election rallies during the campaign, but nothing comparable to the number that converged on Augusta. It is close to twenty miles from the airport to the Augusta National Golf Club, and the road was lined all the way on both sides from two or three deep to fifteen deep. The route was, of course, adequately policed only to a very small extent. Often Ike's car had to crawl along, with an occasional complete stop. The only thing that saved the caravan from serious difficulty was Southern hospitality at its best. The people were there not just to greet Ike, but to show him every consideration. At critical corners, when the weight of those in the back rows forced those in the front too far forward to permit safe passage, numbers of people called out to "open up and let him through." It was an exciting but a long and tiring twenty miles, but Mamie and Ike smiled and waved continuously all the way.

During the flight to Augusta I explained to Ike that the club could offer him improved quarters, but he said that, if Bob Jones's cabin was available, he and Mamie would prefer it. I also explained that I was anxious to obtain from Ike a promise that, whenever he visited the club as President, he would never leave its grounds, except to go to church; that I anticipated many invitations of various kinds and that, if he ever accepted one, both he and the club would be in serious trouble. I elaborated by saying that I believed we could pass the word to the community that the President could always rely on Augusta as the one place where he could go for uninterrupted relaxation. Ike understood and readily gave me his word. And the residents of Augusta understood and extended their co-operation.

Those staying at the club during this November 1952 visit included Mamie's mother, Mrs. J. S. Doud; Mrs. John S. D. Eisenhower and her three children, David, Barbara Anne and Susan; Ike's personal physician, Major General Snyder and Mrs. Snyder; together with Sergeant Moaney and his wife, Delores. Jim Hagerty, the press secretary, the staff people, and the news media all stayed at the Bon Air Hotel.

Ike remained until November 18, a stay of two weeks. During that period practically the entire Cabinet was formed. The reason for all possible speed was Ike's desire to go to Korea before the inaugural ceremony. The work was nearly all done by telephone through a small group in New York. Tom Dewey was the only one of importance to come to Augusta. Ike did not like to talk on the telephone, and had me take and make all calls during the first two days, but this procedure slowed things down too much and left too little time for golf, so Ike began doing his own telephoning.

Through Jim Hagerty I invited the entire White House press group to a dinner at the club, at which time I made a brief talk to the effect that the club wanted to help them do their job, within reasonable limits, if they in turn would respect the fact that the Augusta National was strictly a private

General Eisenhower with his favorite caddie, "Cemetery" (Willie Frank Parteet).

club and wished, as nearly as possible, to remain so. A satisfactory arrangement was worked out so that press conferences would be held at the club instead of the hotel. Pictures could be made on special occasions of the President teeing off, but cameras could not follow him. No information about the President's scores would be supplied. No list of club members would be available. Three newsmen could be nominated to play the course, accompanied by a member, with the understanding that they would report their impressions to all others.

Just before Ike's departure for New York, he and his family posed for a group picture which included every person who could be hurriedly assembled who was a part of the club organization, together with those members who were present at the time. This photograph is one of the most treasured possessions of the club.

Having personally financed all expenses of the trip to Augusta of Ike and his staff, I was soon to learn the rather startling news that the United States Government was not authorized to pay expenses of this sort for a President-elect until he takes office. I was partially reimbursed, however, a year or so later by the Republican party treasurer.

The Eisenhower Cabin

Nineteen fifty-three was the year when the most improvements, by far, were undertaken at Augusta. At the suggestion of the Secret Service, a cyclone fence was installed around the entire property. A new pro shop was built, with suitable quarters on the second floor for the President's office.

On April 8, 1953, the club announced that it would construct a new building to be named the Eisenhower Cabin. On November 25, a second press release included the following:

There is an understandable public interest, as evidenced by a number of inquiries concerning the Eisenhower Cabin. Although the Augusta National is a private club, it is glad to respond to this public interest by supplying information that is deemed to be appropriate. First of all, we might explain that the new building would ordinarily be described as a cottage or a house, as it is of sufficient size to accommodate eight persons. We call it a cabin, the same as we do other club units, in keeping with a Southern custom, when ref-

The Eisenhower Cabin.

erence is made to separate smaller buildings used for living quarters and which are apart from the main house. It is owned and will be maintained and operated by the Augusta National. When not occupied by the Eisenhower family, it will be available for use by other club members. Mrs. Robert T. Jones, Jr., wife of the club's President, assumed the responsibility for the interior arrangements.

I might elaborate a bit on the press release by explaining that, when I first told Ike about the proposed cabin, he said he was most happy, but deemed it necessary to stipulate that it must not be set aside for his exclusive use. He wished it to be as available as all the other cabins to all the members. At the time, he also especially requested that I find some way to cause

The First Lady, Easter Sunday, 1953, at Augusta National.

Mrs. John Doud.

Mamie to feel that she was definitely a part of his participation in the Augusta National.

No one was permitted to inspect the building until Mamie and Ike had seen it. Later, they invited the news media to visit the place. Having in mind Ike's admonition to me about Mamie, I stated to several of the reporters that, as we had a fishpond named for Ike, this new structure might be called "Mamie's Cabin" by the members. This name has probably been used more widely than the official title, the Eisenhower Cabin. And the cabin was, in fact, designed principally to please Mamie. Mary Jones and her decorator friend, Mrs. Edith M. Hills, used colors and materials which they knew in advance were Mamie's favorites.

Fifty members of the Augusta National bought building certificates in a total amount sufficient to cover the cost of all the improvements. Each subscriber signed a written agreement that he would not divulge to anyone his participation in this 1953 financing of the new facilities at the club.

In carrying out Ike's wishes, the club found itself in an unusual situation. Men only are members of Augusta National. Then, too, the club has five stag parties each year when members only are allowed on the grounds. This rule had to be overlooked in favor of the First Lady whenever the President and she occupied the Eisenhower Cabin during one of the stag party periods, and Mamie is the only wife of a member who has been permitted to stay at the club during the stag gatherings. Such a situation would ordinarily be expected to bring about friction. I know that it may seem hard to believe, but I have yet to hear a single complaint about this most unusual arrangement, even though it has continued to the present day. The members of the Augusta National are indeed most happy that Mamie feels so much at home in her cabin that she still uses it a large part of the time the club is open each year.

The building might be described as a story-and-a-half construction, plus a basement floor that is not visible from the front because of sloping ground. This bottom floor contains a full-scale kitchen, two bedrooms, and a security room equipped with communication facilities, gunracks, and floodlight switches. The ground floor has a large living room, dining room, small barroom, and two large double bedrooms, each with a dressing room. One was for Mamie and one was named Min's room, for Mamie's mother, Mrs. John Doud, who made a number of trips to Augusta. She was full of fun and very lovable and popular, especially with Colonel Bob Jones, since she joined in with his efforts at song festivals. I do not know the derivation of her cognomen, but Min belied all tales of unpopular mothers-in-law. Ike adored her, so much so that he urged her to spend some time in Paris, at Augusta, and at the White House, all of which she did.

The upstairs floor has a living room and what might be called a bedroom

Mrs. R. T. (Mary) Jones.

and a half on either side. The north side was Ike's bedroom, with a big bed and a mattress as hard as concrete, as was his preference. The connecting half-room was Ike's studio where he spent many hours painting. This little room faced exactly in the right direction for good lighting.

Mamie and Ike provided certain items which are to remain in the cabin. Among these is a painting by Ike of David, his grandson, when David was about five years of age. At the time, David was trying to swing a golf club from a set Bob Jones had had made up for him. Another item that will remain is a painting by Ike of the Augusta National's sixteenth hole.

The two most notable mementos obtained by the club are groups of photographs. One group was assembled for the club by the Air Corps, and shows every one of the twenty-three homes in which Mamie and Ike lived. Most of the buildings, which were, of course, army installations, no longer exist. The other group of photographs in Ike's bedroom are nine pictures of Mamie when she was a young girl. They were gotten together for the Eisenhower Cabin by Mamie's mother.

The First Four
Presidential Visits

Prior to becoming President, Ike made five trips to the Augusta National. As President he made twenty-nine such trips, four of which occurred in 1953. The dates of the first Presidential trip were February 26–March 1; the second occurred April 13–21; the third November 24–29; and the fourth December 26–January 3.

When Ike was elected President, all of us automatically began addressing him as "Mr. President." It was a little awkward at first, but, after a few lapses, mostly by me, we indicated our respect for our friend's high office in a natural and correct fashion.

The President was accompanied by Mamie and her mother on his first 1953 visit to Augusta. On the second and third visits, the President brought Mamie and her mother and also Barbara Eisenhower and her three children, and by the time of the third visit their cabin was ready for them to see and to use. It was the nearest thing to a home they could call their own in their entire married life. Bob Jones and I met them at the airport. We could have driven them by car directly to the back door of their cabin, but we preferred

President Eisenhower with Senator Taft, wearing "Don't ask what I shot" buttons originated by a golf magazine.

them to enter through the front door. This was accomplished by asking them to walk through the clubhouse and then across the lawn. Bowman accompanied them to the front door and departed. We thought it a good idea to leave them to themselves while they had a look at the place. They were genuinely pleased—as happy as two kids. Indeed, I have never known two grown people to show so much emotional enthusiasm over a present.

The fourth and final 1953 excursion to the club included Mamie and her mother, Min, and John and Barbara Eisenhower and their three children.

Beginning with this report, I shall not list the press secretary, the doctor, or the staff people who accompanied the President.

A number of working parties arrived from Washington, one of which numbered nine, on December 31. These groups had to do with the State of the Union report, proposed legislation, and other government business. The President worked an average of five hours each morning and once an entire day. On all other days he played golf in the afternoon and usually bridge in the evening. One important reason for the President's endurance capacity was his ability to dismiss problems and to relax once the day's work was done. I was several times reliably informed that, even during the war, he could, when he had a chance, fall soundly asleep on a moment's notice.

On New Year's Eve I invited all the news media, the Presidential staff, and three members of the Cabinet who were present, to have dinner with me at the club. The President and Mamie had cocktails with us, and then departed to their cabin for a family dinner which included the grandchildren.

The President as Artist

One of our members, William H. Danforth, of Boston, commissioned Thomas E. Stephens to do an oil painting of Francis Ouimet. When finished it was presented to the United States Golf Association. In the portrait, Francis is wearing the traditional red coat of the Captain of the Royal and Ancient Golf Club of St. Andrews, Scotland.

Thomas Stephens is the artist who made a total of twenty-four portraits of President Eisenhower, and he is also the person who caused the President to become interested in trying to paint. As I am the one who recommended Stephens to do the Ouimet portrait, a color photograph of it was sent to me by Stephens. I showed it to the President in 1954 and, as I hoped, he was attracted by the red color in the coat and decided to make a copy of the portrait.

I believe I should explain that the President sat for several portraits while at Columbia University. So far as I know, he had never shown any aptitude or interest in artistic endeavor. I understand that at West Point he had not done very well in making drawings or sketches. But he did become interested in how Tommy Stephens produced the desired shade of color by mixing several other colors. Finally, Stephens made a point, before leaving one afternoon, of inviting his subject to try mixing paints and daubing the end result on blank paper left on the easel. The President was soon trying to paint as well as mix colors. He found it very difficult at first to produce anything that even remotely resembled the thing he was trying to copy. But he discovered that he became completely absorbed in the effort, and therefore mentally relaxed.

While the President always belittled his accomplishments, he became able to make good copies of paintings done by others. In addition, he occasionally produced something original, usually with the aid of photographs, that came close to being comparable in quality to the works of his friend Winston Churchill. Most assuredly, the portraits he did of friends, when presented to those friends, to them possessed quality beyond that of any artist who ever lived.

When the President finished his copy of the Stephens painting of Francis Ouimet, I suggested he give it to the Royal and Ancient Golf Club. He liked the idea but did not dare break his rule not to give a painting to any kind of an organization. I then proposed that he give the painting to Bob Jones, who might see fit to loan it to St. Andrews. All this was done with the aid of Bob's close friend, Roger Wethered, of London, and the picture hangs today in the Royal and Ancient clubhouse at St. Andrews. Moreover, it is likely to always remain there.

Anyone viewing this painting cannot help but notice the word "COPY" printed in bold letters with a paint brush in one corner of the portrait. The President explained to me that he wished to make certain no one was led to think the portrait by D.E. was an original. If I had known he intended to write "COPY" in such big letters, I would have tried to persuade him that smaller letters would suffice.

The President arrived for his first 1954 visit on April 13, bringing the First Lady and her mother, Min. John and Barbara Eisenhower and their three children came over, after a few days, from Fort Benning, Georgia. The President's arrival was delayed one day because of a Monday play-off in the Masters between Ben Hogan and Sam Snead. The President and I had an understanding from the beginning of his club membership that it would not be wise for him to undertake to attend the Masters. His great popularity, I was sure, would create so many problems that it would be difficult to operate the tournament. He understood this because he had once tried to attend a golf tournament in Denver, where all the spectators preferred to watch the General rather than the contestants. After a half-hour of not being able to see any of the action, and realizing that he had totally disrupted the tournament, the General departed. It is a pity that the President could not have seen some of the 1954 Masters, because it was a year of great excitement when an amateur, Billy Joe Patton, of North Carolina, nearly won the tournament.

Upon his arrival in Augusta, the President told us he would remain for twelve days except for a two-day trip, on April 22–23, to Washington and New York and then three stops in Kentucky. At the conclusion of this two-day trip he seemed severely fatigued, and General Snyder noticed a skip in his pulse. The doctor advised the President to go ahead and play golf, but to use one of the fifteen new electric carts the club had acquired (they represented a big improvement, I might add, over the first electric cart we had designed and built for use by Bob Jones).

Despite the McCarthy problem, concern over Indo-China, and necessity of a trip to Augusta by Secretary Dulles, the President looked and acted better than when he first arrived.

Field Marshal Montgomery

The President and Mamie arrived for their second 1954 trip to Augusta on Wednesday, November 24, to spend five days, including Thanksgiving Day. Bob and Mary Jones were present for Thursday evening dinner, the total attendance being about forty. Field Marshal Montgomery had made an appointment to see the President in Washington November 24, but, in order to leave early that day for Augusta, the President brought Montgomery along. He remained for only two days, but, as the President had some unexpected work to do on Thanksgiving Day, he gave me the responsibility of looking after his guest. He did this partly because I had previously met the Field Marshal at NATO in Paris, where he served as a representative of Great Britain.

Montgomery did not play golf and he seemed to prefer to talk rather than to spend much time looking at the club property. It seemed to me that his conversation was mostly of the order of making historical pronouncements. It was all very serious, no light talk at all. I recall very clearly what he said about the political advice he gave General Ike in Paris. I already knew about it, because the General had been so surprised about Montgomery's complete change of heart that he told me about it almost immediately after Montgomery unburdened himself. The two versions were exactly the same, so I shall try to put Montgomery's words down verbatim:

I have several times advised you to always remember that you are a professional soldier, and you should never listen to the political siren. But I now realize I have been giving you bad advice. You must return to the United States and take the Presidency. It's our only chance of salvation for the free world. I know one of your worries is myself. An American must succeed you at SHAPE. You will want Gruenther to be named. But I am, politically speaking, almost indispensable at NATO, and Gruenther is quite inferior to me in rank. I now want to assure you that I'll happily serve under a new American supreme commander despite the matter of rank, if only you will take the the U. S. A. Presidency—and save all of us from disaster.

The Marshal went on to tell me that he had come to the United States principally to deliver just two thoughts to the President, which he had done on the previous day. One was to the effect that General Gruenther was doing a good job at SHAPE and should be allowed to stay, and that he (Montgomery) would remain as long as Gruenther did. The second thought was that the President must stand for re-election in 1956, four years being too short a time to make important headway in solving the world's problems.

I can offer no explanation for some of the surprising comments made by the Marshal in later years. I am able to say, however, that in 1954 he was fervidly devoted to his boss in the main part of World War II and again at SHAPE.

Re-election Proposals

Immediately after the President arrived in Augusta on his second 1954 visit (November 24–29), he told me that he wanted to talk to me at the first opportunity about politics. Friday morning, just after Montgomery left, the President sent for me and disclosed that he was being strongly importuned by three important friends to privately agree to run again in 1956. He wanted my advice on what reply to give. He stated that he was in no mood to make any commitments, private or otherwise, but did not want to say so bluntly. The reason I was consulted was because I knew well all three of the people who had approached him, and could rather accurately gauge the extent of their influence.

The Chief already understood the advantages of having capable friends laying the groundwork for renomination and re-election. Likewise, he knew that, if he told anyone he definitely would not run again, and the word got around, he would then be weakened for the next two years by a lame-duck classification.

In the course of the discussion, the President gave me the impression that his job in Washington was less trying than the one he left in Paris. His position as the head of the American government gave him a better opportunity to achieve some constructive results, as he had a certain amount of authority, plus leeway to act. The NATO assignment and title were impressive, but he was obliged to cater to the whims and fancies of thirteen governments, some of which were headed by temperamental individuals.

In the end, the President decided he would decline, for health reasons, to consider the matter for another year, regardless of the consequences. I felt that this was the right decision, and said so. At my suggestion Ike also decided to make a promise to his friends that he would provide active leadership during the next eighteen months in an effort to revitalize the Republican party.

"Tame" Quail

On December 23, 1954, the President, Mamie, and Mrs. Doud arrived in Augusta for an eleven-day visit. It was the first time the President had ever visited the club without my accompanying him or being on hand to greet him. I reached Augusta one day after his arrival. Perfect golfing weather prevailed ten out of the eleven days.

The President was taking for the first time the "India" drug, rauwolfia, to combat his high-blood-pressure tendency. It had been prescribed by an army heart specialist, according to General Snyder.

Offers to the club of quail-shooting facilities for the President were more numerous than any other. Being concerned that the Chief might have heard of some of these proposals, I suggested one day that he and I go quail shooting on the club property. The idea, of course, was to make it easier for him to keep his promise not to leave the club grounds. As he knew, there were five or six coveys inside our border fences. But on that particular day we couldn't find one bird, although we had the assistance of a hunter and two good dogs.

Early the following day, one of our members gave us fifty quail that he had raised, and these were duly placed in areas near the fairways. The President was invited to try again, and we were careful not to tell him about the special arrangements, thinking he would never know the difference. Promptly several birds were flushed and he shot two of them, but right away he wanted to know who planted the tame birds. I might mention, incidentally, that, when quail shooting, the Chief preferred to use a .410 shotgun.

On Christmas Day, miscellaneous gifts were being passed around. I received an important one, the fourth portrait of myself by the President.

The President returned to Washington on January 2, 1955.

Two More 1955 Visits

The President departed Washington Saturday morning, January 29, for a quick trip to Augusta. He made a sudden decision to go there, and I was the only one asked to accompany him. After two rounds of golf we left Sunday

Byron Nelson, President Eisenhower, Ben Hogan, and Clifford Roberts in the mid-fifties. The two Masters champions had stayed over following the tournament to play with the President at his request.

afternoon in time for the President to attend a 7 P.M. Security Council meeting in Washington which had been hurriedly called concerning Formosa.

The President informed me that he had made a date for a three-day trip to George Humphrey's quail-shooting place in South Georgia on February 10, and that he wanted the same foursome as last year, which meant Pete Jones and myself.

Another visit by the President that year began on Tuesday, April 12, after the close of the Masters. He had typical Eisenhower luck on weather, eight perfect days in a row, and took full advantage of it by playing golf every day. Mamie had a strep throat and could not make the trip.

During this visit, Senator George, Democrat of Georgia, called on the President, who was one of his great admirers. Senator George and Colonel Bob Jones were lifelong friends. When F.D.R. undertook to purge Senator George, I raised some money in New York, at the Colonel's request, to help the Senator. On this occasion, the Senator made a point of once more thanking me. Upon hearing the story, the President said that he wanted to add his thanks to me. The Senator's great speech in favor of the resolution authorizing the defense of Formosa was regarded by the President as the decisive effort.

Bob Windfohr, a member from Fort Worth, Texas, was at the club and met the President for the first time. I recruited Windfohr to help in the Citizens for Eisenhower congressional election efforts in 1954. He declined a title but raised far more money than any other individual. I offered several times to introduce him to the President, but he always replied that he admired the man too much to impose upon his time unnecessarily.

156

"The Colonel"

Bob Jones was not a "Junior," his father's name being Robert Purmetus Jones. I'll explain that Bob's grandfather, of Canton, Georgia, a quite well-to-do owner of a cotton mill, was the original Robert Tyre Jones. He failed to give his name to his oldest son, Bob's dad, who was to become a prominent attorney in Atlanta. Bob knew that his dad, known as "The Colonel," had always been unhappy about not being named Robert Tyre. His dutiful and only son therefore tried to heal the wound by signing himself Robert T. Jones, Jr., and continued to do so as long as he lived. In turn, Bob named his only son Robert Tyre, who properly signed himself Robert Tyre Jones III.

"The Colonel," Bob Jones's father.

Old friends of the Colonel told me about his buying a place out in the country which happened to border one of the fairways of the East Lake Golf Course, near Atlanta. Young Bob was age six or less at the time, and the Colonel's stated reason for the country home was to benefit his son's health. It is true that Bob was not a very robust youngster during his early years, but some wondered if the Colonel's love for the game of golf was not equally as important a reason for the East Lake house as his desire to provide fresh air for his only child.

The Colonel himself has told me about Bob's unusual ability as a child to mimic the peculiarities of the golf swings of various individuals. After a golf game, Bob would respond with alacrity when called upon to entertain the Colonel's foursome as they enjoyed refreshments on the porch of the East Lake home. His mimicry of each member of the foursome was highly entertaining.

Bob was very devoted to the Colonel and treated him with the utmost respect. The Colonel was extremely proud of his son, and was always ready to make any financial sacrifice that might be necessary in order that Bob could travel to golf tournaments as much as he liked. The same thing applied to Bob's wishes about schooling. I doubt if Bob could ever have done anything that pleased the Colonel quite as much as when he once declined a fine home in Atlanta that had been offered to him, as a present, by some well-meaning and generous-minded friends.

Enjoying their very close father and son relationship, both the Colonel and Bob were anxious to spend as much time together as possible. But their inclinations and attitudes were decidedly dissimilar in some respects. The Colonel might properly be described as an extrovert in that he was outgoing and friendly with everyone, including strangers, and was invariably the leader at group gatherings in fun making, storytelling, and singing. Bob on the other hand was definitely a conservative, and on a number of occasions, when the Colonel was unusually rambunctious, was made to feel uncomfortable or even embarrassed.

The place where the Colonel liked best of all to hold forth was in the locker room after golf. He had a deep and powerful bass voice that was suited to "Ol' Man River" and a host of similar songs. Whenever a foursome or more were ready to join in, the Colonel never needed to be coaxed. In fact, he would lead off by himself, after his first bourbon, if no one proposed a song.

The Colonel was one time described as the greatest orator in the South, either standing up or sitting down. With little or no advance notice, he could make an entertaining talk on most any topic. As a teller of humorous tales he had no equal, especially from an endurance angle. One of the happiest and longest evenings I've ever experienced was listening, in turn, to the

Colonel and Grantland Rice. The former told stories and Grant recited poetry.

When I first knew the Colonel, he could play to a handicap of about eight. When he played worse than that it was the fault of the ball, the way some green had been mowed, a divot hole, an unraked bunker, or some bad luck demon. On such days he was prone to express his feelings with swearwords; not just the usual kind of swearing, but original, lengthy, and complex imprecations that were classics. Numbers of people who were regular companions felt disappointed when the Colonel played well, as they always looked forward to a prolonged blast of cussing that they had never previously heard. Bob was one of those who perpetually wondered what his dad might come forth with next. As is well known Bob had a temper of his own in his teens which he learned to control. The difference between him and the Colonel was that Bob became angry only at himself.

One of the incidents I'll always remember concerning the Colonel occurred at the twelfth hole during one of the early Masters Tournaments. We were shorthanded with respect to officials who knew the Rules of Golf, and before play started I asked Bob about using the Colonel. Bob replied, "Go ahead and make him an official if you find it necessary. He is not thoroughly familiar with the rules, but, as you know, Dad is practical and fair-minded, and if he gets involved in some difficult situation, you can count on him to find a practical solution."

Playing the twelfth hole during the last round, one of the old-time champions topped his tee shot, which came to rest on wet ground short of Rae's Creek. The old-timer, playing in Bob's tournament for the first time, was anxious, if he did nothing else, to conduct himself in a proper fashion. Spotting the Colonel with an official badge, he asked for a ruling as to whether he was entitled to a free drop on the basis of casual water. Instead of replying, the Colonel asked, "How do you stand at this point?" "Eighteen over," replied the old-timer. Said the Colonel, "Then what in the goddamn hell difference does it make? Tee the thing up on a peg for all I give a hoot!"

When the club was in the planning stages, the Colonel made it known that he was in favor of the project, and he did so in his usual emphatic fashion. The matter of a charter and the club's bylaws were being discussed. The Colonel broke in with a statement that the legal matters were too important to be entrusted to any inexperienced attorney, or to a hired hand who had no personal interest. Accordingly, he had decided to do it himself.

The Colonel became a great pal of one of our quite popular members, C. J. Schoo, of Springfield, Massachusetts, who was better known as "Schooie." On one occasion the Colonel and Schooie elected to play together as a team in a club contest. On this particular day Schooie could do nothing right. The more he tried, the worse he got. The Colonel, meanwhile, was

Augusta National Golf Club

struggling manfully, in spite of the complete lack of help from his partner, to keep the team from losing all bets. Finally, as they were walking down the eleventh fairway, Schooie, who was feeling very badly, decided to seek a word of encouragement from his partner. He sidled up to the Colonel and said, "At this rate, I know you are likely to decide that I am the worst partner you ever had." The Colonel replied, "Yes, you yellow-bellied old bastard—and you haven't got far to go."

The Colonel, Bob, and I decided to attend the U. S. Open in Philadelphia in 1934, the year when Olin Dutra won. We were given an immense living room and three connecting bedrooms. Numerous friends began gathering in our living room each evening. On Saturday night Bob noticed that the Colonel was missing. After looking in all our bedrooms he suggested that we make a further search in the hotel. First we went to the bar, with no success. Then we peeked in the ballroom, where a large crowd was dancing. Bob took one look and a horrified expression came over his face. He said, "Oh, my God! Go and get him, please!" The Colonel, baton in hand, was directing the orchestra, and at the same time singing the words for the music that he was conducting.

A Denver Gathering

A few of us had started going to Denver for a long weekend when the General was at Columbia University. He asked me to come and bring two more who played golf and bridge. He and Mamie stayed at her mother's home, where we played bridge in the evenings. We three stags stayed at the Brown Palace Hotel. Unless something interfered, the four of us played golf every afternoon at the Cherry Hills Golf Club. After 1952, the group going to Denver grew to six or eight as the President's friendships expanded within the Augusta membership.

Along toward the middle of 1955, the President started talking about getting "the gang" together for a long Labor Day weekend in Denver. He proceeded to make up the list, and when he finished it was four times as long as the previous Denver gatherings. On top of that, he proposed that ladies be included so as to make the party more enjoyable for Mamie. Every name on the list was an Augusta National member.

To the extent possible, I avoided publicity. We merely happened to meet the President for lunch at Cherry Hills, a private club, where we were joined by some of his local friends. I was anxious to avoid the Augusta Na-

Clarence J. Schoo.

Freeman Gosden, onetime Amos of the Amos and Andy radio show, and a popular Augusta National member.

tional becoming a political liability to the President. The basic qualification for membership at our club was a genuine interest in the game of golf, but many members possessed leadership qualities and were, therefore, better known than the average. Naturally, the President was attracted by the leader type, and this usually meant big business. If the news media began calling attention to the President surrounding himself in Denver with Augusta members, it might hurt him, or so I thought. Then, too, several of us were already suffering a bit from some uncomplimentary articles, and were not anxious to give writers unfriendly to the President any extra ammunition. Drew Pearson, the columnist, singled me out for special criticism. This was probably because I often met the President on his arrival at Augusta, and had been mentioned by him as his personal financial adviser. I might add that, when meeting the President upon his Augusta arrivals, the members I chose to accompany me were locals who could not very well be classified as "tycoons" by unfriendly news media. Neither Bob Jones nor I wanted the privacy of our club to be invaded unnecessarily.

Unfortunately, Bob Jones was unable to join us in Denver. He was the sort of person about whom it was almost impossible to invent a plausible smear story, as one of the President's opposition leaders found out a few years later when his unfounded charges boomeranged with a vengeance due to Bob's popularity.

I was, however, several times able to include Freeman Gosden, onetime Amos of the Amos and Andy radio team. Freeman was an Augusta member who was greatly liked by the President. In one sense Freeman took Bob Jones's place, because it would be rather difficult to make the public believe that Gosden would undertake venal designs of any sort by reason of his friendship with the President.

The President appreciated my concern about public relations, but he refused to be worried about what the press might say. So long as they were respectable people, and friends of his, he saw no need for alarm. Maybe this frame of mind was one of the reasons why the voters believed in his rugged integrity and elected him by a margin of 10 million votes.

After some discussion the President reluctantly agreed to reduce his much-too-long list and to then split it into two sections: the first a mixed party, and the second a stag gathering. The first party added up to fifteen members plus twelve ladies, without counting those from Denver who were included, and I am afraid we imposed a bit on the Cherry Hills club. The manager of the Brown Palace Hotel set aside a whole floor, which included the Presidential suite. Present were executives of three large oil companies, one liquor company, one well-known capitalist, and the heads of the three largest U.S. manufacturing companies in their respective fields. This was, of course, just too much to go unnoticed, and consequently the news media rather widely advertised our presence. Then, too, the left-wingers wanted to know why the President chose people of wealth for playmates. Several of our group greatly regretted this adverse publicity, but, if the President knew about it, he said nothing. It was his practice, I might point out, to waste little time in reading the papers or magazines, and he seldom looked at TV. He preferred to go through the special news items selected by his staff for his attention.

The stag group assembled Thursday, September 15, and departed the following Monday. It totaled fourteen Augusta members, including the President, and included six big business names. But the presence of Francis Ouimet and Charlie Yates helped to make us a little less vulnerable to unkind news comment. One labor publication did, however, note the absence of any labor leaders among the President's pals.

Heart Attack

Shortly after the conclusion of the golf party, the President left Denver for a fishing trip at the camp of a long-time personal friend, Axel Nielsen, situated about 8,500 feet above sea level.

On September 24, 1955, it was announced that the President had suffered a heart attack during the previous night. Mrs. Ann Whitman, Ike's personal secretary, phoned the particulars to me in New York. General Snyder and another army doctor from Fitzsimons Hospital were in charge. In the absence of the press secretary, his assistant, Murray Snyder, issued General Snyder's statement. Colonel Mattingly, of Walter Reed Hospital, was en route to Denver. He had examined the President only a few weeks previously and found him to be in good health.

The illness of one person probably never before caused such great repercussions world-wide. The press coverage included all details available. There are a few circumstances and happenings known to me, however, that might be worthy of mention at this time. Accordingly, I shall recite them and comment briefly.

The President told Mrs. Whitman that he retired quite early the previous night at the camp, slept exceptionally well, and had breakfast at 5:30 A.M. He arrived at his Denver office at 7 A.M., and, after about two and a half hours of work, left for the golf club. The President played twenty-seven holes of golf with the professional Rip Arnold, stopping after eighteen holes for a hamburger with two large slices of raw onion. Rip reported that the President was playing well but complained that his lunch did not agree with him.

Herbert Brownell and Sherman Adams were in Europe. Lucius Clay had just undergone major surgery upon his return to New York from the Denver stag party. When I learned that no civilian heart specialist had been called in, I felt a serious mistake was being made and contacted several top administration people, including George Humphrey and Jerry Persons. Finally, Dr. Paul White, the noted heart man, was dispatched from Boston, much to the relief of the general public. Dr. White turned out to be a good public relations man as well as a good doctor. In due course he indicated that the President would recover sufficiently to continue actively in public life.

It was only four months afterwards, I might mention, that the President returned the compliment by sending Dr. White to see me when I experienced a mild attack of the same order.

It was more than a coincidence that Lucius and the President, long-time friends, should be knocked out at the same time. Neither one knew how to take it easy during working hours, nor could they just loaf even when an opportunity presented itself. They had to be actively doing something every wakeful moment. The President, particularly, never liked to sit down, even at a meeting. He had to get up and walk about as he thought or talked. He had to work or play constantly, unless he was completely tired out. More than once after eighteen holes of golf I've wanted badly to stretch out and rest, only to have Sergeant Moaney come and tell me as I stepped out of the shower, "The Boss is ready to play bridge."

Looking back, I can easily see that, after the strain of World War II, General Eisenhower was richly entitled to take life easy, assuming it was possible for him to unwind to that extent. His job at Columbia University was enough to keep him sufficiently occupied. Instead, he was brought back to Washington to help place the four armed services under one top command. Next, he was called upon to help organize the North Atlantic Treaty Organization (NATO) and to serve as Commander of Supreme Headquarters Allied Powers, Europe (SHAPE). Subsequently, he was elected President of the United States. These postwar assignments took their toll despite his being a remarkably rugged physical machine. The first signal of serious trouble was the ileitis attack in Washington.

In this connection, Ed Eisenhower, Ike's brother, once told me that he suffered the same kind of attacks for several years. At the time he was quite active as a lawyer, representing clients in labor-contract negotiations. On his doctor's advice he withdrew from the stress and strain of this part of his law practice. The ileitis attacks ended and Ed enjoyed good health for the balance of his life.

The next danger signal was the General's ileitis attack in Paris. Then came the high blood pressure. In the President's case there seems to have been a connection between stomach upsets and heart strain, not only with his illness in Denver, but in subsequent heart attacks. After only a few years in the White House the President had lost his ability to shut everything out of his mind and take brief naps. His intense concentration on the business of hitting a golf ball, or playing a hand of bridge, represented for him quite complete relaxation. The same was at least equally true with respect to the time he devoted to his painting.

In response to a summons from the Denver White House I arrived in Denver on October 19, where it was announced I was to be the first one, aside from his family, to pay a visit to the President. Before seeing him on October 20, I was briefed by three doctors, General Snyder, Colonel Pollock, and Colonel Powell. The principal idea was to avoid serious subjects, particularly political topics. However, the first thing the President asked me, once the nurse had departed, was, "Do you think George Humphrey would be a candidate for President if we all asked him to run?" I answered by saying that George and I had initiated a gentlemen's agreement which required a moratorium on political discussion involving the 1956 Presidential nomination until the Chief was recovered and had taken his place at the head of the table. The President said he was happy to know of the understanding and would support it.

A Second Term

The President and Mamie arrived in Augusta on April 9, 1956, the day following the end of the Masters, for a one-week stay. A year had gone by since their last trip to Augusta. They were accompanied by Mrs. Doud, John, and David.

There was little doubt in my mind about the President accepting the nomination for another term. The principal reason was the lack of a good candidate who could win to take his place. He had previously asked my opinion, but he brought up the subject again in Augusta. It was my thought that, if the doctors said all right, he might be better off to continue as President. This was on the theory that he would suffer torturously on the sidelines watching everything go down the drain he had so far accomplished if a socialistically minded man should succeed him. Then, too, he was the only Republican who had a chance to win control of the House and the Senate.

Once more the Chief ran through his list of seven Republican Presidential possibilities, but in the end he admitted that he had been unable to develop any considerable amount of enthusiasm for a single one. Worst of all, the experienced politicians he had consulted assured him that the two men he rated highest in ability had no chance whatsoever of being elected.

Another Crisis—and
a Quick Recovery

On June 6, 1956, General Snyder telephoned me in New York to inform me the President had suffered another ileitis attack and was to undergo surgery within a few hours. The type of operation is called ileo-transverse colostomy. The President's heart behaved all right, the operation went well, and once more we were treated to another display of amazing recuperative powers. The Chief was out of the hospital and back at work somewhat sooner than was at first thought possible. Once more, everyone began beating the drums for a quick nomination at the San Francisco Convention in August.

Everyone seemed to think that the President made an excellent acceptance speech in San Francisco. I was further reassured when he proposed a short golf outing at the Cypress Point Golf Club before returning East. About twenty responded, mostly Augusta National members. The President surprised all of us by playing eighteen holes a day for the three days, and got in a little bridge as well. I am sure Lloyd's of London would have given long odds, less than two months earlier, against all these miraculous occurrences ever taking place.

The Republican candidate and I made a firm date, the same as in 1952, to leave for Augusta the day after the election, regardless of the outcome. The only difference was that I did not need to charter a plane.

Some ten or twelve of us were with the President in Washington the night of the election. He did not, however, go on to Augusta the next day as planned: one reason was war clouds, and the other was the need to cause some studies to be made promptly on the congressional and senatorial results. The Chief referred to his personal triumph as being a hollow victory in view of losing in both houses of Congress.

The President was able to go to Augusta on November 26 and remain until December 13. Mamie and Min accompanied him. With excellent weather, he played golf every day, in addition to hitting practice balls. Then,

Charles R. Yates, the long-serving Masters official who in 1938 won the British Amateur Championship.

The tree at number seventeen which gave General Eisenhower so much trouble.

too, he held good cards at bridge. The President looked and acted as strong as when he first came to Augusta.

A club governors' meeting was scheduled during the President's stay, and I reminded him that he was a governor and suggested he attend. This he was glad to do. The Augusta National has a large board, so being a governor serves as an excuse to go to the club. Additionally, every member who is on hand is invited to attend board meetings. Sensing that this meeting, with a President of the United States actively serving on the board, would become a historical occasion, every member on the grounds was present. The total was more than forty.

Charles R. Yates had just been made club secretary to succeed Fielding Wallace. I opened the meeting by asking the new secretary to rise and "Advise us what is on the agenda for today." Good-natured Charlie looked perplexed and finally blurted out, "Why, nothing at all, Mr. Chairman!" When quiet was restored, I made the mistake of seriously trying to explain why things had gone wrong in the club's effort to substitute a new type of green on the eighth hole. The President immediately broke in with, "Explanations will not be submitted, because none will be acceptable." After the laughter at my expense had subsided, the President went on to tell us about the origin of his comment—an old army order.

The President once again took over by announcing, in a most serious vein, that the chief torment and concern of his life was the big pine tree located in the left center of the seventeenth fairway. He stated that it acted as a magnet to his drive. No matter where he aimed, he always hit this tree. The President went on to demand that the offending tree be chopped down forthwith. At this point, I decided the only way to protect the club's property would be to declare the meeting adjourned, which I did.

Somewhere in between the tomfoolery we did manage to attend to one important piece of business. At my request, James M. Hull had prepared a resolution eulogizing Colonel Bob Jones, who had recently died. I showed it to the President before the meeting and, as he rewrote a part of it, he is recorded as the author. He also is the one who proposed the resolution. It reads as follows:

BE IT RESOLVED *by the Board of Governors of Augusta National Golf Club that we record the death of our beloved friend and associate, Robert P. Jones, with great sorrow and a deep sense of personal loss to us and to the entire membership of the Club.*

By the genuine warmth of his personality, the unaffected charm of his companionship and the many fine qualities of ability and integrity which were the dominant traits of his character, he won the admiration and affection of his fellow members and his visits to the Club were always welcomed and enjoyed.

As one of the planners and developers of the Augusta National Golf Club, who served continuously as a member of the Board of Governors and as a member of the Executive Committee, his vision and initiative, his wise counsel and his constructive work contributed greatly to the prized fellowship of this Club. He unfailingly supplemented and supported the incomparable leadership and invaluable services of his distinguished son, the honored President of this Club, Robert T. Jones, Jr. To them, we owe a great debt of gratitude and thanks which can never be repaid.

BE IT FURTHER RESOLVED *that these resolutions be recorded in the Minutes of the Meeting of the Board of Governors held this 8th day of December, 1956, and that copies be sent to Mrs. Robert P. Jones and to Mr. Robert T. Jones, Jr., as a sincere, although inadequate, expression of the high esteem, the cherished friendship and the appreciative sentiments set forth therein.*

The President's final 1956 visit was a two-day stag affair, December 28–30.

George M. Humphrey

The President arrived at Augusta on the morning of February 2, 1957, and left in the afternoon of the following day. He played one round of golf each day. He also attended a special dinner Saturday night given in honor of a member. A half-dozen spoke but the President was not called on at all, and partly for that reason he enjoyed himself immensely.

The President and Mamie arrived again in Augusta on April 18. He remained until April 30, although Mamie returned to Washington on the twenty-seventh. Shortly after they arrived, Secretary of the Treasury George Humphrey and his very lovable wife, Pam, joined them for a four-day visit. It was their first appearance at the Augusta National and a happy occasion for everyone.

The President arrived with a cough, but, after thirteen days of warm sunshine, he left without the cough and looked the picture of good health. General Snyder commented that the President responded better to this vacation than any other since he had known him.

The close relationship between George Humphrey and the President makes George a good subject for special attention, and I shall try to do him justice.

The Secretary of the Treasury became the top favorite of the President for a combination of reasons, one being exceptional ability and another his talent for reducing complicated problems to simple terms and solutions. Additionally, George was a rugged and plain-spoken sort of person who was personally popular with most everyone with whom he came in contact. The President mentioned to me several times how often other members of the Cabinet liked to consult with Humphrey. The only trouble with George was the President's problem of trying to make a pal out of him. Unfortunately he was not a golfer, and, as a bridge player, he was not even entitled to a mediocre rating. George had played very little bridge and he lacked natural card sense.

The President was determined to somehow make a bridge player and golfer out of George. He began by warning him about the dangers of riding a horse, George's regular practice. Next, I noticed that George was often included at the bridge sessions in the White House. No matter if George repeated the same error the same evening, the President would patiently explain the second time just why and how to correct the mistake. For his part,

George M. Humphrey.

George would earnestly endeavor to understand and to improve because he was devoted to the President.

When the problem arose of making George a golfer, the President enlisted my assistance. In 1954 I bought and sent to George in Washington all the necessary equipment—not just a set of clubs and bag, but everything imaginable, including golf balls, a golf glove, tees, cap, rain suit, umbrella, sweater, spiked shoes, socks, and a miniature library of golf instructional books. I received such a warm letter of thanks from the prospective golfer that I expected some results, but nothing happened until 1957, when the President was at the club and, by agreement, George also. Moreover, George brought his elaborate set of clubs and immediately undertook to learn how to hit a golf ball. He did well for a sixty-eight-year-old beginner. On his last day at the club, George scored a bogie five on a par-four hole, and we felt sure he was bitten hard by the golf bug, so much so that he was invited to be a member of the club, which he promptly accepted. Bob Jones and I had agreed that no governmental official would be taken in as a member, so that the place could remain a haven for the President. But, in this instance, the Chief wanted George to be taken in and, also, we were aware that George would soon be leaving Washington.

The press secretary called a meeting of the news media at the club, on November 17, 1957, at which time the President and George Humphrey were on hand. The following press release is self-explanatory:

THE WHITE HOUSE
Augusta, Georgia

Following is an exchange of letters between the President and Clifford Roberts, chairman of the Executive Committee, Augusta National Golf Club—and Mr. Roberts and George M. Humphrey of Cleveland, Ohio, member of Augusta National Golf Club and former Secretary of the Treasury.

The President's letter to Mr. Roberts follows:

July 25, 1957

Dear Cliff:

Last evening I gave a farewell stag dinner for George Humphrey. Those present were members of the Cabinet and a few staff officers. In addition, we had George's successor, Bob Anderson.

During the evening there was only one man who felt impelled to "rise to his feet" to make a talk. That was George. And his effort took a strange turn.

He described at some length his recent visit to the Augusta National. The incident or occasion that had impressed him most was a Sunday morning visit we had sitting in the golf shop. I do not recall the identity of those present, but George and I were sitting with three or four others scattered around the shop.

The informality of the occasion, the free exchange of views among good fellows with no pressures or exhortations marring the quality of a pleasant conversation left an indelible imprint on George's mind. As we left the golf shop that morning, I remember him remarking, "The greatest deliberative body this country has ever known was the old country store. This morning's experience was almost a replica of the thousands of such meetings that took place only a few years back, sitting around a round-bellied stove, and with a cracker barrel always handy from which a man could extract a soda cracker to nibble on while he listened."

George recited this whole experience at some length to the dinner guests and said that from the moment he had such a pleasant conversation in the golf shop, he had determined to provide a cracker barrel for the Augusta National. This he did, and he brought the result to the dinner and told the party about it.

The barrel has been made on special order. It is beautifully bound with brass hoops and has a lid which is fastened to the keg itself by a chain. On the side is a little brass plate which reads: "The Eisenhower Cracker Barrel, presented to the Augusta National Golf Club by G. M. Humphrey, in 1957." George of course intends that the cracker barrel shall be actually installed in the golf shop and he says that it is your responsibility to keep it properly supplied with crackers.

Of course you would know nothing about cracker barrels and country stores. I understand you were raised as a city boy. But the glee that at least two-thirds of the dinner guests expressed upon hearing George's description of the cracker barrel, the sand box and the hot stove, provided ample evidence that most Americans are well acquainted with the old grocery story discussions.

I suggest also that on the basis of this letter you write to George, now in Cleveland, and tell him that you are looking forward to seeing his gift at the Augusta National.

As ever,

D.E.

The Eisenhower Cracker Barrel, presented to the club by the President's friend and colleague, George M. Humphrey, in 1957.

Mr. Roberts' letter to Mr. Humphrey follows:

July 29, 1957

Dear George:
The President has informed me of the White House unveiling by you of the Eisenhower Cracker Barrel and I hasten to make appropriate response on behalf of the Augusta National. To this end I have, by making use of the telephone, risked being accused of violating the spirit of your project. But by utilizing this modern instrument to confer with Bob Jones, I am able to promptly say to you that your barrel now has a home.

*Over the years the Augusta National had declined to accept golf librar-
ies, Halls of Fame and a museum. But a Cracker Barrel is something we can
enthusiastically embrace because we understand it and like it and everything
it implies. May its sturdy staves and strong bindings long offer the munching
material for companionable gatherings and salty observations.*

*In humble gratefulness I accept the role you assign to me. Henceforth,
my personal fortune and my best efforts shall be dedicated to measures designed to keep our Cracker Barrel well filled at all times.*

*I join with the President in suggesting the fall of the year as the proper
season for the installation of the Cracker Barrel. Its exact location in the
Golf Shop requires study by all of us.*

Long live the donor of the Eisenhower Cracker Barrel.

Most sincerely yours,
Clifford Roberts

The President wrote me a second letter on July 31, a very personal letter,
which was not made available to the news media. My only excuse for making
it a part of this book is to illustrate the warmth of the Chief's praise when
someone performed in a manner that met with his approval. Such praise
came only, however, on rare occasions.

July 31, 1957

Dear Cliff:

*I have a sense of astonishment that in spite of some years of intimate as-
sociation and friendship with you, I have never truly appreciated your ability
to mix humor, exposition and a bit of philosophy into a "thank you" note in*

such fashion as to make it a piece of literature.

*By this I mean to say that your letter to George is a masterpiece. I sin-
cerely hope that the Cracker Barrel ceremony can come off as planned, and
that you, George and I, together with a substantial portion of the "gang,"
can all attend.*

*One piece of incidental news. Yesterday I played nine holes and hit the
ball straighter and farther than I have since I was ill last year. At least I was
good enough so I am planning to go out tomorrow to try again.*

As ever,
D.E.

The President's letter to me, as released to the press, clearly illustrated
his great liking for George Humphrey and the importance he attached to any-

thing proposed by him. It seemed to me, too, that the proposal made by George at the White House dinner revealed the nature of the man and his philosophy better than any description by another person.

I should add that the staves of the club's cracker barrel are timber that came from the White House when it was being rebuilt in the 1940s.

J. Gordon Gilfillan

No history of the Augusta National could ever be complete unless it described Gil Gilfillan, of Le Roy, New York, who was one of the founders of the club. Gil had been spending the winter season at the Bon Air Vanderbilt Hotel for a period of years prior to the time our club was formed. He was not very skillful as a golfer, but was always available to make up a foursome.

Gil began his business career working for a family that sold patent medicines. The products were widely distributed by horse-drawn wagons. Each wagon was driven by a trained salesman, who was sometimes called the barker. Gil was a star performer who was prepared to stop and reel off his sales pitch wherever he could get the attention of a group of three or more people. On rainy days at the Augusta National it was never difficult to induce Gil to entertain us in his onetime role as a barker. Re-enacting the sale of remedies capable of curing anything from a headache to fallen arches seemed to be just as enjoyable to him as it was to us.

The owners of the patent medicine business developed a product called Jello, which became so profitable that the medicine business was sidetracked. Gil was a hired hand who never owned any stock, but he was made president of the Jell-O Company. He earned this title, and a good salary, because he was the best barker. Further, he retained the title until it was time for him to retire.

When it came to golf, Gil was easygoing as regards the negotiations about strokes and stakes. But he worked out a system whereby he seldom lost any money playing the game. It was not too difficult to defeat him, but collecting any money was another matter. Let us assume that you, the reader, have won your individual match against Gil and you are at the eighteenth tee. You now must play him double or quits on the eighteenth hole. Also, assuming you win, you must run the gauntlet of three more double or quits. One involves flipping a coin, heads or tails. If you have won again, you now cut the deck for high card. Finally, if you are still alive, you face the final hurdle of spinning a wheel for the high number.

Gil did lose, of course, once in a great while, and when this happened it was the chief topic of conversation for days on end. The other side of the coin is that Gil had the fun of doing his opponents out of their hard-earned winnings over a considerable period of time.

Most golfers make a friendly bet and, if they lose, they pay up and that's the end of it. But when Gil lost, that was just the beginning of the most important part of the contest. I think he got more fun out of golf bets than anyone else I know. And why did everyone fall for his double or quits series? That's easy to answer. Gil was such an agreeable and likable old barker that no one ever thought of refusing to go along with his proposals.

The Little Rock Crisis

I spent a few days at the Newport naval installation in September 1957, where the President and Mamie were vacationing. After playing one round of golf at the only nearby golf course, I could more easily understand why the Augusta National was so greatly appreciated by the Chief. The Newport course was operated as a private club, at least during the summer months, but there were five places where a golf hole bordered a public road. This meant that the President was playing exhibition golf five times each round for a considerable number of sightseeing spectators. He remarked to me how much he wished the Augusta National could be operated on a year-round basis.

Middle East problems, plus the Little Rock crisis, made the President at that time a commuter between Washington and Newport. The surprise decision by the Supreme Court requiring integrated schools gave the President the responsibility of enforcing a most difficult ruling. He wondered out loud to me if he would be welcome in the future in Augusta. I tried to reassure him, but I myself had misgivings, as the sending in of federal troops was, for a period, like starting up another Civil War. The unpopular consequences were pristine clear in advance to the President, but his sense of duty to enforce the law made his action mandatory. Moreover, he knew, from an international point of view, the importance of an image of Uncle Sam respecting the legal rights of the colored races.

When the President and Mamie arrived in Augusta on November 15, 1957, for a six-day stay, the mayor, the mayor-elect, the county commissioner, and a dozen other prominent local leaders were on hand at the airport. They constituted a special welcoming committee. I was especially pleased that the son of the publisher of the Augusta *Chronicle* was on hand as the representative of his father, who was critically ill. The Eisenhowers' presence was widely publicized by radio and television, as well as by the newspapers. A number of individuals took action in various ways to discourage any tendency toward an unpleasant incident. While there were relatively few people along the motor route to the club, no open unfriendliness was evidenced.

I made it a point to go to Augusta well ahead of the President's planned arrival, and at first I was shocked and discouraged by the bitter attitude of the local people. The area newspapers that heretofore had supported the President enthusiastically were attacking him in the news columns and editorially.

The President had told me in Washington that he was concerned about making the trip to Augusta for fear he might transfer some of his personal unpopularity in the South to the Augusta National. The club became a party to the issue, because I used the argument with those who were open-minded that any discourtesy to the President would hurt the club and in turn harm the Masters Tournament. James M. Hull, an Augusta member, deserves much credit for his help in organizing the welcoming committee.

I am happy to say that in a matter of months rather than years President Eisenhower's popularity in the Augusta area was restored, not by any particular action on his part but rather by the good common sense of the people. I'll go so far as to say that, if Augusta had been given another ballot-box opportunity, its people would have (for the third time) voted in favor of our distinguished club member.

Stroke

I was in a New York hospital for an annual checkup on November 25, 1957, when a television announcement was repeated to me which ended by saying that the President was to be re-examined by a team of specialists to determine his condition. As I could not get through the switchboard to anyone in the White House office, I asked for Mrs. Eisenhower's secretary, Mrs. McCaffrey, who promptly connected me with the First Lady. Mamie conveyed the whole story to me by saying, "Ike has suffered the same thing which happened to Gummy" The "Gummy" referred to by Mamie was W. Montgomery Harison, an Augusta member who had recently experienced a light stroke which had impaired his speech.

Shortly afterwards, General Snyder told me there was an outside chance that the President had suffered only a spasm induced by a chill, in which case he would quickly recover. But Snyder went on to say that complete and prolonged rest might be required. The General then added that the President had been pushing himself too hard and, being unable to unwind, had failed to derive any benefit from his last trip to Augusta.

For me it was a repetition of the same thing that occurred after the Denver heart attack, meaning lots of phone calls from the President's friends, including several from Europe, who thought I might be a source of accurate information. Another repeat occurrence took place shortly afterward in Gettysburg when I saw the President. He had surprised everyone by going to church in Washington with Mamie on Thanksgiving morning and then driving to Gettysburg Friday. I had a visit with the President Saturday. Once again it had been suggested to me that I refrain from discussing any serious subjects.

Two neighbors were present when I arrived. Just as soon as they departed, the President immediately started to tell me about his stroke. In this instance, I suspected he might feel the need to unburden himself to someone, so made no effort to stop him. He hesitated or groped for a word only occasionally.

The President explained that he had experienced no pain; how he first fumbled and dropped his glasses in his office and was unable to recover them; how he could think clearly but couldn't talk coherently to Ann Whitman when she responded to his buzz; and how cold his feet got when they put him to bed.

The President then started to discuss a decision he needed to make in a matter of days. He was scheduled to go to Paris for a special NATO conference, and the question was whether he should go or send the Vice President. At that point I broke in with the suggestion that he not consider the problem at all until the medical people gave him their final report on his future capabilities. He did pursue the subject briefly, however, by saying that his preference was to let the Paris trip become the test of his ability to continue in office. He added that we were going through a perilous period, and he was possibly better able to keep open warfare from breaking out than anyone else.

After the medical reports were in, the President decided to go to Paris. Howard Snyder complained to me afterward that, when he urged that Nixon be sent, the President responded with, "I am the one who will decide what must be done." The faithful doctor was really elated about the prospect of the President "getting away with it," but he thought the gamble to be an unnecessary one.

The Nine-Hole Par-Three Course

As is well known, Bob Jones selected the architect and then assisted him in designing our golf course. I like to lay claim to similar fame with respect to our nine-hole par-three course. Some of our members, I must confess, disrespectfully referred to it as a "Tom Thumb course." Others thought of my pet project as a waste of money. But this new facility, when completed, was so very attractive and useful that it became even more popular than any of us who originally supported it ever thought possible.

The Augusta National par-three course was built in 1958. George W. Cobb, the architect, and I set out to develop something outstanding as a practice facility and an enjoyable golfing diversion. The first tee is only about one hundred yards from the clubhouse. Total yardage is 1,075, the shortest hole being 75 yards and the longest 160.

A decision to construct a three-and-one-half-acre pond is responsible for much of the beauty of the course, and also for the fun of playing it. Six of the holes either border the pond or require a carry over its waters. The pond is located just above "Ike's Pond," the view of which adds to the charm of the area. Both ponds are fed by a dependable spring which borders the course to the north. While the nine holes plus the pond occupy only about ten acres, there are another fifteen bordering acres that provide much color from flowering trees, plants, and wisteria vines. Some of the best specimens of longleaf pine trees on the club's property complete a very pleasing nature-made background for the golf holes.

Many of our members use the par-three course in the morning to warm up prior to playing the big course. The oldsters who do not care to undertake the regular course every day find the little layout a pleasant change. The Masters participants regard it as a very worthwhile practice facility, almost the entire field playing around the nine holes at least once each day during the tournament practice rounds. On Wednesday, the day preceding the start of the Masters, a tune-up event is staged on the par-three course. Only trophies and souvenirs are offered as prizes, but the competition is keen and the contest attracts large numbers of patrons. It is, in fact, much more popular than the clinics, driving and iron-play contests, and trick-shot entertainment staged on Wednesdays prior to the existence of our par-three course.

We are convinced that the principal reason our short course is popular with all types of players is that it is not too easy. It is a good test of short-

181

Augusta
National
Golf Club

game accuracy, in which hazards of one type or another are encountered on each hole. Every green is undulating to some extent, and three are severely contoured.

Par-three courses have become very popular in the United States since ours was built in 1958. We are informed by an authoritative source that there are now in this country approximately 1,440 par-three golf courses and 900 "executive"-type courses, the latter being presumed to mean principally par-three holes. Based on our experience, we would not hesitate to recommend to anyone who is building a new regulation-size golf course that a separate short course be included. As little as seven or eight acres will suffice for nine par-three holes.

In addition to the advantages previously cited, a par-three facility at most clubs offers an opportunity for youngsters to learn the game. We do not have any junior members at the Augusta National, but there are numbers of oldsters who consider our par-three course to be quite essential. More often than not, some of them prefer to play it.

1958 and 1959 Presidential Visits

The President made five trips to Augusta in 1958, the dates being January 31–February 2, March 22–23, April 11–13, April 26–28, and November 20–December 3.

The first visit occurred after the President and Mamie attended the funeral in Kansas City, Missouri, of the President's elder brother, Arthur. The Chief played golf for the first time since his stroke, but only for a partial round the first day, as it was cold and windy. His next three visits were even briefer, and Mamie understandably skipped all of them. Flying had always made her quite uncomfortable, and there was no point in her enduring distress by traveling for such short stays. During the thirteen days in November, Mamie, Min, John, Barbara, and the three grandchildren all went along. John was also present in March.

To me, the most remarkable part of all five of the 1958 trips was how well the President looked and acted.

The following year the President made four trips to Augusta, as follows: April 7–21, October 21–25, November 10–23, and December 27–January 4.

Mamie made all the visits except the short one in October. In April the Chief was obliged to make a one-day trip back to Washington. Otherwise,

General Eisenhower's painting of his grandson, David, when David was about five years of age. The youngster is attempting to swing with a golf club from a set Bob Jones had made up for him.

The portrait of General Eisenhower which hangs over the fireplace in the Trophy Room.

The Trophy Room portrait of Clifford Roberts by Thomas Stephens.

The Thomas Stephens portrait of Bob Jones that hangs in the Trophy Room.

Clifford Roberts on the occasion of his eightieth birthday introduces the four senior Augusta National staff members, from left to right, Robert Reynolds, Ben Smalley, John Milton, and Bowman Milligan.

Clifford Roberts' eightieth birthday dinner party on May 10, 1974.

The 1975 Jamboree.

The 1975 Masters Club Dinner. Clockwise around the tables from the bottom of the long table: Jack Burke, Jr., Claude Harmon, Billy Casper, Doug Ford, Herman Keiser, Bob Goalby, Tommy Aaron, Charles Coody, Arnold Palmer, Byron Nelson, Clifford Roberts, Gary Player, Gene Sarazen, Jack Nicklaus, Jimmy Demaret, Sam Snead, Cary Middlecoff, Ralph Guldahl, Art Wall, Jr., Henry Picard, Gay Brewer and George Archer.

The dinner for the players at the 1975 Masters. FIRST TABLE: (left) George R. Wislar, Hugh Baiocchi, Eugene M. Howerdd, Jr., Victor Regalado, Sam M. Fleming, Maurice Bembridge, Joseph C. Dey, Bob Charles, Isaac Grainger, Henry C. Poe, (right) J. Haley Roberts, Brian Henning, Dale Hayes, John L. Murray, Jr., Lu Liang-Huan, Peter Menk, Bobby Cole, Robert W. Berry, Graham Marsh. SECOND TABLE: (left) Theodore N. Danforth, Frank Chou, Masashi Ozaki, Phillip May, George R. Cockburn, Bruce Devlin, David M. Lilly, (right) David L. Davis, William T. Gary, Isao Aoki, E. Val Hastings, Roberto de Vicenzo, Gerald H. Achenbach, Bruce Crampton, Hord W. Hardin, Gerald H. Micklem. HEAD TABLE: Tony Jacklin, Gary Player, Clifford Roberts, Sir John Carmichael, Harton S. Semple, Deane R. Beman.

The dinner for the amateur contestants at the 1975 Masters. FIRST TABLE: (left) John W. Fischer, Jr., Charles H. Davis III, Robert W. Berry, W. M. Miller, John M. Winters, Jr., George Burns III, Gerald H. Mickelm, (right) Hugh Sprot, P. J. Boatwright, Jr., David L. Davis, K. R. T. Mackenzie, John P. Grace, Charles R. Coe, John L. Crist, Jr. SECOND TABLE: (left) Arthur W. Rice, John S. O. Haslewood, James R. Hand, Curtis Strange, Joseph C. Dey, John D. Ames, Eugene S. Pulliam, (right) Frank B. Edwards, Gordon H. Ewen, Jerome K. Franklin, Will F. Nicholson, Jr., Gary Koch, Alan Turner, Howard J. Carey, Jr., John Williams. THIRD TABLE: (left) Elbert S. Jemison, Jr., William H. Lane, G. Jeffrey Agate, Richard L. Siderowf, Kenneth Cameron, Isaac B. Grainger, (right) John T. Lupton, Craig Stadler, William D. Kerr, Harry W. Easterly, G. R. Cockburn, Jerome K. Pate, Sir Peter Allen. HEAD TABLE: Gerald H. Achenbach, Charles R. Yates, Sir John Carmichael, Clifford Roberts, Harton S. Semple, the Earl of Derby, Hord W. Hardin.

General Eisenhower's copy of Thomas Stephens' portrait of Francis Ouimet, which hangs in the clubhouse of the Royal and Ancient Golf Club of St. Andrews.

The fourth hole.

The sixth hole.

The twelfth hole.

The eighteenth hole during the 1974 Masters.

The thirteenth hole of Augusta National.

This painting by General Eisenhower of Augusta National's sixteenth hole hangs in the Eisenhower Cabin, along with his painting of his grandson, David.

The seventh hole from the tee.

Tenth hole vista.

Second shot on the eleventh hole.

Second shot on the fifteenth hole.

Par-three course—looking across the pond
from the rear of the eighth green.

Par-three course—looking across the pond
towards the sixth green.

nothing marred the fourteen days of ideal weather, as well as the beautiful spring flowers at the height of their bloom, notably the redbud, azaleas, and dogwood. Mamie missed the last three days of this stay because of an appointment in Washington which could not be canceled.

When Churchill made his last journey to the United States, the President gave a dinner for him at the White House on May 6 to which I was invited. I also heard the President speak another time at the Waldorf in New York on May 14. Not once in either instance did he falter or stumble over a word. He would occasionally stutter or slur a word and stop to correct himself, but this seemed to happen only during casual conversations with a few friends. This meant that the President could, on important occasions and through intense concentration, overcome all the adverse effects on his speech caused by the stroke.

I received a telephone call from the President on October 20 asking if the club could accommodate him the following day. He explained that he was most anxious to get out of Washington for a few days, and wanted me to go with him to Augusta. The course was not scheduled to be opened for play until October 30, but the greenskeeper, the housekeeper, and others responded to my telephone calls. Moaney did all the cooking for us in the Eisenhower cabin kitchen. Accordingly, we managed to have a one-man temporary preseason opening. When the Chief realized all the extra work that had to be done to accommodate him, and to what extent he had thrown a monkey wrench into the scheduled order of opening preparations, he was not only concerned but apologetic.

Every one of the four days was cloudy and cool with occasional showers —the worst stretch of weather the President ever experienced in Augusta. However, he played eighteen holes, twenty-seven holes, thirty-six holes, and eighteen holes. On top of that, he did little work on the practice tee and played bridge every night. Howard Snyder was very unhappy about the thirty-six holes of golf in one day, the only time the President had undertaken such a thing since his Denver heart attack.

An announcement was being prepared stating that the President would soon make a nine-nation trip in nineteen days (this was also decided without General Snyder's approval). Possibly the President's activities in Augusta were to prove to himself, and to the doctors, his capacity to do the things he believed he needed to do.

For the November excursion, the President and Mamie had thirteen days of absolutely perfect weather with no rain or strong winds. This gave the Chief the exercise and rest he needed for the upcoming 22,000-mile itinerary. Not too much bridge was played, as he quit early and went to bed most of the time.

The day the President and Mamie left for Augusta in December, I was starting extended travel to South America and therefore saw nothing of them at that time.

Bob and the Later Years of the Masters

When Bob Jones first became lame he could himself still operate a golf cart. By this means he was able for some years to see something of each Masters Tournament. As he lost strength in his arms, as well as in his legs, someone would do the driving for him, with Bob strapped to his seat. His mind was never adversely affected, and he participated in the deliberations of the tournament rules committee when difficult decisions needed to be rendered. Bob chiefly officiated at the presentation ceremony at the conclusion of each tournament. His inimitable style, and his wonderfully well-worded tribute to the winner and the runners-up, put him in a class all by himself as a master of ceremonies.

One of the most important contributions made by Bob to the Masters was his thoughtfulness in recognizing good behavior on the part of the patrons. It was not all praise, however. On occasion he would point out how our patrons might improve things for the players or for each other. The Masters is said to have the most knowledgeable and considerate galleries of any golf tournament. If this be true, it is due in large part to the efforts of Bob Jones.

As an illustration, we reproduce a message, written in 1967, which is still printed on all the Masters Tournament series badges:

Augusta National Golf Club

Message From: ROBERT TYRE JONES, JR. *President Augusta National Golf Club*

In golf, customs of etiquette and decorum are just as important as rules governing play. It is appropriate for spectators to applaud successful strokes in proportion to difficulty but excessive demonstrations by a player or his partisans are not proper because of the possible effect upon other competitors.

Most distressing to those who love the game of golf is the applauding or cheering of misplays or misfortunes of a player. Such occurrences have been rare at the Masters but we must eliminate them entirely if our patrons are to continue to merit their reputation as the most knowledgeable and considerate in the world.

Bob Jones presiding over one of the last Masters Club dinners he was able to attend, in 1956. From left to right, the diners are Cary Middlecoff, Henry Picard, Craig Wood, Gene Sarazen, Claude Harmon, Byron Nelson, Jones, Sam Snead, Ben Hogan, Jimmy Demaret, Horton Smith, and the author.

When television came along, it was Bob who interviewed the top finishers in a brief green coat ceremony for the television audience. And it was Bob who laid down the rule that, while the professional announcers attend to the televising, it must be the responsibility of a club member to recognize the winner and award the trophies.

It had always been the practice at this club to give its president an opportunity to say the last word on any matter of substance. This applied especially to club policy, and to any changes or refinements on the golf course. Bob's illness never interrupted this established procedure. As long as he was able to read his mail, or use the telephone, he was kept informed.

A number of those who knew Bob intimately during this period believed that his keen interest in the club, and especially in the Masters Tour-

Augusta
National
Golf Club

nament, might have prolonged his life by as much as ten years. This special interest provided him with a mental exercise in making plans for each tournament. It required a struggle to get himself together and to be on hand yearly. Although every trip to Augusta was undoubtedly a severe strain on him, there was an important compensating factor in the form of a string of callers at his cabin from among the players and writers. These visitors included some of the younger element, as well as the oldsters.

Oscar Bane Keeler

The above name would have registered with almost no one but the parents of this famed writer. But "O.B.," his first two initials, was widely known as meaning Bob Jones's "Boswell."

O.B. was such a remarkable and talented person that I wish here to describe some of his qualities and customs. He could write entertainingly and authoritatively about a number of sports, and a range of other subjects. At the beginning his father wanted him to be a businessman, and obtained for him a job as a bookkeeper. After a brief period of this O.B. announced that, rather than do that sort of work, he would prefer to throw a rock in the river and forget to let go of the rock.

O.B. applied to the Atlanta *Georgian* for a job as a writer in 1909. When asked about his experience he admitted that he had had none, and he was given a job with a commensurate amount of pay. The first piece he wrote was used on the front page. O.B. went to work for the Kansas City *Star* in 1910, and was the first person to be given a by-line by that publication. He became a most versatile reporter and at one point in his career was made an Associated Press staff member. In 1913 he joined the Atlanta *Journal* and remained there until he retired in 1950.

He not only wrote poetry, but committed to memory large volumes of poetry written by others. Some said he had a tar-bucket mind: everything stuck that arrived. He was noted for his conviviality and matchless flow of words. His gift for telling stories was equal to his genius as a writer. His friend Ed Miles wrote that "he possessed a thousand funny yarns and he retold them a thousand times, and, like wine, they improved with age and repeated sippings."

He became interested in Bob and started writing about him when the promising young amateur was only twelve years of age. He is believed to have accompanied Bob on every golfing trip made by him during the following sixteen years. One might say that O.B. made a career of Bob's career. Despite the difference in their ages, they were close friends. They co-authored a book on golf, titled *Down the Fairway*. In 1953 Grantland Rice wrote *The Bobby Jones Story*, which was a compilation of the writings of O. B. Keeler. The preface of the book, contributed by Robert Tyre Jones, Jr., reads as follows:

O. B. KEELER AND I ENJOYED A VERY REAL PARTNERSHIP *for the better part of twenty years. We traveled thousands of miles together, we lived our golf tournaments together, we wrote a book, did a radio series, and two motion picture series, all in the closest and most harmonious collaboration. I doubt if ever such a relationship existed between performer and reporter in sport or elsewhere.*

The ebb and flow of a player's confidence is one of the strange phenomena of competitive golf. I have discussed this angle with all the great players of my own and later eras and none deny or can explain the periods of uncertainty that occasionally come in the midst of the most complete assurance.

In the first qualifying round for the Amateur Championship at Minikahda in 1927 I posted a 75. I never wanted to win qualifying medals— a sort of superstition I suppose—and I had tried to coast along and do a modest, comfortable score. But I had slipped a stroke here and there and perhaps had been lucky to score 75. Suddenly I began to see that another slack round with a stroke or two more gone might leave me out of the tournament.

So I set out to find Keeler.

"O.B.," I said, "the only way for me to get out of this thing is to go out this afternoon and try to win the medal, and I need you to walk with me for a few holes until I get calmed down."

I wanted just the satisfaction of having an understanding soul with me to get over that feeling of aloneness which comes when your confidence is gone. It worked like a charm. I let O.B. go after the fifth hole, finished the round in 67 for a course record and the medal, and went on to win the championship.

This is just one of the things I owe to Keeler. The bigger thing no one knows better than I or than the boys who were writing sports in those days. To gain any sort of fame it isn't enough to do the job. There must be someone to spread the news. If fame can be said to attach to one because of his proficiency in the inconsequential performance of striking a golf ball, what measure of it I have enjoyed has been due in large part to Keeler and his gifted typewriter.

I am asked now to say that I am willing to leave the record of my golfing activities to the words this man has written. Why in Heaven's name shouldn't I be? He never once gave me anything but the best of any argument.

During the early days of the Masters, when we employed most every means of coaxing people to buy a ticket, O.B. was one of several who contributed well-written stories about the tournament. These we distributed to sports writers with permission to publish them as their own. One story by O.B., prepared in 1940, still appears annually in the "Masters Green Booklet," which contains tournament data for the news media.

O.B. could recite prose by the hour, sober or otherwise. Alcohol seemed to sharpen his memory rather than to dull it. No one ever knew him to fail, or even falter, on a line of classical prose.

On one occasion, during the early days of the Masters, O.B. was giving a recital in the barroom, which was then located on the second floor of the clubhouse. It became late in the evening and O.B. had been summoned for the third time to come downstairs. He elected to use the stairway that was then on the east side of the old manor house. One of his great admirers and an Augusta member, W. Montgomery (Gummy) Harison, was in the group being entertained by O.B. Gummy had not inbibed, and therefore realized that O.B. was in no condition to negotiate the long flight of steps. Moreover, O.B. was handicapped by a stiff leg which would not bend at the knee. Accordingly, Gummy placed an arm around his friend and undertook to assist him down the steps. O.B. was quite agreeable, and placed an arm around Gummy. Unfortunately, O.B.'s stiff leg scooted out from under him at the first step and the two of them rolled head over heels together all the way to the bottom. O.B. landed on top, of course, without a scratch or a bruise, while the completely sober good Samaritan had to be taken to the hospital for extensive repairs.

A Thank-You Letter and Party

President Eisenhower arrived in Augusta on four separate occasions for visits at the club in 1960 (April 11–18, April 18–21, November 9–22, and December 9–12). During the first trip in April he was accompanied by John, Barbara, and the children, as well as by Mamie. On April 18 the President flew

Photograph sent by the President.

DDE

Dear Cliff:

As you know, for almost eight years I have lived in ignorance of the identity of the individuals who so thoughtfully and kindly provided the means by which was built the house at Augusta, now known as Mamie's Cabin. But now that my tour in the Presidency is ending, I am glad you have given me the names of the donors so that I might, even after this long delay, express, in some measure, the gratitude my wife and I feel to each of you.

The house has enabled Mamie and me, when in Augusta, to entertain good friends in a family atmosphere and, when we so chose, to live in complete privacy. The consideration of the group in assuring that the house would be available to us through our lifetime, rather than merely during my service as President, doubles its value to us, particularly on the sentimental side.

I shall hope, at some future time, to have an opportunity to thank you more intimately and personally. But I did not want to leave this office without making a written record of my gratitude. Incidentally, you will find along with this letter a picture of Mamie and me standing in front of the Cabin.

As to the one week end in the late spring when we might gather at Augusta for a real get-together, I would ask that you delay making any firm plans until I can straighten out my affairs as I undertake the job of living as a private citizen. This I have not done in half a century. But I will let you know the prospects as soon as I can.

With warm regard,

As ever,

(signature)

Mr. Clifford Roberts

Thank-you letter from Eisenhower to the author.

to Washington on an errand and returned to Augusta the same day. On November 9, Mamie accompanied the President. On December 9 none of the family made the trip to Augusta.

The General's last journey to Augusta as President was on January 7, 1961, and he returned to Washington on January 8. I told him in some detail for the first time how the several club improvements were accomplished in 1953 in order to make the place usable by him as President. Likewise, I informed him about the members who were involved. We discussed the idea of inviting all those who had participated to attend a party at the club so that he could personally express his thanks. I was therefore surprised to receive shortly afterwards a letter from the General indicating the extent of his appreciation. The date of the letter makes it obvious that it was one of the final things he did prior to leaving the White House. It was likewise obvious that the letter was intended for all the members who had supplied the necessary funds.

On May 6, 1961, the planned dinner party took place. Nearly forty members who had subscribed to the special improvements fund were alive and able to attend, and this unusual occasion was celebrated in a fashion that was enjoyable to everyone. Nothing was said about it at the dinner, but, to me, the principal thing to celebrate was the character of the membership of our club. As recited earlier, the fifty subscribing members signed agreements not to disclose their participation in the financing. So far as I know, not one made such a disclosure to the President, or to anyone else.

Golden Wedding Anniversary Party

When President Eisenhower left Washington, he communicated with a number of his intimates asking that he be reinstated on a first-name basis. Almost no one complied and he was usually addressed as "Mr. President," although a few called him "General." In order to avoid any possible confusion in this book between our distinguished member and any of his successors in office, or with any other general, I shall hereafter discontinue the name of President and use the term General Ike.

In addition to a two-day visit in January, General Ike made two trips to Augusta in 1961. He made two more in 1962, three in 1963, and one each in 1964, 1965, 1966, and 1967, making eleven in all after he left the White House.

Mamie and the General were married July 1, 1916. A number of the club members decided that a celebration was in order prior to the fiftieth anniversary of their marriage. Holding such a party at Augusta meant taking over the entire facilities of the club, and it was decided that the best date this could be done was October 27, 1965. The invitations were in the form of a combination birthday and wedding celebration, the General's birthday being October 14 and Mamie's November 14. Accordingly, October 27 fell in between those two dates.

I was given the responsibility of selecting a suitable gift for the couple we wished to honor. Asprey of London accepted an order from me to make a gold bowl. Ordinarily they would have required one year's time to complete the work that was required. But when the firm was informed as to the recipients of the gift, they agreed to cut that time in half. This was accomplished by rotating extra craftsmen, and the bowl was completed in time for the scheduled celebration. A description by Asprey & Company follows:

The 18ct. yellow gold Bowl and cover was especially designed and hand-made in the finest tradition of goldsmithing by craftsmen of Asprey & Company in London.

The theme of decoration is based on the State flowers of the birthplaces of The General and Mrs. Eisenhower, and the State where they were married. These three flowers, Blue Bonnet of Texas (The General), Wild Rose of Iowa (Mrs. Eisenhower) and the Columbine of Colorado are finely chased and pierced, and when repeated form the cover of the Bowl. At the base of the symbolic Eagle are engraved the following dates—opposite the appropriate flower:

October 14th, 1890   *(The General)*
November 14th, 1896   *(Mrs. Eisenhower)*
July 1st, 1916   *(When they were married)*

Engraved around the flange of the Bowl are the twenty-two homes where the Eisenhowers have lived. The White House and Mamie's Cabin being larger than the others and all are framed with white gold batons.

Weight of Bowl 84.5 ounces Troy
Width 12¼ inches—Height 7 inches

The Bowl is housed in a dark green Niger leather case with 18ct. gold catches and gold tooled with the Augusta National Club Emblem and the appropriate initials.

A sketch of the gold bowl presented to General and Mrs. Eisenhower at the golden wedding-birthday dinner at the Augusta National.

A finely bound book containing the presentation inscription and the donors' names, hand lettered on vellum is contained in a plinth under the Bowl.

The bowl arrived in Augusta just two days prior to the dinner. It had been sent over by special courier. No one other than myself had seen it until after it had been presented. Mamie arranged to put it on display the day following the dinner, so that the donors of the gift could see it in the daylight.

Eighty-six of the Eisenhowers' close friends took part in the plans. Nearly that many were able to be present at the Augusta National on October 27, 1965. A few problems arose, however. George Humphrey was to make the presentation of the gold bowl, but he suffered a heart disturbance only a few days before the party. Accordingly, I was the one who was nominated to take his place. Bob Jones was to be the master of ceremonies. He and Mary arrived by car from Atlanta in good time, but the trip was too much of a strain on Bob and he was at once put to bed. A doctor was called and he advised his patient not to attempt to attend the dinner. This meant still another assignment for me, as insufficient time remained to brief another toastmaster on the planned schedule.

The third disappointment was an equipment failure. Elaborate arrangements had been made to play during the dinner hour various recordings of political campaign songs which were known to be favorites of the couple we were trying to honor and to entertain. This part of the proceedings had to be abandoned after a half hour of screeching attempts to produce music and song.

Once the dinner dishes had been cleared away, I introduced Oveta Hobby, the first head of the Women's Army Corps, an active officer of Citizens for Eisenhower in 1952, and the first to hold the cabinet post of Secretary of Health, Education and Welfare. Oveta's assigned role was to talk about the General. In my introductory remarks, I suggested that this was her opportunity to unburden herself about things the General, her long-time boss, had done that might not have suited her. Mine was, of course, an attempt to keep things on the light side, but Oveta would have none of it. She came to Augusta to praise the General, and she did just that—in the most glowing terms any of us had ever been privileged to hear.

The next speaker on the agenda was General Gruenther. It was his assignment to talk about Mamie. Al responded to my introduction with his very best wit and humor. This meant that Mamie was made very happy, while all others present were better entertained than by any speech-listening experience at previous functions.

The gold bowl was duly presented, after which the General expressed appreciation on behalf of Mamie and himself. He then proceeded to make a brief but entertaining speech. To me, the highlight of his remarks concerned the matter of relating funny stories. He explained that he was quite aware that speakers are usually expected to tell a funny story, and that he would like to tell several, as Al Gruenther had done. The trouble was that, although he had heard many, he could never remember them. There had been, however, one exception, and he was prepared, on this special occasion, to tell the one story he remembered.

The story was about the mate on a sailing vessel. The captain had recorded in the ship's log that the first mate had been drunk on duty the previous night. The mate begged the captain to remove the charge, as it would seriously damage his career, but the captain refused. The mate thought hard for many days as to what he might do to get even with the captain. Finally, after a night's watch, he wrote in the log of the ship: "The captain was sober today."

Augusta National Golf Club

General and Mrs. Eisenhower at the combined golden wedding anniversary and birthday party given to them by members of the club on October 27, 1965. General Al Gruenther is to Mamie's right.

PART FOUR

Second Heart Attack

During the 1965 stay at the club, General Ike and Mamie accepted an invitation to have dinner in Aiken, South Carolina, with Mr. and Mrs. Barry Leithead. I was not at the club at the time and did not arrive until the next day. General Ike had either forgotten his agreement with me about not accepting engagements off the club grounds, or he decided, since he was no longer in office, that there was no point in further compliance. At any rate, he had become very devoted to Barry, and when Barry invited him to his home for dinner on November 8, General Ike gladly responded. The Leitheads had a couple who were quite capable in preparing and serving food. The guest of honor had a good appetite, as usual, and ate heartily. As I was told later, General Ike had two helpings of a very rich dish composed mainly of avocado pear.

That same night, November 9, around 12:30 A.M., our member Dr. Louis Battey was summoned because General Ike was stricken with chest pains. Next came Dr. Harry T. Harper, who was followed by a medical team from Fort Gordon. They moved the patient to the Fort Gordon Hospital about an hour later. The only heart monitor-defibrillator in the area at that time was loaned to Fort Gordon by St. Joseph Hospital, and it might have been the means of saving General Ike's life. The patient was transferred to Walter Reed Hospital in Washington, D.C., on November 22.

The reason I mention the rich avocado pear dish is the repeat indication that there might have been some connection, in General Ike's case, between indigestion and heart trouble. When I visited him at Fort Gordon, and later in Washington, I found the same concern about others rather than himself that I had noticed in Denver after his first heart attack. And, also, the same determination to recover.

199

*Augusta
National
Golf Club*

Post-Presidential Activities

Shortly after General Ike finished his second term as President, he decided to spend the winter months, particularly January and February, in the desert in California. His doctors advised him to avoid the cold. I was one of those who urged him to go to Palm Springs, or rather the Eldorado Club at Palm Desert, where a number of the Augusta National members spent some time during the winter.

The weather pattern had changed considerably in the Southeast section of the country since the 1920s when I first knew Augusta. In those days, January and February provided much good golfing weather and snow was unknown. But, during the 1960s, Augusta quite often registered temperatures that were just too cold for golf, and snow was no longer a curiosity during January and February. Sometimes cold waves would extend to south Florida and drive temperature readings down to thirty or lower. Some say the change was caused by the jet stream moving farther south. Whatever the reason, the change was very real. We now have one compensating factor, however, at Augusta, which is that the spring and fall seasons are more delightful than ever. And who knows?—the jet stream might decide to move back to the north again.

Each winter General Ike would organize an Augusta National gathering at the Eldorado Club. Eight or ten would go from the East and join up with the half-dozen West Coast members who had been invited. The management of all the details would be ably looked after by Freeman Gosden. General Ike would usually cook one of his famous steak dinners during the course of these long-weekend parties. Leonard Firestone was a dinner host at his desert home on several occasions. Bob Hope was one of the few invited for golf who was not a member of the Augusta National. Golf every day and bridge every night were routine, and nothing was allowed to interfere. These were stag gatherings, and Mamie co-operated by arranging her annual trip to Main Chance on the same dates General Ike was holding his parties.

There continued to be a close association between General Ike and members of the Augusta National from the time he left Washington until he died in 1969. He did not go to Augusta as often, especially after his heart attack in 1965. But a number of us saw him occasionally in New York and at Gettysburg, in addition to the visits in California.

General Ike in these years did considerable writing. He also followed

Augusta
National
Golf Club

through on several charitable and patriotic organizations with which he had become identified while serving as President. Each one of these organizations needed money, of course, and they all made special appeals to those who were known to be personal friends of the General. Many of us went right along with whatever project in which General Ike became involved. Aside from the Red Cross, Freedoms Foundation, USO, and others, a notable example of more direct personal involvement was the Eisenhower Exchange Fellowships. In this instance, it became necessary for a number of the Augusta group to serve on the board. Another personal interest in which many of us participated was the Eisenhower Library, in Abilene, Kansas.

After the presidency, General Ike gave his blessings to two more projects in worthy fields: Eisenhower College, at Seneca Falls, New York; and Eisenhower Medical Center, at Palm Desert, California. Bob Hope and I helped to organize a nationwide effort to obtain many small gifts on a fifty-fifty basis for these institutions through a vehicle called "Golf's Tribute to Ike." Although every member of the Augusta National and the Burning Tree Club in Washington, D.C., made a contribution, the over-all results were nothing to boast about.

A number of Augusta members made gifts directly, over a period of years, to Eisenhower Medical Center. They provided much more, however, for Eisenhower College—probably a total of several millions. One member alone gave in excess of half a million dollars. This was because the General had indicated that the college was his favorite undertaking, and also because the college needed substantially more money than the California hospital.

Third Heart Attack

On June 17, 1968, General Ike suffered a heart attack for the third time. It occurred in California. As soon as his condition had stabilized, he was flown to Walter Reed Hospital in Washington. As a result of heroic efforts on the part of the doctors and nurses, he lived until March 28, 1969.

I saw the General briefly several times at Walter Reed, as did a number of his friends. He was alert and quite apparently was being kept informed on world news. He wanted to talk about Augusta, investments, and politics. At one point there was some discussion about allowing him to be moved to a nearby apartment or house. Such a plan never materialized because he continued to experience slight chest pains occasionally.

The one matter that seemed to greatly concern General Ike was Eisenhower College. He knew it was in trouble financially. I had declined an invitation from the organizers to serve as a trustee, and had not been enthusiastic about the project because I was afraid it would become too burdensome to the General. Also, I felt it might keep him from doing some of the things I knew he was anxious to accomplish, such as writing quite fully about Churchill and General Marshall.

When I realized the extent of General Ike's apprehension about Eisenhower College, I tried to put his mind at rest by assuring him that I would tackle the problem. I had no idea at the time where to find the needed funds. My first step was to get three friends to join me in making an immediate gift of $25,000 cash to the college, with instructions to let the General know what I had done as a starter. Next, I prepared for the college a very much-needed slogan, as follows: "Dedicated to the character, principles and patriotism of Dwight David Eisenhower." Later came the "Golf's Tribute to Ike" campaign which, as I have said, was not the success we anticipated but which did produce around $1 million. The 50 per cent share received by the college was very helpful.

In 1970, Congress approved the minting of the Eisenhower dollar. A $1 coin, a $3 uncirculated coin, and a $10-proof coin were authorized. The United States Treasury estimated a $470 million profit from the sale of the Eisenhower uncirculated and proof coins. I therefore proposed that Congress be asked to give Eisenhower College a part—say 10 per cent—of this most unusual potential profit. The Eisenhower Memorial Bill was duly introduced, General Ike having referred to the college as a "living memorial" and therefore something especially acceptable.

Here again, numbers of Augusta National members became involved in what some might call a political effort that concerned the club's most illustrious member. Many asked congressmen or senators to support the legislation. We anticipated no great difficulty but, because of unforeseen complications, three years of effort was required before the bill was finally passed by both houses of Congress and signed by the President. It provided $9 million for Eisenhower College. This was not as much as was hoped for, but sufficient to cover the needs of the college for the time being.

I will state quite frankly that the legislative effort could never have been successful except for the active support of Mr. George Meany. When we first spoke to him about the problem, his instant response, as nearly as I can recall, was as follows: "Although I never voted for President Eisenhower, I admired him immensely as a great and warmhearted American and I liked him personally. I'll be happy to assist in honoring him by giving support to Eisenhower College."

Operating under the Eisenhower creed, General Ike's college has an opportunity to wield a constructive influence beyond what might be expected from a small educational institution. Thousands of fine people have given it their support. It will need gifts, however, from additional thousands who admired President Eisenhower and the things for which he stood, because another twenty years must elapse before Eisenhower College will have an alumni from which it can expect financial support.

The Trophy Room

The principal room where food is served at the Augusta National is called the Trophy Room. The reason for this name is because it contains a glass-enclosed case which displays the club's most treasured possessions. The following is the legend on a printed card within the case:

Eleven of the golf clubs exhibited here were used by Robert T. Jones, Jr., during the Grand Slam year of 1930. The twelfth club, a putter, is the original Calamity Jane model which was not used after 1924. The complete set of sixteen clubs represented final selection after more than one hundred clubs had been used and discarded during previous years. The remainder of the set not displayed here are accounted for as follows:

(1) *A Driver, made by Jack White of Scotland, an uncle of Jimmy Thomson, now in the Museum of the Royal and Ancient Golf Club, St. Andrews, Scotland.*

(2) *A Brassie, made by George Duncan, which was presented to the James River Museum, James River, Virginia.*

(3) *A Putter, a copy of the original, in use during 1930, is now a part of the United States Golf Association Museum Collection in Far Hills, New Jersey.*

(4) *A Run-up Club which was lost.*

(5) *A Sand Wedge carried during 1930 which was used to play only two tournament shots.*

All the clubs are, of course, wood-shafted. Likewise, all are known by a name rather than a number.

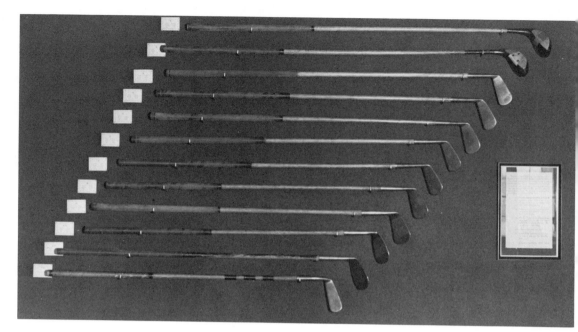

Bob Jones's clubs displayed in the Trophy Room.

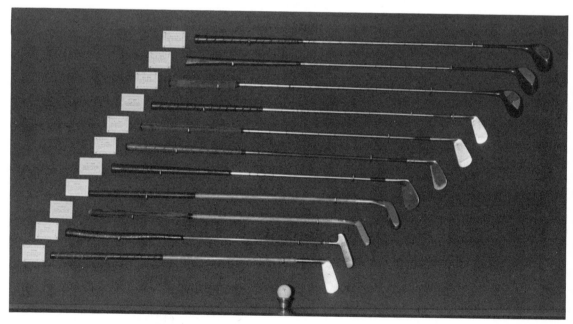

Masters champions' clubs displayed in the Trophy Room.

A second case in the Trophy Room contains eleven golf clubs. Ten of these clubs were presented to the Augusta National by the earliest Masters champions. All were described by the donors as being the most helpful to them in winning the tournament. The eleventh is Lloyd Mangrum's putter, used by him to establish, in competition, the official Augusta National course record of 64 in 1940 (since equaled by Jack Nicklaus in 1965, Maurice Bembridge in 1974, and Hale Irwin in 1975). Also exhibited here is the golf ball used by Gene Sarazen in scoring a double-eagle on the fifteenth hole in the 1935 Masters Tournament.

There are three portraits in the Trophy Room, all done by Thomas Stephens. One is of President Eisenhower, which hangs in the most prominent place—over the fireplace. One is of the club president, Bob Jones, which hangs at the east end of the room. The third is a likeness of myself at the west end of the room. The portraits were done, however, in the reverse order of my listing, and the reason for this might be mildly interesting.

In 1949, a few members thought I deserved to have my portrait hung in the Trophy Room, one of Bob already being there and appearing to be a bit lonesome in such a large room. An artist had been tentatively commissioned when General Ike heard about it. He at once insisted that Tommy Stephens was a better portrait painter and should be engaged. When my portrait was finished by Stephens, everyone thought it such a good likeness that the smaller portrait of Bob appeared dwarfed and inferior. Accordingly, Tommy was commissioned to do one of Bob. When both were hung, we realized that the empty space over the fireplace was an ideal location for the General's portrait, and Tommy was once again pressed into service. Happily, our club came into possession of the finest Stephens portrait of President Eisenhower. We realize that twenty-three other owners of such paintings feel sure that theirs is the finest, but we are positive ours is the best because the President is shown wearing his green club coat.

The Masters Club

During the 1952 tournament, the defending champion, Ben Hogan, gave a dinner for all previous winners. At that time he proposed the formation of the Masters Club, with its membership limited to Masters champions past, present, and future. Nine of the eleven who were eligible were present and they voted favorably on Ben's proposal. They also voted to extend honorary memberships to Bob Jones and to me.

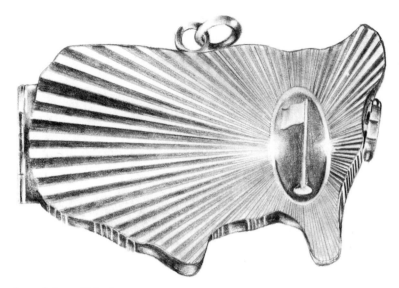

A drawing of the gold locket presented as certificate of membership to the Masters Club.

Ever since its organization, attendance at the Masters Club dinner has been remarkably good. In 1975, twenty-one of the twenty-two living Masters champions were present. Bob Jones never failed to attend as long as he was able to make the trip from Atlanta. I have never missed one of the dinners. Each year the new champion pays the dinner check, and receives as his certificate of membership a suitably inscribed gold locket in the form of the club emblem. The presentation is usually made by Ben Hogan or Byron Nelson. The dinners are always held on the Tuesday evening during the week of the Masters. Everyone wears his green jacket.

It was Ben's idea that the Masters Club meet annually merely for the purpose of enjoying each other's company. It was to be a time to reminisce, to hear Sam Snead's latest story, to dine well, and generally to promote good fellowship among the members of the club. Over the years no one has been immune to banter and mildly sarcastic comments, including the management of the tournament. While socializing remains the dominant theme, the Masters Club has served some highly useful purposes.

Merely because of their identity, the members of the Masters Club automatically contributed to the development of the tournament. Their stature as players, and as men of character, has added greatly to the prestige of the event. Equally important has been their active efforts in helping to make improvements. This applies to tournament procedures, tournament equipment, the golf course, player invitation regulations, course conditioning, and the designing of various facilities. A number of Masters champions are not only golf course architects or consultants but are students of engineering, agronomy, and horticulture.

I believe it is rather well known that the Augusta National has, from the beginning of the tournament, welcomed suggestions for improvements from all sources: golfing fans, patrons, players, architects, and golf association officials. I also believe I can best explain my admiration for the members of the Masters Club by stating that they have probably provided more practical suggestions for improvements than the combined total from all other sources.

The End of Bob's Suffering

Bob Jones died on December 18, 1971. If it is ever appropriate to say that death came as a blessing, this was such an occasion. Bob had for many months been almost completely helpless. I was told that his weight was only about sixty pounds. He had so little flesh on his bones that he could not lie in one position longer than about two hours without aching pain. By then he was so weak that it was necessary for someone to turn him over. The last time I went to Atlanta to see him, it hurt me deeply to see how badly he appeared, and to watch him struggle in an effort to talk to me. I know of several close friends who wished to see him who received a message that he looked and felt so badly he thought it best they not come.

The wonder of it is that Bob lived as long as he did. So many complications had developed that it was impossible to make him comfortable. He was capable of suffering, uncomplainingly, but that was about all. Many wrote wonderful tributes to Bob's courage. To me, one by Herbert Warren Wind summed it all up in a splendid fashion:

> As a young man, he was able to stand up to just about the best that life can offer, which is not easy, and later he stood up with equal grace to just about the worst.

On April 12, 1966, the Augusta National at its annual stockholders' meeting adopted a resolution which reads as follows:

ROBERT TYRE JONES, Jr.

It has been well and truly said that "Every great institution is the lengthened shadow of a man." So it is with the Augusta National Golf Club: the man being Robert Tyre Jones, Jr.

His was the established and unique leadership position coupled with remarkable ability which was principally responsible for the organization and development of the Augusta National Golf Club and the Masters Tournament. He exemplifies the highest standards of sportsmanship and his position is pre-eminent throughout and beyond the golfing world.

Bob Jones, as he is affectionately known to his fellow members, has served as President of the Augusta National Golf Club from its very beginning, being unanimously elected each succeeding year, and it is desired that the distinction of being the only President of the Club be preserved by changing the By-Laws so as to provide for his election as President in Perpetuity. More especially, it is desired that the spirit of his principles, his acts of good sportsmanship, his innate modesty and other admirable and lovable qualities shall forever guide the policies of the Augusta National and the Masters Tournament.

NOW, THEREFORE, BE IT RESOLVED, That the By-Laws be amended to provide for the position of a President in Perpetuity as a lasting tribute to Robert Tyre Jones, Jr., and that he be the only person ever to be elected to that position.

RESOLVED, FURTHER, That the name of Robert Tyre Jones, Jr., President in Perpetuity, be carried on the letterhead and masthead of the Augusta National Golf Club as long as it continues in existence.

I am the one who proposed the idea of making Bob President in Perpetuity. I was also the co-author, along with James M. Hull, of the resolution that did so. In view of this, and my many expressions in these passages of high regard and affection for Bob Jones, I shall not try to describe my sense of personal loss. Any such effort, I feel, would be redundant.

Our News Fraternity Friends

The Masters Tournament has been favored with unusually good relationships with all segments of the news fraternity. This was true at the beginning, and I am confident that it exists today. In my opinion this happy relationship was founded on the firm friendships that existed between Bob Jones and the golf reporters.

At the outset, a policy was established of issuing press releases during a

The sketch of Charles Bartlett that hangs in the lounge named for him in the Press Building.

period of some eight weeks prior to the beginning of each tournament. They contained merely factual information. No professional talent was employed to prepare these releases. The only exception to this custom was in the form of a few articles prepared, without pay, by friends of Bob during the earliest years of the Masters.

Each year an effort was made to improve the facilities for the news media. As I have noted, a permanent and large building was constructed which was reserved in its entirety for their use. It features a number of conveniences that are not always available at golf tournaments. One of the decorative features of the Charles Bartlett Lounge is a photograph of each president of the Golf Writers Association of America.

It was here at Augusta that the technique was developed of bringing the players to the press, rather than having the press chase the players when they headed for the locker room after completing their play. This procedure is now willingly accepted by both the players and the reporters, and no one seems interested in returning to the old system. Our Press Committee can usually determine which players are wanted for interviews, and each one of the desired contestants is then met at the eighteenth green and conducted in a golf cart to the Press Building. The interviews take place in the Charles Bartlett Lounge, where the working press only is permitted to participate. The player is seated on an elevated platform, the questions posed are repeated by a member of our Press Committee, and the player then makes his reply. Everyone, including those in the radio and TV section of the building, can clearly hear each question and answer by means of amplifying equipment. Closed-circuit television coverage is likewise provided. Since the original Press, Radio and TV Building was constructed in 1953, it has been enlarged and extended several times. Additionally, separate space is provided in a large trailer for private interviews. Another separate facility provides space for Western Union and SportsComm.

In 1972 a system was initiated for the immediate posting of all scores of the entire field on both the press scoreboard and the large official scoreboard which is located adjacent to the Press Building. In 1973 a special news information service was begun which permits newspapers and TV and radio stations that do not have a representative on the grounds to call by telephone and hear recordings of up-to-the-minute tournament developments.

We feel certain, however, that the most appreciated facilities for all of the news media are the ones provided on the golf course for our patrons. The club operates more than twenty scoreboards and an equal number of scoring standards, which means that the reporter who is covering the tournament on the grounds can readily keep abreast of developments no matter in which direction his steps may take him. Eight special towers are erected for the

To my friend
Jerry Franklin.
With warm regard,
Sincerely,
Bob Jones

Bob Jones liked this photograph and inscribed it to his friend Jerry Franklin.

official photographers, and a reserved section is set aside for both photographers and the working press in the spectator stands.

Jerome A. Franklin

The present-day membership of the Augusta National has much reason to be grateful to Jerry Franklin. Without question, he has spent more hours doing both big and little chores for the club than any other member.

Jerry was in the organic chemical business and, being a resident of Augusta and one of our original members, he has served on the Local Operating Committee ever since it came into existence. I doubt if anyone has more faithfully attended the meetings.

Jerry is one of those rare individuals who is liked by everyone he meets. He has a host of friends and no enemies. In selling an idea on behalf of the club, he has a very high batting average. In talking with a recalcitrant person where plain and forceful language was necessary, he has always been able to make his point without creating resentment. I doubt if Jerry ever thought of himself as a diplomat, but I've never witnessed a better day-to-day example of how to get things done without rancor. Probably one of the reasons for his constructive accomplishments on behalf of the club was the complete absence of any self-seeking motives.

Some years ago Jerry began keeping me informed on how many were left of the original members. He does not remind me about it any more, since he and I are the only two left. Maybe that has developed an even stronger bond of friendship between us, a friendship that began close to fifty years ago. Then, too, I am finding Jerry very helpful in my efforts to write this book. Being eight years my junior, I find that his memory is less fuzzy than mine.

My Eightieth Birthday Celebration

I remarked earlier in these pages that I have been overpaid for my services to the Augusta National. All things considered, this is not as fictional as it might sound. One reason is the expressions of appreciation that have come

Jerome A. Franklin.

my way, and another is the several tangible tokens of my association. One such item was an especially fine pocket watch that was presented to me in 1939 by twenty-two members. Another was a gold cigarette box given to me by 110 members during the 1964 Jamboree Party. The gift related to my having achieved the age of seventy, and the occasion resulted in an unusually good attendance at the Jamboree.

Ten years later it was suggested that my birthday be again celebrated. I agreed, provided it would serve some useful purpose such as beefing up what is called the Closing Party. This particular gathering of members had never drawn more than twenty-odd participants because it is held near the end of the season in the month of May. A committee was formed to organize the birthday aspects of the 1974 Closing Party. Much to the unexpected delight of everyone concerned, including myself, 109 members arrived at the club to help me celebrate my eightieth birthday at a special dinner on May 10. No one seemed to mind that the actual date of my birthday was March 6. In fact, the dinner drew—by a considerable margin, I am proud to report—the largest gathering of Augusta National members ever assembled at one time.

Members from twenty-three states attended the birthday party. Three came from Canada, and two made a special trip from Europe. I doubt if anyone was ever made happier than myself through this kind of an expression of friendship. A wonderfully worded scroll was presented to me. It had been written by James M. Hull, who was within one year of reaching the age of ninety. Other long-time friends spoke eloquently of my good traits, and rather gently chided me about my bad ones. There were several highly pleasing surprises that had been provided for the occasion.

At the end, when it came my turn, I brought in my own surprise in the form of four members of the club organization who had begun serving the Augusta National at its inception in 1931. I shall name and describe each one:

Robert Reynolds, of the golf course crew, whose age at the time of my birthday party was ninety-one. His brother, Ed, had been a part of the club's nursery crew from the beginning until his death a few years earlier. Their mother was still alive, age 107.

Ben Smalley, one of our caddies, age seventy-one, who was the favorite of Bob Jones. He continues to operate his own small farm with the aid of an ox.

John Milton, our head chauffeur, age seventy-two, who is privileged to drive the Cadillac limousine rather than the station wagon.

Bowman Milligan, our club steward emeritus, age seventy-two, who has the responsibility to select each year the proper-size green coat to fit the new Masters Champion.

Each one was given a present and a special award in recognition of his many years of loyal and especially capable service to the club, and I do not believe I exaggerate when I say that this period of the evening was enjoyed more by the members than any other part of the proceedings. After all, there are not many golf clubs that have been blessed with the devotion of stalwarts such as Bowman Milligan, John Milton, Ben Smalley, and Robert Reynolds.

Tournament Organization

Operating a baseball, football, or basketball game, or other such athletic contest, is relatively simple when compared to a sizable golf tournament. The former take place in a limited area and the spectators are seated within close range. In a golfing contest, play occurs in an area upwards of two hundred acres. The spectators want to see what is taking place, and they require creature comforts to some extent throughout this extensive playing field. Then, too, the galleries require a limited amount of control, as well as scoring reports at all parts of the golf course.

For a number of years approximately two thousand individuals have served in the Masters Tournament organization. The exact figure for all workers of every type in 1975 was 2,206. Of these, only ninety-four were club members. Approximately 95 per cent of the 1975 personnel had served previously. As experience is very important in the operation of a golf tournament, ours enjoys a considerable advantage over those that find it necessary to function each year at a new location with a group of new workers.

As in the beginning, only a small fraction of the total tournament organization can be drawn from the club's widely dispersed membership. There is a large number of nonmember volunteers, patrons of the game, who serve without pay. The majority of the workers, however, are paid for their services, it still being our policy that those who will accept pay should receive compensation, as it means better control.

There are several hundred essential tournament chores that are routinely performed each year by the club staff. A total of twenty-five important tournament functions require special committees. I shall briefly describe ten of these committees, each one of which is unique and seldom duplicated at other golfing events.

Rules Committee. This committee is regarded as the most important on the list. Forty-seven experts on the Rules of Golf served in 1975. This is about the usual number that come to Augusta annually as volunteers at their own expense. They may be classified as the largest, most distinguished group of golfing officials that are drawn together anywhere. The Captain of the Royal and Ancient Golf Club of St. Andrews was present, and acted as the 1975 Honorary Chairman. The President of the British PGA and the President of the United States Golf Association accepted the same designation. A former president of the USGA acted as Chairman of the Masters Rules Committee, while three other former USGA presidents served as vice-chairmen. By coincidence, all seven of these officials in 1975, we are proud to say, were members of the Augusta National Golf Club.

The President of the Professional Golfers' Association of America, together with four former presidents, served on our 1975 Rules Committee. The Commissioner of the Tournament Players' Division and four other active or retired PGA officials were also on hand.

Twenty-four active or former members of the USGA Executive Committee served on the 1975 Masters Rules Committee. The same was true of two USGA staff officers, and one former staff official of both the USGA and the PGA.

One former captain, five currently active or former officials, and the top staff officer of the R and A also assisted our Rules Committee to function in a proper fashion in 1975.

Our club is indeed proud to have the leading golf officials, both professional and amateur, use the Masters Tournament annually as a common meeting ground. Over the years, much constructive discussion has occurred at Augusta. Those who are working together to help operate one particular golfing event seem to find it easier to formulate plans designed to promote the general good of the game of golf.

Technically, the Augusta National Golf Club is the sole sponsor of the Masters Tournament. But, in actual practice, the tournament is directed and supported by representatives of a number of golfing associations, notably the USGA, PGA, and R and A. Our tournament was founded on a format predicated on scoring records established in the three major championships operated by these three golf associations.

Additionally, there are many hundreds of leadership-type golfers who assemble at the Masters each year. They are officers of clubs, or representatives of tournaments being planned or being held. They make the trip to learn about new procedures, to exchange ideas, or just to mingle with kindred spirits. They come from every state in the Union, and from many of the foreign countries where golf is played. Our tournament is directly benefited by the presence of these golfing leaders, as well as by the working assignments that are accepted by nationally and internationally recognized authorities on rules, customs, and etiquette. All are deeply devoted to golf, and the atmosphere they generate is constructive and wholesome.

In the early days of the Masters, it was sometimes difficult to assemble a half-dozen officials who were adequately versed in the Rules of Golf. Later, our tournament was the first to station a qualified official at each of the eighteen holes. Our Rules Chairman now has sufficient top-rated talent to place two officials at each hole. And this is often done so that the pair can confer or provide relief for each other, as necessary.

Tournament Improvements Committee. A second unusual committee is named the Tournament Improvements Committee. As the name implies, its members search for opportunities to make improvements. Each year this committee submits for further study a list of possible improvements in such areas as the golf course, tournament procedures, equipment, beautification, course conditioning, patrons' conveniences, and organization.

Seven club members and ten Masters champions now compose this committee, the latter being eligible for life as contestants in the Masters. However, it has become customary for the older champions, who no longer make a serious effort to play tournament golf, to help operate or assist in improving the Masters.

At any given time there are in the neighborhood of fifty improvement suggestions under consideration from a number of sources. Only a modest percentage are ever adopted, of course, but at no point does the club have less than ten or twelve approved projects awaiting their turn for action. The delaying factor is usually limitation of funds. Time can also be very important in this regard, since it is preferable to make any physical changes during the period when the club is closed. This means June, July, August, and September, which limits the amount of work that can be undertaken in any one year.

Score Reporting System. This has been to me a favorite tournament department ever since the beginning. In addition to a committee of twelve, 240 mature men are active, all of whom are golfers. They are volunteers each of whom receives a series badge for his wife or girl friend. Many are lawyers, businessmen, or bankers, and all are civic-minded supporters of the game of golf. They are drawn from Augusta, Aiken, and other nearby towns, and many use the week of the Masters as a part of their annual vacation in order to serve in our tournament organization. Needless to say, they are conscientious and dependable. Surprisingly enough, the turnover among this group is less than 5 per cent annually, and the chairman of this very important committee has a waiting list of people who have indicated a willingness to serve equal in number to the present active group.

In addition to men volunteers, there are 235 boys, or young men of late high school or college age, who are paid for their services. They are the ones who are better able to climb the ladders on the scoreboards. Most of them play golf and all are familiar with the game.

Approximately thirty-one circuit miles of underground telephone lines are involved. There are nine separate circuits and fifty-six telephones, each one of which has local battery power. Men are permanently stationed at each hole and take turns in covering each player from the time he leaves the tee until he holes out at the green. A telephone is available near each green which is used to report immediately the score to Scoring Control Room. From there, it is at once transmitted by Telautograph to the Press Building and the official scoreboard, the latter being available to our patrons. If the score relates to one of the ten leaders, it is posted on the numerous leader boards. As each team completes play on one of the holes, their scores are relayed to the scoring standard on the succeeding hole.

We prefer the telephone as the most reliable means of reporting scores under adverse conditions. Walkie-talkies are in use by several other of our tournament committees, which make it doubly desirable to let the telephone handle the large volume of score-reporting information. The men who observe play at each hole can report correct scores without going inside the spectator ropes or disturbing the patrons. Any time they are in doubt, they can check their tally with the player's caddie. All reported scores are double-checked at the ninth and eighteenth greens.

Our club is credited with having pioneered in providing scoreboards around the golf course. Until the Masters began, it was customary to operate only one scoreboard, its location usually being near the clubhouse. The numerous boards provided on the Augusta National course are called leader boards, and they supply the patrons with immediate scoring reports on the ten tournament leaders, plus special bulletins concerning others in the field.

Since the beginning, two important improvements have been made in the leader boards. The first is the previously described over-and-under-par scoring system, in which the scores are shown on a cumulative basis by using red and green numerals. The second is the system of posting scores from the back rather than the front of the board that was developed in 1969. The prior method often deprived the patrons of a clear view of the board, because of the interference by those who were posting the scores, or by ladders and other paraphernalia. Our "new" method, it should be explained, is merely a belated copy of a practice that has long been in use at baseball games. The major problem in adapting the baseball system at a golf tournament is the many more numbers that are involved. However, when the idea was first advanced, it was obviously so very simple and worthwhile that we felt chagrined at our failure to think of it sooner.

Three sizes of leader boards are used on the course: small, medium, and large. The back-of-the-board score posting was so immediately popular that all of the large- and medium-size boards were replaced with new ones. They are constructed of steel frames with aluminum panels. Considerable weight is involved, and the large-size boards each require eight-foot concrete footings. The dimensions of the three leader boards are as follows: small, eight feet by sixteen feet; medium, twelve feet by twenty-four feet; large, seventeen feet by thirty-four feet. The club operates a total of twenty-three scoreboards, including those in the clubhouse, Tournament Headquarters, and the Press Building.

Erecting and dismantling our system of scoreboards each year, we must admit, is quite a chore. We would not advise anyone to duplicate our equipment unless, first, they were quite certain of being able to write off the original cost over a period of years; and, secondly, they were willing to have their course in a state of disarray for a three-week period prior to the tournament and another two weeks at the conclusion of the tournament. It should be said, however, that other needed equipment must be erected, used, and dismantled during the same period of time, the most notable example at Augusta, next to scoreboards, being spectator stands.

Grounds and Litter Control Committees. Other quite unusual committees, we feel, are the Grounds and Litter Control committees. The former is under the direction of a retired brigadier general, a major general, and a lieutenant colonel. They organize the staff that distributes the pairings sheets and spectator booklets; the staff that looks after our twenty-one rest rooms, all of which are of concrete-block construction and equipped with modern plumbing; and the operation of the seven check stands.

Litter control is under the direction of seven individuals from Ohio who spend a week each year at Augusta and take pride in their work. All are friends of our manager, who is from Ohio. They do an outstanding job with a staff of about fifty, and have made numerous improvements since they joined our organization in 1968. The clean-up operation has been a feature of the Masters since its inception, and our patrons now co-operate to a remarkable extent. For example, it is not at all uncommon to see a spectator go out of his way to pick up a paper cup, or some other form of litter, and then place it where it belongs in a trash bag.

When the Masters first began, a pick-up crew was equipped with sharp, steel-tipped sticks and told to stab and retrieve all pieces of litter immediately after they hit the ground. One of the golf writers cautioned his readers never to drop paper cups near where they stood, as they might get stabbed in the foot. Later we dressed all the clean-up crew in natty uniforms. I do not know if they ever stabbed any feet, but they did acquire a sense of pride in their uniforms and in keeping the course clean.

Official Pin Setters and Tee Markers. This committee is composed of eight members with a very small staff. It performs three important tournament functions. One is the placement of the tee markers each day, which is done in accordance with the direction of the wind and the condition of each tee. Next is the placement of the pins, and usually the only variable factor here is the condition of each green. There are a minimum of four areas on each green that are not too undulating but that represent a good test of putting skill. Also, these areas are not easy to reach, except by a well-struck approach shot from a preferred fairway location. The same areas are used year after year. The players know in advance just about where the four holes will be cut on each green, but the one thing they do not know is which particular location will be used on which day.

Much has been written about the degree of difficulty of the pin placements at Augusta on some particular days. In truth, the committee tries to rotate the several areas on the greens so that the average degree of difficulty of the course is the same for each of the four days of play. Moreover, it should be explained that the club members normally play the same pin placements that are used during the tournament. And I might add that most of the members prefer those areas on the greens because they make the course more interesting.

The third responsibility of this committee is to operate a new system whereby each contestant may acquaint himself on each tee as to the location of the cup on the corresponding green. This is done through the use of a placard on all tees, excepting the par-threes. The pin location as shown on the placard is calibrated to attain accuracy. It is more reliable than information furnished by runners sent out by some of the contestants prior to the start of each day of play. Then, too, our service is free, and it most certainly is fair to all.

Advance information on where the hole is cut can be quite helpful on a number of holes on the Augusta National. Knowledge of where best to place the tee shot on the par-fives is important to the player who is trying to make the green in two. Likewise, tee-shot placement needs to be co-ordinated with the pin location on most of the par-fours. Also, several of our greens slope away from the player, and it is therefore difficult—even when only a short-iron approach shot is called for—to determine the exact location of the pin by sight alone.

Furnishing accurate pin-placement information in advance eliminates the need for a player to waste time by walking far ahead of his ball to examine closely the pin location on the green. The service accordingly tends to speed up play.

Concession Committee. We believe that one of the reasons the Masters is popular with patrons of the game is because they can obtain good food and drink at reasonable prices at various concession stands on the course. Our Concession Committee is composed of three members who are in the food business. The same concessionaire who was originally selected served for fourteen years. Upon his death, his son succeeded him, and we are highly pleased with his efforts.

The club owns, maintains, and provides free of rental numbers of permanent concession buildings. Our committee retains control over quality and prices, and there has never been any difficulty about terms, since the club wishes its concessionaire to be adequately compensated for assembling each year a host of capable workers and a considerable amount of equipment. The club receives a modest percentage of sales, which arrangement was designed primarily to cover the cost of making available noontime meals for the large groups of tournament employees.

Caddies. The Augusta National is one of the clubs that are still fortunate enough to have caddies. Moreover, they are good caddies. We cling to the notion that a round of golf can be more pleasurable if the player has a caddie with whom he can confer on club selection and the line of putt. Our members can take a caddie or a cart, or both. All want a caddie, although many prefer to walk.

The club has a capable caddiemaster, with an assistant, in charge of the caddie house. Our two professionals help to provide instruction for new caddies. The snack counter in the caddie house makes lunch items available on a low-cost basis. Card tables, a TV set, a pool table, and a shower room are provided. The "regular" caddies who report for assignment but who do not get a job are given a modest stipend. All caddies who are eligible for assignment are furnished with a uniform, a cap, and a pair of rubber-soled shoes, plus locker space. Our caddies are believed to be the first to be outfitted in this fashion, and we find it advantageous for several reasons.

An important inducement to caddie at our club is the possibility of getting a job during the Masters, and hopefully an assignment to work for the next champion. Several caddies from the Augusta National have become professional caddies on the tour. One, by the name of Jim Dent, became a prominent and popular tour player, and is now acknowledged to be the longest driver in the professional ranks.

Television and Radio. This important committee comprises seven individuals, six of whom are members of the club. I say important because possibly two thousand times more people see or hear the Masters through aerial transmission as can attend the tournament. Nine golfing countries, in addition to the United States, view the Masters through television. The club is especially anxious to have the telecasts done in a first-rate fashion, because the best opportunity to render a service to the game of golf is through television. The efforts of so many people, and the sacrifices made by the members, could not be justified unless such a service to golf is provided.

Accordingly, the club foregoes about 65 per cent of the television rights fee that are attainable. By so doing, the telecasts are sponsored by only two advertisers and the commercial announcements are limited. This contractual arrangement justifies the network in burying all cables and in erecting eighteen towers that are set in concrete, both of which aid in the sending of steady, clear pictures.

When the Masters Tournament began, the professional tournament golfer was probably the poorest-paid athlete in the United States, and our tournament provided its full share of leadership in bringing about a significant improvement. On the theory that too much emphasis on money may not now be in the best interests of the game, we recommend to the network that televises the Masters that it is not necessary to discuss money prizes at all: to let the emphasis be placed, instead, on titles and trophies. It is our feeling that all professional golfers are amateurs at heart, and that they will support whatever policy they deem to be the best for the game.

Our TV Committee further believes that the television pictures clearly indicate that the Masters is a well-attended tournament, and therefore suggests that attendance estimates by the announcers are unnecessary. Another reason for this policy is the absence of accurate figures. At golf tournaments people are coming and going all day long, and it would be impossible to make an accurate head count of bona fide spectators.

Finance and Admission Credentials. The three Finance Committee members, the tournament director, the two tournament secretaries and their staff have had no problem in a number of years in finding buyers for all the series badges that are authorized to be sold. Daily admission tickets are no longer sold, except for the three days of practice rounds. Each year, on January 2, everyone on our Patrons List, as earlier described, is mailed an application form for series badges. By the middle of January orders in hand exceed the available supply. The books are kept open long enough to give consideration to all orders postmarked not later than January 31. After allotments are made, very large sums of money must be returned to those whose orders cannot be filled at all or only in part.

There are considerable numbers on our Patrons List to whom the club has so far never been able to make an allocation of series badges. Before too long the attrition rate of the older patrons will enable the committee to supply these individuals. In the meantime, several thousands who have applied have had their names placed on a waiting list for the Patrons List.

The club is indeed fortunate to receive orders year after year, without any sales effort on its part, for all the series badges that can be made available. Many problems stem from this excess of demand over supply. For example, the club finds it difficult to explain to groups in various foreign countries who wish to charter jets and attend the Masters why we cannot supply admission credentials. The new players who qualify for the Masters each year do not understand at first why they cannot buy all the admission credentials their friends ask them to obtain. Much pressure is also put on our members and on the various news media and golf association officials, as well as our tournament organization.

The club regularly tries, through the news media, to warn golfing fans not to come to Augusta unless they have in hand the necessary tournament entry badges. But a lot of people arrive each year with nothing other than cash and a determination to somehow see the Augusta National course and the tournament that is played on it. The result is a black market for series badges, where prices are bid up as high as five times the amount received by the club. Some of the local motels charge substantially more than normal rates for accommodation during the week of the tournament. The club does everything within its power to discourage the black market in series badges, while public-spirited citizens urge all types of business people never to raise prices during the week of the tournament.

Motion Picture Committee. The first documentary movie of the Masters, made with the approval of the club, was produced by an independent company in 1960, and the same was true the following year. In 1962, the club became the producer of the Masters movie, with Reginald Wells as the director. The movie has now become quite an important part of the tournament, requiring twenty-four towers to be erected each year for the exclusive use of movie-camera operators.

At the present time, sixteen-millimeter color prints of the film are sold annually for nontheatrical use to three United States sponsors. The movie is likewise being shown in ten or more foreign golfing countries, at golf clubs, luncheon clubs, and at business and social gatherings.

A committee of three club members looks after the business end of the movie. The largest sale of prints occurred in 1974, when 785 copies were marketed. Those who view the movie can readily see more of the important tournament action each year than by any other means. This is true although the running time of the film is little more than a half hour.

Tournament Organization Outings. The Augusta National regularly closes its golf course for the summer during the latter part of May, the last day the members could use their course in 1975 being May 24. However, nonmembers who serve the Masters Tournament are invited each year to play the course following the closing date during a four-day series of outings. The first day the club entertains the scorers, the second day the nearby radio, TV, and press personnel, and the third day the gallery, communications, and miscellaneous workers. The final day is devoted to the caddies.

As a thank-you gesture for the volunteer efforts that help to operate the Masters, the club entertained in 1975 a total of 757 golf-playing guests.

The Masters—Its Future

Someone once quite proudly told Dr. Mackenzie, our golf course architect, that no one had ever been able to break par on a golf course located in the doctor's home town. "Good heavens!" exclaimed Doc. "What on earth is wrong with it?"

The foregoing explains quite clearly the attitude Bob Jones and Mackenzie had in mind when they were planning the golf course that was named the Augusta National. Both spoke and wrote about their desire to produce something that would give pleasure to the greatest possible number. This same philosophy was applied to the Masters Tournament when it came along a few years later. To quote from a Masters Tournament spectator booklet written by Bob Jones in 1949: "The course is not intended so much to punish severely the wayward shot as to reward adequately the stroke played with skill—and judgment."

It has been proven, at least to our own satisfaction, that those who patronize the Masters get more pleasure and excitement watching the great players make birdies than bogies. It would be easy to set up the Augusta National so that no one could break 80 on it. But, if this were done, we doubt if the players would like it. And we are certain such a policy would be unpopular with the patrons.

We firmly believe that the rating and the general appraisal of our course have been benefited by the subpar scoring records that have been established here. Most assuredly, Mackenzie and Jones would have been disappointed if good scores by capable players had not been forthcoming. The club officers, and many others, like the practice of permitting the Masters field to compete under the same playing conditions that are normal for members' play. Many of our members are low- or medium-handicap players. They enjoy testing their golfing capacity occasionally by playing from the championship tees, with the knowledge that the pin locations are as difficult, or nearly so, as during the Masters Tournament. Guests are often especially anxious to try playing the championship tees.

There are various theories as to the best method of providing a proper test of golfing skill. Our club has no quarrel with any of them. We merely assert that our course and our tournament policies are usually suitable to those who participate in the Masters, who help to operate it, or who support it in the various ways a golf tournament requires support.

In the late 1920s, several of the best tournament players of that period were having a lively discussion as to the relative advantages of hitting drives with a draw versus a fade. Bob Jones was present, and, when asked for his view, stated simply that he saw nothing wrong with hitting a straight ball. I like to recall this incident when trying to make the point that, if the player is accurate, all he needs to do at Augusta is to hit a straight tee shot in the right direction in order to reach the favored fairway location. There are a number of holes that invite a draw or a hooked shot, but none that require it. There are several that invite a fade, but it is not necessary to play a left-to-right tee shot in order to score well.

The rolling terrain at the Augusta National makes it highly desirable for a player to be able to execute almost every conceivable kind of fairway shot from downhill, uphill, and sidehill as well as level lies. Good putters have an advantage because there are a number of severely contoured greens, and, while others are moderately contoured, there is not a single green on the course that could be classified as flat.

Long hitters with courage and accuracy have an advantage, because all four of the par-fives are reachable in two shots. No one, however, should mistakenly exaggerate the importance of this particular advantage. The records of the Masters reveal a large number of double bogies on the par-fives, due to encounters with water and woods. We might point out that the great record of success achieved by Jack Nicklaus on the Augusta National is due to strokes gained on the par-threes rather than on the par-fives.

Those who can skillfully maneuver their approach shots to greens that are both undulating and firm likewise have an edge. Sometimes rain will interfere, but it is always our policy to try to provide greens that are fast, and this requires surfaces that are firm almost to the point of hardness.

Players who are capable of executing chip shots accurately have a better opportunity, because everyone in the field is going to occasionally find his ball a little off the putting surface. Our largest green, the thirteenth, measures 8,400 square feet. The smallest, the seventh, is 3,600 square feet. The average is approximately 5,600 square feet. This means that our greens are quite generous in size, but they will not hold a poorly struck approach shot. To quote Bob Jones again: "The spectator should appreciate that, careful greenskeeping notwithstanding, a player may encounter a 'heavy' or too-grassy lie, even in the fairway, from which a ball cannot be played with severe backspin, no matter how skillful the player. A clean contact between club and ball is the first requirement for this kind of shot. Sometimes an unsatisfactory lie for a quick-stopping shot will induce the expert to play a running approach, which type of shot a number of our greens are designed to accommodate—especially, I might say, numbers five and fourteen."

The principal thoughts I personally wish to convey about the course where the Masters is played are, first, that it is designed to bring to the front those who are most skillful and who exercise the best judgment; and, second, that it does not favor any particular kind of player, but rather rewards the well-rounded player. A year-by-year list of winners of the Masters Tournament (see Appendix II) is, in itself, the finest tribute that can ever be paid to our golf course.

Golf is used, and rightly so, to serve many purposes. The sale of merchandise and real estate, the raising of charitable funds, and the promotion of various projects. The Masters is operated for the single purpose of benefiting the game itself. We try to eliminate all forms of commercialism, except on TV and in our movies. Network sponsorship is necessary in order to serve a ten-nation audience. The same is true of the movies. But the commercials are held to a minimum.

Officials of the leading golf associations regularly meet at the Masters. They lend their support and assist in directing the event, and, as far as I am concerned, they own it. All are deeply devoted to the traditions of the game and to its continued popularity. So long as these things are true, the Masters is useful and worthwhile to everyone involved.

I would like in conclusion to make the observation that those with talent who give unselfishly of themselves just because they love golf are entitled to one uncomplicated place where they can feel completely at ease.

APPENDIXES

APPENDIX I

Author's Note

Because of the fifty-year span that this book covers, its preparation was necessarily quite largely a singlehanded undertaking. I am the only one left who took an active part in all phases of the organization of the Augusta National. The same is true with regard to establishing the Masters Tournament.

"First Person Singular" might have been a suitable name for my book, except that it has no golfing connotation. I say this because the pronoun "I" has, I am afraid, been overworked a bit, although I have made an effort to avoid this error.

Several times during my two years of writing effort, I have been tempted to take the easy way out and engage an experienced writer of books to put my recollections into words. Had I done so, the result, from a literary point of view, would definitely have been superior. The reason I determined to adhere to my original plan is because the members of the club, and many other friends, know only too well my customary manner of expressing myself. They will readily realize, without any reassurance from me, that this book is unmistakably mine. To the others who may peruse these passages, I can only hope that my method of translating my thoughts and related information is understandable. I also hope that my sincerity and my efforts at accuracy will compensate for lack of skill.

Mrs. Wilda Gwin and Mrs. Kathryn Murphy, executive secretaries at the Masters Tournament headquarters, have tirelessly done research work, and have corrected errors in grammar, punctuation, and spelling. They have made most valuable suggestions, as well as doing much typing and retyping. Philip Wahl, our club manager, and his secretary, Mrs. Maureen Juwig, have assisted in digging out from the club's records much of the needed information. My secretary in New York, Miss Mary Haldeman, also helped during the initial stages of the project. During the summer of 1974, in the Blue Ridge Mountain area near Linville, North Carolina, Mrs. Virginia Foxx gave me a considerable amount of secretarial assistance. One of Bob Jones's law partners, a club member, Francis M. Bird, of Atlanta, supplied some special information. Another member, William S. Morris III, publisher of the Augusta *Chronicle* and the Augusta *Herald*, caused his newspapers to supply old news items and photographs.

A nephew of mine, Kenneth L. Roberts, of Seattle, read a considerable part of the manuscript and made a number of useful suggestions. I found it necessary to call on more than twenty friends in various parts of the country for bits of information or verification of dates. I know they will forgive me for not listing their names. Likewise, I asked three club members to read parts of the manuscript, as I prepared it, to find out if my efforts were producing material that might be readable as well as factual. I am greatly obliged to them for their encouragement, whether or not their complimentary appraisals were justified.

As photographs occupy an unusually large space percentagewise of the pages of this book, the quality of the photography is vitally important. Mr. Frank Christian, of Augusta, is the only person who could ever have been considered to undertake this responsibility. I state this because of his talent and also his interest in our club. He has been the club photographer for many years, and his father, a photographer for the Augusta *Herald*, covered the club's activities from its beginning. Frank's brother, Anthony, has done much of the club's architectural work, and his sister, Patricia, has done interior decorating for the club. One might say there is a family relationship with the club, and one which I consider to be quite important.

I am also indebted to Mrs. Ann Whitman, General Eisenhower's long-time personal secretary, and to the Dwight D. Eisenhower Library, of Abilene, Kansas, for verification of dates and other special information concerning travel schedules of President Eisenhower.

APPENDIX II

Masters Winners and Runners-Up

Year	Winner	Score	Runner-Up	Score	
1934	Horton Smith	284	Craig Wood	285	
*1935	Gene Sarazen	282	Craig Wood	282	
1936	Horton Smith	285	Harry Cooper	286	
1937	Byron Nelson	283	Ralph Guldahl	285	
1938	Henry Picard	285	Ralph Guldahl, Harry Cooper	287	
1939	Ralph Guldahl	279	Sam Snead	280	
1940	Jimmy Demaret	280	Lloyd Mangrum	284	
1941	Craig Wood	280	Byron Nelson	283	
*1942	Byron Nelson	280	Ben Hogan	280	
1946	Herman Keiser	282	Ben Hogan	283	
1947	Jimmy Demaret	281	Byron Nelson, Frank Stranahan	283	
1948	Claude Harmon	279	Cary Middlecoff	284	231
1949	Sam Snead	282	Johnny Bulla, Lloyd Mangrum	285	*Augusta*
1950	Jimmy Demaret	283	Jim Ferrier	285	*National*
1951	Ben Hogan	280	Skee Riegel	282	*Golf Club*
1952	Sam Snead	286	Jack Burke, Jr.	290	
1953	Ben Hogan	274	Ed Oliver, Jr.	279	
*1954	Sam Snead	289	Ben Hogan	289	
1955	Cary Middlecoff	279	Ben Hogan	286	
1956	Jack Burke, Jr.	289	Ken Venturi	290	
1957	Doug Ford	283	Sam Snead	286	
1958	Arnold Palmer	284	Doug Ford, Fred Hawkins	285	
1959	Art Wall, Jr.	284	Cary Middlecoff	285	
1960	Arnold Palmer	282	Ken Venturi	283	

Year	Winner	Score	Runner-Up	Score
1961	Gary Player	280	Charles R. Coe, Arnold Palmer	281
*1962	Arnold Palmer	280	Gary Player, Dow Finsterwald	280
1963	Jack Nicklaus	286	Tony Lema	287
1964	Arnold Palmer	276	Dave Marr, Jack Nicklaus	282
1965	Jack Nicklaus	271	Arnold Palmer, Gary Player	280
*1966	Jack Nicklaus	288	Tommy Jacobs, Gay Brewer, Jr.	288
1967	Gay Brewer, Jr.	280	Bobby Nichols	281
1968	Bob Goalby	277	Roberto de Vicenzo	278
1969	George Archer	281	Billy Casper, George Knudson, Tom Weiskopf	282
*1970	Billy Casper	279	Gene Littler	279
1971	Charles Coody	279	Johnny Miller, Jack Nicklaus	281
1972	Jack Nicklaus	286	Bruce Crampton, Bobby Mitchell, Tom Weiskopf	289
1973	Tommy Aaron	283	J. C. Snead	284
1974	Gary Player	278	Dave Stockton, Tom Weiskopf	280
1975	Jack Nicklaus	276	Johnny Miller, Tom Weiskopf	277

* Won in 18-hole play-off.

APPENDIX III

*The Tournament Record and
Other Performances of
Robert Tyre Jones, Jr.,
1911–42*

Compiled by Bill Inglish

Note: For many years Mr. Bill Inglish, of *The Daily Oklahoman,* has been compiling statistical information concerning the Masters Tournament. Shortly after the death of our club president, the Augusta National requested Mr. Inglish to prepare a complete record of tournament play by Robert T. Jones, Jr. This was done, and at the same time Mr. Inglish also supplied some other interesting information that is pertinent to the career of Bob Jones.

The documentary by Inglish required considerable research, and it may well be the most complete thing of its kind in existence. Every item, we are assured, has been carefully substantiated. The officers of the Augusta National therefore feel an obligation to make the information available to the news media and through them, to the golfing public. Accordingly, they have granted permission for me to include it as an appendix to this book.

Those who find something of interest in my account of the Augusta National can have a better understanding of the character and remarkable talents of the chief founder of the club by reading the material assembled by Bill Inglish.

Bob Jones's name is indelibly linked with the Augusta National. For this reason, I can think of no better way to assure a long life for his club and his tournament than to keep fresh the recorded evidence of Bob's great qualities of mind and heart. The same thought can be applied to the future popularity of the game of golf.

Clifford Roberts

Beginning in 1916 at the age of fourteen, and ending in 1930 at the age of twenty-eight, Robert Tyre Jones, Jr., played in thirty-one major championships for which amateurs are eligible. His first victory came in the U. S. Open in 1923 at the age of twenty-one. During eight consecutive years, 1923–30, he held one or more major titles every year. In those eight years he entered a total of twenty-eight tournaments, an average of only 3.6 per annum. Twenty-one of these tournaments were major events, an average of 2.5 per annum. He won thirteen of the twenty-one major tournaments.

Jones won the U. S. Amateur five times in thirteen starts, the U. S. Open four times in eleven starts, the British Open three times in four starts, and the British Amateur once in three starts.

Jones averaged 73.61 strokes for fifty-six rounds in the two National Opens, not counting play-offs, and won fifty-nine matches in match-play while losing only ten—almost six out of every seven.

In 1930, Jones captured all four major championships, the British Amateur, British Open, U. S. Open, and U. S. Amateur, in that order. This was golf's Grand Slam. He then retired from competition at the age of twenty-eight.

However, a finer achievement than the Grand Slam, in the opinion of O. B. Keeler, was Jones's performance in the two National Open Championships.

In the last nine years of his career, from 1922–30, Jones played in twelve National Open Championships, nine in this country and three in Britain. He finished first or second eleven times in those twelve starts. The only exception was the U. S. Open at Oakmont, in 1927, in which he tied for eleventh place.

234   *Jones the Man—a Biography*

Augusta National Golf Club

Born   March 17, 1902 (St. Patrick's Day) in Atlanta, Georgia, the son of Robert P. and Clara Thomas Jones

Schools   Woodbury School and Tech High School, Atlanta

Colleges   Georgia Tech (BS in Mechanical Engineering, 1922); Harvard (BS in English Literature, 1924); Emory University Law School, 1926–27. He was admitted to the Georgia Bar in 1928.

Fraternity   Sigma Alpha Epsilon

Married   Mary Malone on June 17, 1924, in Atlanta

Children   Clara Malone (Black), Robert T. III, and Mary Ellen (Hood)

Honors   Executive Committee, United States Golf Association, 1928–29–30. (He was a long-time member of the USGA Museum Committee.)

  • Sullivan Award as Nation's Outstanding Amateur Athlete, 1930

- Honorary Vice-President of the Professional Golfers' Association of America 1931 (until his death)
- Georgia Tech's Distinguished Service Medal, 1937
- Certificate of Distinguished Achievement, Atlanta Chamber of Commerce, 1939
- His Grand Slam was voted the outstanding all-time sports achievement in an Associated Press poll, 1944
- Honorary Chairman, USGA Amateur Public Links Championship, 1948
- An overwhelming choice as the Greatest Golfer of the Age by the nation's sports writers and sports broadcasters in a fifty-year poll of the Associated Press, 1950
- Commended by the Georgia Legislature for his sportsmanship and character, 1951.
- Voted the top amateur golfer of half century in PGA poll, 1952
- Silver Buffalo Award, Boy Scouts of America (scouting's highest national award)
- Man of the South by *Dixie Business Magazine*, 1953
- Gold Tee Award of the Metropolitan (New York) Chapter, Golf Writers Association of America, 1953
- The USGA's Award for Distinguished Sportsmanship in Golf was conceived and named for him, 1955
- Richardson Award of the Golf Writers Association of America for consistently outstanding contributions to golf, 1957
- Freedom of St. Andrews, Scotland, 1958. (Only one other American—Benjamin Franklin—has been so honored.)
- Named Man of the Age in Sports by the Sports Lodge of B'nai B'rith, 1960. (One of nine so honored.)
- Walter Hagen Award for the most distinguished contribution to the furtherance of Anglo-American golf, 1962
- State of Georgia Athletic Hall of Fame, 1963. (One of three original inductees.)
- An overwhelming choice in a 1973 poll of the Golf Writers Association of America as one of the five greatest golfers of all time. (The others: Walter Hagen, Ben Hogan, Jack Nicklaus, and Arnold Palmer.)
- The Inaugural Lecture of the Robert Tyre Jones, Jr., Memorial Lecture on Legal Ethics was given at the Emory Law School on October 31, 1974. The presentation was by Mr. Justice Harry A. Blackmun, of the United States Supreme Court, who said in part:

Of his career at the bar and of his physical distress in later years, the general public knows less. He seldom engaged in litigation of the type that attracts notice and publicity. His practice was largely an office one. But his legal and business activities and interests were substantial. A partner has stated, "It was always recognized in this office that his judgment . . . was superlative and dependable." I therefore am aware, as you people of Atlanta and of Georgia have long known, that he was an upright laborer in the vineyard of the law, an accomplished journeyman in the profession we serve, a partner in a good firm, a servant of the interests of his clients, and a member of an old and an honored bar.

And so, to summarize these sketchy references to Bob Jones, we find: (1) talent, (2) personality, (3) achieved mastery of self, (4) a focus on a significant target, and (5) a desire for something more in life than participation in the sport he had dominated.

What, however, is the sixth factor that stands out, silent and impressive? It is, it seems to me, the complete absence, so far as I know or have read, of any besmirching or demeaning or unethical aspect in his legal or extra-legal career.

Business Interests (in addition to the practice of law)
    Director of the Southern Company
    Director of the Jones Mercantile Company
    Director of the Canton Textile Mills of Canton, Georgia
    Director of the First National Bank of Atlanta, Georgia
    Coca-Cola interests
    Director and later Vice-President of A. G. Spalding & Brothers. (He was a distinguished club designer.)
Military Record   Captain, U. S. Army Organized Reserve, 1931; Captain, U. S. Ninth Air Force, 1942; Major, 1943; Lieutenant Colonel, 1944, serving in England and Normandy
Clubs   Augusta National Golf Club, Atlanta Athletic Club, Capital City Club, Druid Hills Golf Club, Piedmont Driving Club, Peachtree Golf Club (Atlanta, Georgia), Royal and Ancient Golf Club of St. Andrews, Scotland.
Other Sports   Baseball (catcher), touch football and track as boy, tennis, ordinary and deep-sea fishing, hunting, and trapshooting. He also was a faithful Georgia Tech football fan.
Author   *Down the Fairway* (with O. B. Keeler), 1927
    Golf Is My Game, 1960
    Bobby Jones on Golf, 1966
    Bobby Jones on the Basic Golf Swing (with Anthony Ravielli), 1969
    In addition to these books, he also authored countless newspaper and magazine articles on the game.
Deceased   December 18, 1971, in Atlanta.
Interred   December 20, 1971, in Oakland Cemetery, Atlanta. Golfers from both sides of the Atlantic attended a memorial service for him in Holy Trinity Church, St. Andrews, Scotland, on May 4, 1972.

A Man of Intellect

Roger Wethered recognized a little-known quality of Robert T. Jones, Jr.—his intellect—at the memorial service for Jones in St. Andrews, Scotland. Paying tribute to his old friend and rival in an address at Trinity Parish Church, Wethered remarked: "I do not think we realized the exceptional mental caliber that lay beneath Bobby's quiet, reserved manner."

Jones was a fine student and scholar. He was graduated from high school at the age of sixteen, took his first college degree (in mechanical engineering at Georgia Tech) at age twenty, his second degree (in English literature at Harvard) at 22, and passed the Georgia State Bar Examination after completing only two semesters at Emory University Law School. His writings and public speeches reflected this rich background.

At Georgia Tech, Jones was elected to Koseme and Bull Dog honor societies. He also was a member of the Pan-Hellenic Council, of ANAK, and the informal varsity golf team which he and his friend, Perry Adair, formed. In addition, he was secretary of his senior class. Walter Coxe, a classmate at Tech, says: "Jones was a fine, clean, friendly, healthy, fun-loving, smart, modest and hard-working man on campus. He always rated highly in his classes." Some say he was so devoted to his studies that his schoolmates nicknamed him "Deac."

The mechanical engineering curriculum at Tech was packed with courses in mathematics, chemistry, physics, geology, and drawing, in addition to engineering —with no electives—yet Jones maintained good marks. He scored 98, 96, and 95 in math; 97 in geology; two 90s in English; 91, 89, 84, and 83 in chemistry; 85 in physics and 85 in electrical engineering. He fared poorest, by comparison, in mechanical engineering, although maintaining a high over-all average for the four years. In the years ahead, he utilized his training in mechanical engineering as a designer of golf clubs.

At Harvard, he logged mostly B's in French, German, English history, German prose, History of the Roman Republic, and History of Continental Europe from 1815–71, and in his major study. His English courses included Comparative Literature, English Composition, Dryden and his Time, Swift and his Time, and Shakespeare. He had eleven different instructors in elementary German, six in elementary French. Although he was not eligible for varsity golf, he was awarded an honorary "H"—a signal honor.

Jones took only one course—Public Utilities—in his first semester in law school and six the second—Agency, Contracts, Damages, Pleading and Practice, Property, and Torts. He scored three A's, three B's, and one C, earning the Callaghan and Company prize. He withdrew from Emory during his third semester, in the autumn of 1927, and passed the bar examination shortly thereafter. He won his first federal case (a petition for a preferred claim) at Macon, Georgia, on May 17, 1929, after being admitted to practice in federal courts only a day before he came to Macon. He had launched his practice of law in Atlanta in January 1928.

A Part-Time Golfer

Although he was the most outstanding golfer of his day, Robert T. Jones, Jr., played a very limited tournament schedule. He devoted most of his time to his schooling, his family, the practice of law, the playing of charity matches (he probably played more exhibitions than any other amateur in history), and his civic responsibilities.

In his thirteen years in competition in the major championships, he was a student—either high school or college—in nine of those years. He took part in only fifty-two tournaments in that span, an average of only four per year. He won twenty-three. The most he entered was eight as an eighteen-year-old in 1920; the fewest was two in later years. He captured six of seven tournaments in which he started in 1930, his final year of competition.

For the most part, the major championships (the U.S. and British Amateurs and Opens), and an occasional appearance elsewhere, were the only events in which he appeared. In some years, he participated in only the U. S. Open and Amateur Championships.

For each of these events, he had to come out of months of retirement. He did not have the chance to keep competitively conditioned on the tournament trail. He played no serious golf between the National Amateur in 1922 (at Brookline) and the National Open in 1923 (which he won at Inwood). He had entered Harvard University in the autumn of 1922, and did not touch a club until early the following summer, when he returned home to Atlanta to prepare for the Open.

Following the 1928 U. S. Amateur at Brae Burn in September, he played only six or seven informal rounds until the next April. After the 1929 U. S. Open at Winged Foot (which he won after 108 holes of competition), he said he felt as if he had just started hitting the ball and could use a lot more golf.

Fortunately, he had the type of swing that responded quickly to a few rounds in competition.

He altered his limited schedule to include another tournament only once. After tying for eleventh in the U. S. Open at Oakmont in 1927 (his worst showing in this Championship), he hurriedly filed his entry for the British Open at St. Andrews in an effort to redeem himself. He triumphed at St. Andrews with a classic performance. Then he said: "I will not return to England until 1930 when I go back as a member of the Walker Cup team. I cannot afford to make another trip sooner than that." This was the only time he mentioned his finances, either directly or indirectly. (In 1928, he refused a $50,000 home offered by Atlanta friends and admirers, although W. C. Fownes, president of the USGA, said the gift would not have affected his amateur standing.)

"To my knowledge, Jones never made reference to his limited tournament schedule," says Watts Gunn, a fellow Atlantan whom Jones defeated in the final of the 1925 U. S. Amateur. "Every round he played as though he were in a championship match."

Thirty years after his retirement from competition, Jones made a brief comment about his limited play. In *Golf Is My Game*, a book he authored in 1960, he wrote: ". . . For a great many of the years when I had been winning championships, I had played only two tournaments a year."

Other friends remember him not only as a great golfer but also as a husband, father, friend, and outstanding citizen of Atlanta. He headed the Community

Chest drive the first year it went over the top, and also chaired successful Red Cross drives.

"Bob always stayed close to and spent a lot of time with his three children," Ivan Allen, Jr., says. "There were many trips to the beach, the movies and the circus. In addition to attending PTA meetings, he was always available to help with homework."

Joe Dey, former USGA Executive Director and Commissioner of the PGA Tournament Players Division, said: "He was thought of as a person first and a golfer second."

In one of his last interviews, Jones said: "My wife and children came first, then my profession. Finally, and never in a life by itself, came golf." In sum, he treated golf as a game rather than as a way of life, and kept it in proper perspective among his varied pursuits.

His limited tournament schedule and his effectiveness in competition are underscored by the following chronological listing of his performances:

Age	Year	Tournaments	Finishing Position
14	1916	Georgia Amateur	Winner
		USGA National Amateur	Quarter-finalist
17	1919	Yates-Gode Tournament	Winner
		Canadian Open	Tied for second
		Southern Amateur	Semifinalist
		Western Amateur	Defeated, first round
		USGA National Amateur	Runner-up
		Southern Open	Runner-up
18	1920	Georgia Amateur	Semifinalist
		Davis-Freeman Tournament	Winner
		Southern Amateur	Winner
		Western Amateur	Semifinalist
		USGA National Open	Tied for eighth
		Morris County (N.J.) Invitation	Winner
		USGA National Amateur	Semifinalist
		Southern Open	Runner-up
19	1921	British Amateur	Defeated, fourth round
		British Open	Withdrew, third round
		USGA National Open	Tied for fifth
		Western Open	Tied for fourth
		USGA National Amateur	Quarter-finalist
20	1922	Southern Amateur	Winner
		USGA National Open	Tied for second
		USGA National Amateur	Semifinalist
21	1923	USGA National Open	Winner
		USGA National Amateur	Defeated, second round

239

Augusta
National
Golf Club

Age	Year	Tournaments	Finishing Position
22	1924	USGA National Open	Runner-up
		USGA National Amateur	Winner
23	1925	West Coast of Florida Open	Sixteenth
		USGA National Open	Runner-up
		USGA National Amateur	Winner
24	1926	West Coast of Florida Open	Runner-up
		British Amateur	Defeated, sixth round
		British Open	Winner
		USGA National Open	Winner
		USGA National Amateur	Runner-up
25	1927	Southern Open	Winner
		USGA National Open	Tied for eleventh
		British Open	Winner
		USGA National Amateur	Winner
26	1928	USGA National Open	Runner-up
		Warren K. Wood Memorial	Winner
		USGA National Amateur	Winner
27	1929	USGA National Open	Winner
		USGA National Amateur	Defeated, first round
28	1930	Savannah Open	Runner-up
		Southeastern Open	Winner
		Golf Illustrated Gold Vase	Winner
		British Amateur	Winner
		British Open	Winner
		USGA National Open	Winner
		USGA National Amateur	Winner

USGA *National Amateur Championship*

1916 *Merion Cricket Club, Ardmore, Pennsylvania, September 4–9*

Jones, at age 14, qualified with 163 (74 on the west course, 89 on the east). The 74 led the field of 157. William C. Fownes, Jr., was medalist with 153.

Jones defeated Eben M. Byers, the 1906 champion, in the first round, 3 and 1, and Frank W. Dyer in the second round, 4 and 2. He was defeated by Robert A. Gardner, the 1909 and 1915 champion, in the quarter-finals, 5 and 3.

All matches were at 36 holes on the east course. Eventual champion was Chick Evans, who defeated Gardner in the final, 4 and 3.

1919 *Oakmont Country Club, Oakmont, Pennsylvania, August 16–23*

Jones qualified with 81-78—159, one stroke behind the tri-medalists, Jimmy Manion, Paul Tewkesbury, and S. Davidson Herron, a home-course player.

Jones defeated Manion in the first round, 3 and 2; Gardner in the second round, 5 and 4; Rudolf Knepper in the quarter-finals, 3 and 2; Fownes, the 1910 champion, in the semifinals, 5 and 3; then was defeated by Herron in the final, 5 and 4. All matches were at 36 holes.

1920 *The Engineers' Country Club, Roslyn, New York, September 6–11*

Jones was medalist with 79-75—154, defeating Fred Wright for the honor by matching cards in their quarter-final match.

He defeated J. Simpson Dean, a fellow Atlantan, in the first round, 5 and 4; Dyer in the second round, 5 and 4; Wright in the quarter-finals, 5 and 4, then was defeated by Francis Ouimet, the 1914 champion, in the semifinals, 6 and 5.

All matches were at 36 holes. Eventual champion was Evans, who defeated Ouimet in the final, 7 and 6.

1921 *St. Louis Country Club, Clayton, Missouri, September 17–24*

Jones qualified with 76-75—151, over the 6,351-yard course, seven strokes behind Ouimet, the medalist.

He defeated Clarence Wolff in the first round, 12 and 11; Dr. Oscar F. Willing in the second round, 9 and 8; then was defeated by Willie Hunter, 1921 British Amateur champion, in the quarter-finals, 2 and 1.

All matches were at 36 holes. Eventual champion was Jesse P. Guilford, who defeated Gardner in the final, 7 and 6.

1922 *The Country Club, Brookline, Massachusetts, September 2–9*

Jones qualified with 72-73—145, one stroke behind Guilford, the medalist and defender.

He defeated James J. Beadle in the first round, 3 and 1; Gardner in the second round, 3 and 2; William McPhail in the quarter-finals, 4 and 3; then was defeated by Jess W. Sweetser in the semifinals, 8 and 7. This was Jones's worst defeat at match-play.

All matches were at 36 holes. Eventual champion was Sweetser, who defeated Evans in the final, 3 and 2.

1923 *Flossmoor Country Club, Flossmoor, Illinois, September 15–22*

Jones was medalist with 75-74—149, one over par, on the 6,704-yard course. Evans equaled the 149 but Jones won the play-off, 72–76.

Jones defeated Tom B. Cochran in the first round, 2 and 1, but was defeated by Max Marston in the second round, 2 and 1.

All matches were at 36 holes. Eventual champion was Marston, who defeated Sweetser on the 38th hole.

1924 *Merion Cricket Club (East Course), Ardmore, Pennsylvania, September 20–27*

Jones qualified with 72-72—144, two strokes behind the medalist, D. Clarke Corkran.

Jones defeated W. J. Thompson of Canada in the first round, 6 and 5; Corkran in the second round, 3 and 2; Knepper in the quarter-finals, 6 and 4; Ouimet in the semifinals, 11 and 10; and George Von Elm in the final, 9 and 8.

All matches were at 36 holes.

1925 *Oakmont Country Club, Oakmont, Pennsylvania, August 31–September 5*

Jones qualified with 75-72—147, two strokes behind the medalist, Roland R. MacKenzie, whose 145 was one over par for the 6,872-yard course.

Jones defeated William M. Reekie in the first round, 11 and 10; Wolff in the quarter-finals, 6 and 5; Von Elm in the semifinals, 7 and 6; and Watts Gunn, a fellow Atlantan and clubmate, in the final 8 and 7.

Only 16 qualified for match-play and all matches were at 36 holes.

1926 *Baltusrol Golf Club, Springfield, New Jersey, September 13–18*

Jones was medalist with 70-73—143 (the 70 led the field by six strokes).

Jones defeated Richard A. "Dickie" Jones, Jr., in the first round, 1 up; Reekie in the second round, 5 and 4; Evans in the quarter-finals, 3 and 2; Ouimet in the semifinals, 5 and 4; but was defeated by Von Elm in the final, 2 and 1. This was his last defeat at 36 holes.

The first two rounds were at 18 holes, the others at 36.

1927 *Minikahda Club, Minneapolis, Minnesota, August 22–27*

Jones was medalist with 75-67—142, two under par for the 6,679-yard course, to tie the record set by D. Clarke Corkran at Merion in 1924.

Jones defeated Maurice J. McCarthy, Jr., in the first round, 2 up; Eugene V. Homans in the second round, 3 and 2; Harrison R. "Jimmy" Johnston in the quarter-finals, 10 and 9; Ouimet in the semifinals, 11 and 10; and Evans in the final, 8 and 7.

The first two rounds were at 18 holes, the others at 36.

1928 *Brae Burn Country Club, West Newton, Massachusetts, September 10–15*

Jones qualified with 77-74—151, eight strokes behind George J. Voigt, the medalist, whose 143 was one under par for the 6,643-yard course.

Jones defeated J. W. Brown in the first round, 4 and 3; Ray Gorton, a home-course player, in the second round, on the 19th hole; John B. Beck in the quarter-finals, 14 and 13; Phillips Finlay in the semifinals, 13 and 12; and T. Philip Perkins in the final 10 and 9. (Perkins was the British Amateur champion, Jones the defending U. S. Amateur champion.)

The first two matches were at 18 holes, the others at 36.

1929   Pebble Beach Golf Links, Del Monte, California, September 2–7

Jones and Homans tied for the medal with 145s, one over par for the 6,661-yard links. Jones's rounds were 70-75.

Jones was defeated by Johnny Goodman in the first round, one up, in an 18-hole match.

Eventual champion was Johnston, who defeated Dr. Oscar F. Willing in the final, 4 and 3.

1930   Merion Cricket Club, Ardmore, Pennsylvania, September 22–27

Jones was medalist with 69-73—142, two over par for the 6,565-yard course, to tie the record held by himself (1927) and Corkran (1924).

Jones defeated C. Ross "Sandy" Somerville in the first round, 5 and 4; Fred G. Hoblitzel in the second round, 5 and 4; Fay Coleman in the quarter-finals, 6 and 5; Sweetser in the semifinals, 9 and 8; and Homans in the final, 8 and 7.

The first two rounds were at 18 holes, the others at 36.

18 of Jones's U. S. Amateur Records Still Stand

Jones was the outstanding performer in the USGA National Amateur Championship when it was conducted at match-play, and still holds these records:

1   The most titles: five won in 1924-25-27-28-30.
2   The most frequent finalist: seven times, in 1919-24-25-26-27-28-30.
3   The most frequent finalist in successive years: five, in 1924-25-26-27-28.
4   The youngest quarter-finalist: he was only 14 at Merion in 1916.
5   The most frequent medalist: six times in 1920-23-26-27-29-30 (this record is shared with Walter J. Travis).
6   The lowest 18-hole score in the qualifying rounds at the championship proper: 67 at Minikahda in 1927. (D. Clarke Corkran set the original record at Merion in 1924, W. B. "Duff" McCullough tied it at Winged Foot in 1940, Skip Alexander at Omaha Field Club in 1941, and Skee Riegel at Baltusrol in 1946.)
7   He never failed to qualify for the championship, either sectionally or at the championship proper.
8   He won the highest percentage of matches: .843 (he won 43, lost eight).
9   He won his 43 matches by the average margin of 6.1 holes.
10   All eight of his defeats were at the hands of national champions.
11   He won the most scheduled 36-hole matches: 35.
12   He won his scheduled 36-hole matches by an average margin of seven holes.
13   He won the most double-figure victories: eight (career).
14   He won the most double-figure victories in succession: three at Brae Burn in 1928.
15   He won the most double-figure victories in one championship: three at Brae Burn in 1928.
16   He achieved the most decisive victory in a scheduled 36-hole match: 14 and 13 over John B. Beck at Brae Burn in 1928. (He shares this record with

243

*Augusta
National
Golf Club*

Jerome D. Travers, who set the original record at the Country Club of Detroit in 1915.)

17 He was the most holes up on opponents in one championship: 42 at Brae Burn in 1928. (In five matches, he had to play only 108 of a possible 144 holes.)

18 He was 32 up on four opponents at Oakmont in 1925, playing only 116 of a possible 144 holes.

The Amateurs Who Opposed Jones

In his 13 starts in the USGA National Amateur Championship, Jones played 37 different men, 10 of them more than once. He never lost to the same man twice. He won three of four matches from Francis Ouimet; two of three from George Von Elm and Robert Gardner; two each from Frank W. Dyer, Rudolf Knepper, Clarence Wolff, William Reekie, Chick Evans and Gene Homans; and divided two with Jess Sweetser.

Jones's seven defeats at 36 holes were administered by Gardner at Merion in 1916, Davey Herron at Oakmont in 1919, Ouimet at The Engineers in 1920, Willie Hunter at St. Louis in 1921, Sweetser at the Country Club, Brookline, Massachusetts, in 1922, Max Marston at Flossmoor in 1923, and Von Elm at Baltusrol in 1926. All were national champions. Herron, Sweetser, Marston, and Von Elm won the title the years they defeated Jones. Gardner had won in 1909 and 1915, Ouimet in 1914 and again in 1931, while Hunter had won the British Amateur earlier in 1921. Ouimet also took the Open in 1913.

Jones's lone defeat at 18 holes was dealt by Johnny Goodman at Pebble Beach in 1929. Goodman won the Open four years later and the Amateur in 1937.

Two of Jones's defeats came in the finals (1919–26), two in the semifinals (1920–22), two in the quarter-finals (1916–21), one in the second round (1923), and one in the first round (1929).

Jones went extra holes in the Amateur only once, edging Ray Gorton, a home-course player, on the 19th hole in the second round at Brae Burn in 1928.

Jones averaged 148.77 for his 13 qualifying tests at 36 holes.

If some of the leading players in the Amateur Championship were limited to 13 appearances, as was Jones, the won-and-lost records would look like this: Jones 43-8, Charles R. Coe 47-11, Harvie Ward 43-11, Walter J. Travis 39-10, Chick Evans 34-11, Willie Turnesa 34-11, Ray Billows 38-13, Francis Ouimet 30-12, and Johnny Goodman 30-12.

USGA National Open Championship

1920 Inverness Club, Toledo, Ohio, August 12–13
Jones shot 78-74-70-77—299 to tie for eighth place. Edward ("Ted") Ray, of Oxhey, England, was the winner with 295, seven over par.

1921 Columbia Country Club, Chevy Chase, Maryland, July 21–22

Jones shot 78-71-77-77—303 to tie for fifth. Long Jim Barnes was the winner with 289, nine over par.

1922 Skokie Country Club, Glencoe, Illinois, July 14–15

Jones shot 74-72-70-73—289 to tie for second. Gene Sarazen was the winner with 288, eight over par.

1923 Inwood Country Club, Inwood, New York, July 13–15

Jones shot 71-73-76-76—296, a score equaled by Bobby Cruickshank. In the 18-hole play-off, Jones shot 76 over the 6,657-yard, par-72 course to win his first major title. Cruickshank needed 78. Jones was then 21 years of age.

1924 Oakland Hills Country Club, Birmingham, Michigan, June 5–6

Jones shot 74-73-75-78—300 to finish second. Cyril Walker was the winner with 297, nine over par for the 6,880-yard course. He was the only man under 300 among the 85 starters.

1925 Worcester Country Club, Worcester, Massachusetts, June 3–5

Jones shot 77-70-70-74—291, a score equaled by Willie MacFarlane. In the 36-hole play-off, Jones shot 75-73 over the 6,430-yard, par-71 course, losing by one stroke to MacFarlane's 75-72.

1926 Scioto Country Club, Columbus, Ohio, July 8–10

Jones shot 70-79-71-73—293, to win by one stroke over Joe Turnesa. Scioto was 6,736 yards long with a par of 72.

1927 Oakmont Country Club, Oakmont, Pennsylvania, June 14–16

Jones shot 76-77-79-77—309 to tie for 11th, his worst showing in the Open. Tommy Armour was the winner with 301-76 to Harry Cooper's 301-79 over the 6,915-yard, par-72 course.

1928 Olympia Fields Country Club (No. 4 Course), Mateson, Illinois, June 21–24

Jones shot 73-71-73-77—294, a score equaled by Johnny Farrell. In the 36-hole play-off, Jones shot 73-71, losing by one stroke to Farrell's 70-73 over the 6,726-yard, par-71 course.

1929 Winged Foot Golf Club (West Course), Mamaroneck, New York, June 27–30

Jones shot 69-75-71-79—294, a score equaled by Al Espinosa. In the 36-hole play-off, Jones shot 72-69—141, Espinosa 84-80—164 over the 6,786-yard, par-72 course.

1930   Interlachen Country Club, Minneapolis, Minnesota, July 10–12

Jones shot 71-73-68-75—287 to win by two strokes over Macdonald Smith. Interlachen was 6,672 yards long with a par of 72.

U. S. Open Championship Highlights

In his 11 starts, in consecutive years, Jones returned an average score of 295.91 in contrast with an average winning score of 293.18, a difference of only 2.73 strokes. (For the same 11 Opens, Walter Hagen averaged 300.9, Gene Sarazen 302.36.)

In his 44 regular rounds and seven play-off rounds, 51 in all, Jones averaged 73.8 strokes. His best round was 68 in the third round at Interlachen in 1930; his highest 79 in the second round at Scioto in 1926, third round at Oakmont in 1927, and fourth round at Winged Foot in 1929. His first-round 69 at Winged Foot in 1929 was accomplished through a 31 on the second nine. His highest score on one hole was nine on the long fifth at Columbia in 1921.

Jones's 68 at Interlachen was the result of excellent putting. He had 11 one-putt greens, sinking one putt of 25 feet. He needed two pars for 66—a new Open record—but lost a stroke at the 262-yard 17th (perhaps the longest par-three in Open history) and the 402-yard 18th. He also took two fives on the 17th. In contrast, his third-round 77 at Columbia in 1921 included 40 putts.

Jones's best 72-hole score was 287 at Interlachen in his final Open in 1930, his worst 309 at Oakmont in 1927 when he said he attempted to steer the ball away from Oakmont's 273 furrowed bunkers. He shot 69 at Oakmont in practice but no better than 76 in competition.

In nine of his 11 years as an Open participant, Jones was low amateur, the only exceptions being the first two in 1920 and 1921.

Jones called two penalties on himself in the U. S. Open, and one probably cost him an additional title. In the first round at Worcester in 1925, his ball was in long grass at the left of the 11th green. As he prepared to play, his ball moved out of position. Neither the spectators nor the officials thought he had caused the ball to move. It was generally felt that he was too harsh with himself. He also imposed a one-stroke penalty on himself at the 15th hole in the first round at Scioto in 1926. He reported his ball turned halfway over as he grounded his putter. (He went ahead to win.)

Of Jones's 51 rounds in the Open, 11 were subpar, four even par, and 36 over par. Three were in the 60s. (There were only 12 other rounds under 70 in his era.) Seventeen of his rounds—exactly one-third—were 72 or better.

U. S. Open Records Still Held by Jones

Most Victories—Four. (He shares this with Willie Anderson and Ben Hogan.)

Most Frequent Pacesetter at 54 Holes—Six, in 1922 (tie), 1923, 1924 (tie), 1928, 1929, 1930.

Most Play-offs in Which a Participant—Four, in 1923-25-28-29.

Most Play-offs Won—Two, in 1923-29. (He shares this with Anderson.)

Most Play-off Rounds Played—Seven.

Most Decisive Play-off Victory—23 strokes in 1929. He shot 72-69—141 to 84-80—164 for Al Espinosa, a difference of more than a half stroke per hole.

The British Open Championship

1921   Old Course, St. Andrews, Scotland, June 23–24–25

Jones shot 151 for the first 36 holes but picked up after taking 46 on the first nine, then a six on the 312-yard 10th and hitting his ball into a bunker at the par-three 11th hole in the third round. He took two to get out of the bunker, missed his first putt, then picked up. He continued to play, however, and scored an unofficial 72 for the final round.

Eventual champion was Jock Hutchison, U.S., with 296-74-76 to 296-77-82 for Roger Wethered, an amateur, following a 36-hole play-off on the 6,572-yard, par-73 links.

The 10th hole was named for Jones in 1972—the first time a person has been so honored at St. Andrews.

1926   Royal Lytham and St. Annes, June 23–24–25

Jones shot 72-72-73-74—291 to win by two strokes over Al Watrous, the 54-hole leader with 71-75-69, and by four over Walter Hagen, whose 68 led the first round. Jones had led the qualifying rounds with 66-68—134 at Sunningdale June 16–17.

The 291 tied the British Open record set by James Braid at Prestwick in 1908. Jones was the first amateur to win since Harold Hilton won at Hoylake in 1897, five years before Jones was born.

1927   Old Course, St. Andrews, July 13–14–15

Jones successfully defended his title, scoring 68-72-73-72—285, seven under par, to beat Aubrey Boomer and Fred Robson by six strokes. He led all the way, posting 17 birdies and an eagle. He also scored 37 4s, 17 5s, 16 3s, and two 2s. He had qualified with 76-71—147, Cyril Tolley winning the medal with 144.

The 285 was a new record for the Championship, exceeding his own performance of the previous year by six strokes. The 68 tied the St. Andrews record for a single round and marked the first time Jones broke 70 in a national championship. He needed only 29 putts, and holed from 120 feet for an eagle three at the long fifth.

1930   Royal Liverpool Golf Club, Hoylake, England, June 18–19–20

Jones shot 70-72-74-75—291 to capture his third and final British Open. Leo Diegel and Macdonald Smith were two strokes back. Jones had qualified with 73-77—150 at Hoylake, terming the 77 "the worst I ever played in England."

The 70 tied the record for the 7,078-yard Hoylake links, par for which was 72, and stood as the record for amateurs for more than 25 years. The 291 was 10 strokes lower than the 301 Hagen returned when he won at Hoylake in 1924. It resulted from 37 4s, 18 3s, 14 5s, two 6s, and a 7, which came at the long eighth in the final round.

British Open Highlights

Only three amateurs have won the British Open since its inception in 1860—John Ball at Prestwick in 1890, Harold Hilton at Muirfield in 1892 and at Hoylake in 1897, and Jones in 1926-27-30.

Jones's most remarkable scoring came at Sunningdale in the qualifying rounds for the 1926 championship. Writers immediately termed his 66-68 a British record for 36 holes of competitive golf, but the United States Golf Association called it an all-time record for 36 holes of competitive golf.

The 66 included 33 putts and 33 other shots, and broke the record for the 6,472-yard course by four strokes. It was composed of 12 4s and six 3s, and may be ranked as one of the most perfect rounds of championship golf ever played. Jones got down only one long putt, a 25-footer for a birdie three at the fifth. His iron rolled into a shallow pot bunker at the 175-yard 13th, but he chipped out and sank the putt. Otherwise he reached every green with the shot he should have.

This 134 was tied 26 years later by John Panton at Fairhaven and St. Annes in the 1952 Open qualifying rounds, and beaten by Peter Thomson at St. Annes in 1958. Thomson shot 63-70.

After winning at Hoylake in 1930, Jones hinted that his retirement was imminent. He told the Associated Press: "This is my last shot at the British Open. This tournament has taken more out of me than any other I ever played in. It's quite too thick for me. I feel that I'm not strong enough to play in another one."

The British Amateur Championship

1921 *Royal Liverpool Golf Club, Hoylake, England, May 23–27*

Jones defeated G. C. Manford, 3 and 2; E. A. Hamlet, 1 up; Robert Harris (who was to win the British Amateur four years later), 6 and 5; then was eliminated by Allan Graham in the fourth round, 6 and 5.

Eventual champion was Willie Hunter, who defeated Graham in the final, 12 and 11.

1926 *Muirfield, Scotland, May 24–29*

Jones defeated Major C. B. Omerod, 3 and 2; Colin C. Aylmer, 6 and 4; Hugh M. Dickson, 4 and 3; J. Birnie, Jr., 7 and 6; and Robert Harris, 8 and 6, in a match between the U.S. and British Amateur champions; then was eliminated by Andrew Jamieson, Jr., in the sixth round, 4 and 3.

Eventual champion was Jess Sweetser, United States, who defeated A. F. Simpson in the final, 6 and 5.

1930 Old Course, St. Andrews, Scotland, May 26–31
Jones defeated Sidney Roper, 3 and 2, after starting 3-4-3-2-4 (five under par); Cowan Shankland, 5 and 3; Cyril J. H. Tolley (1920 and 1929 British Amateur Champion) on the 19th hole; G. O. Watt, 7 and 6; Harrison R. "Jimmy" Johnston (1929 U. S. Amateur champion), 1 up; Eric Fiddian, 4 and 3; George Voigt, 1 up, after being 2 down with five holes to play; and Roger Wethered (1923 British Amateur Champion), 7 and 6 in the final.
Note: Of the 15 different Britons Jones played in the British Amateur, six played in the Walker Cup series—Aylmer, Fiddian, Harris, Jamieson, Tolley, and Wethered.

The International Match for the Walker Cup
(All matches scheduled 36 holes.)

1922 National Golf Links of America, Southampton, New York (the first match)
Scotch Foursomes, August 28: Jones and Jess W. Sweetser, playing as the No. 3 United States pairing, defeated Willie B. Torrance and C. V. L. Hooman, 3 and 2.
Singles, August 29: Jones, in the No. 2 spot behind Jesse P. Guilford, the U. S. Amateur champion, defeated Roger H. Wethered, 3 and 2.
Team result: United States 8, Great Britain 4.

1923 Old Course, St. Andrews, Scotland
Jones did not compete in the mid-May match, won by the United States, 6–5, being busy with his studies at Harvard University.

1924 Garden City Golf Club, Garden City, New York
Scotch Foursomes, September 12: Jones and William C. Fownes, Jr., playing as the No. 3 United States pairing, were defeated by Hon. Michael Scott and Robert Scott, Jr., 1 up. This was Jones's only defeat in Walker Cup play.
Singles, September 13: Jones, in the No. 2 spot behind Max Marston, the U. S. Amateur champion, defeated Major Charles O. Hezlet, 4 and 3.
Team result: United States 9, Great Britain 3.

1926 Old Course, St. Andrews, Scotland
Scotch Foursomes, June 2: Jones and Watts Gunn, a fellow Atlantan, playing as the No. 2 United States pairing, defeated Cyril J. H. Tolley and Andrew Jamieson, 4 and 3.

Singles, June 3: Jones, playing No. 1 for the United States side, defeated Tolley, 12 and 11, a record margin for the series.

Team result: United States 6, Great Britain 5.

1928 Chicago Golf Club, Wheaton, Illinois

Scotch Foursomes, August 30: Jones, the United States playing captain, with Chick Evans as his partner in the No. 2 pairing, defeated Hezlet and William L. Hope, 5 and 3.

Singles, August 31: Jones, playing No. 1, defeated T. Philip Perkins, 13 and 12, breaking his own record for the most one-sided singles victory.

Team result: United States 11, Great Britain 1.

1930 Royal St. George's Golf Club, Sandwich, England

Scotch Foursomes, May 15: Jones and Dr. Oscar F. Willing, the No. 2 United States pairing, defeated Rex W. Hartley and Thomas A. Torrance, 8 and 7, tying a record for the most one-sided foursome victory.

Singles, May 16: Jones, playing No. 2 behind Harrison R. "Jimmy" Johnston, the U. S. Amateur champion, defeated Wethered, 9 and 8. Jones again captained the United States side.

Team result: United States 10, Great Britain 2.

Walker Cup Highlights

The International Match for the Walker Cup, a match-play competition waged in alternate years by amateurs of the United States and Great Britain and Ireland, grew out of three international matches following World War I. Jones took part in all three.

He was a member of a 10-man United States side that defeated a team of amateurs representing the Royal Canadian Golf Association at the Hamilton (Ontario) Golf Club in 1919, and again at The Engineers Club in Roslyn, New York, in 1920. The scores were 12–3 and 10–4, respectively.

In 1921, he was a member of the American team that defeated the British in an informal contest at Hoylake on the day preceding the British Amateur Championship. The score was 9–3. (William C. Fownes, Jr., assembled all three United States teams.)

In all, Jones participated in five Walker Cup series, sweeping all five of his scheduled 36-hole singles and four of his five Scottish foursomes, also scheduled for 36 holes. (All of his foursome partners were different.) He scored seven of the United States teams' 44 points in that span.

Two of Jones's Walker Cup records still stand: his 13 and 12 victory over T. Philip Perkins at Chicago Golf Club in 1928; and his feat of capturing four singles in successive series. (The latter was tied by Ronald J. White of Great Britain. Bill Campbell later won four straight 18-hole matches.) No one in the era of 36-hole matches came close to his performance of winning nine out of 10 starts.

In 1958, Jones captained the United States side in the first World Amateur Team Championship for the Eisenhower Trophy at St. Andrews, Scotland.

The Grand Slam of 1930, *Step by Step*

British Amateur, Old Course, St. Andrews, Scotland (match-play)
May 26 Jones defeated Sidney Roper, 3 and 2.
May 27 Off day.
May 28 Jones defeated Cowan Shankland, 5 and 3, in the morning; Cyril J. H. Tolley on the 19th hole in the afternoon.
May 29 Jones defeated G. O. Watt, 7 and 6, in the morning; Harrison R. "Jimmy" Johnston, 1 up, in the afternoon.
May 30 Jones defeated Eric Fiddian, 4 and 3, in the morning; George Voigt, 1 up, in the afternoon.
May 31 Jones defeated Roger Wethered, 7 and 6, in the final. The final was scheduled for 36 holes, the other matches 18 holes.

British Open, Royal Liverpool Golf Club, Hoylake, England (72 holes, stroke-play)
June 16–17 Jones shot 73-77—150, tying for twentieth place in the qualifying rounds. Archie Compston, of Great Britain, won the medal with 70-71—141.
June 18 First-round leaders: Jones 36-34—70, Macdonald Smith, United States, 33-37—70; Henry Cotton, Great Britain, 34-36—70.
June 19 Second-round leaders: Jones 70-72—142; Fred Robson, Great Britain, 71-72—143; Horton Smith, United States, 72-73—145.
June 20 morning Third-round leaders: Compston, 73-74-68—215; Jones 70-72-74—216; Leo Diegel, United States, 74-73-71—218.
June 20 afternoon Final scores: Jones 70-72-74-75—291; Diegel 74-73-71-75—293; Macdonald Smith 70-77-75-71—293.

U. S. Open, Interlachen Country Club, Minneapolis (72 holes, stroke-play)
Jones was the defending champion and thus exempt from qualifying.
July 10 First-round leaders: Tommy Armour 37-33—70; Macdonald Smith, 37-33—70; Jones 34-37—71; W. H. "Wiffy" Cox 34-37—71.
July 11 Second-round leaders: Horton Smith 72-70—142; Jones 71-73—144; Charles Lacey 74-70—144; Harry Cooper 72-72—144.
July 12 morning Third-round leaders: Jones 71-73-68—212; Cooper 72-72-73—217; Horton Smith 72-70-76—218; John Golden 74-73-71—218.
July 12 afternoon Final scores: Jones 71-73-68-75—287; Macdonald Smith 70-75-74-70—289; Horton Smith 72-70-76-74—292; Cooper 72-72-73-76—293.

U. S. Amateur, Merion Cricket Club, Ardmore, Pennsylvania (match-play)
September 22–23 Jones shot 69-73—142 to win the medal. George Von Elm was second with 73-70—143.

251

Augusta
National
Golf Club

September 24 morning Jones defeated C. Ross Somerville of London, Ontario, Canada, 5 and 4.

September 24 afternoon Jones defeated Fred G. Hoblitzel of Toronto, Ontario, Canada, 5 and 4.

September 25 Jones defeated Fay Coleman of Culver City, California, in the quarter-finals, 6 and 5 (scheduled 36 holes).

September 26 Jones defeated Jess W. Sweetser of New York City in the semifinals, 9 and 8 (scheduled 36 holes).

September 27 Jones defeated Eugene V. Homans of Englewood, New Jersey, in the final, 8 and 7 (scheduled 36 holes).

Highlights of the Grand Slam

The four triumphs comprising the Grand Slam required 20 calendar days spread over four months, meaning that Jones had to bring his game to a peak four different times.

The feat required 475 holes—152 in the U. S. Amateur, 143 in the British Amateur, 108 in the British Open, and 72 in the U. S. Open. He played 36 holes or was scheduled to play 36 on 10 of the 20 days—half the time.

For his 12 rounds at stroke-play (four in each Open, two in qualifying for the British Open, and two in qualifying for the U. S. Amateur), Jones averaged 72.5 strokes.

Jones won 13 matches in the two Amateur Championships. He was 32 up over nine opponents in scheduled 18-hole matches, an average margin of three and a half holes, and 30 up on four opponents in scheduled 36-hole matches, an average margin of seven and a half holes.

The key shots of the Grand Slam, in Jones's estimation, were:

· British Amateur (St. Andrews): Holing from 12 feet for a birdie 4 at the 467-yard 17th, or Road Hole, after George Voigt had rolled his 50-foot putt dead for his four. Jones won at the 18th after having been two down with five to play in their semifinal match.

· British Open (Hoylake): A bunker shot that finished two inches away from the flagstick at the 532-yard 16th in the final round, assuring a birdie four.

· U. S. Open (Interlachen): A brassie second in a strong crosswind to the long fourth in the final round. The ball stopped just short of the green, setting up a pitch close to the hole for a birdie four.

· U. S. Amateur (Merion): Holing from eight feet, then Sandy Somerville missing from seven feet at the seventh hole—a drive and pitch—in the first round. Jones was one up at the time. Had the results been turned around, the match would have been square. Jones went on to win, 5 and 4.

Other Events in Which Jones Participated

1915 (age 13)

Jones qualified for the Southern Amateur with 83, only one stroke behind the medalists, at the East Lake course of the Atlanta Athletic Club. He lost to Commodore Bryan Heard in the second round.

1917 (age 15)

Jones won the Southern Amateur at Roebuck Springs Country Club, Birmingham, Alabama, defeating Louis Jacoby in the final, 6 and 4.

1918 (age 16)

Red Cross Matches: he toured the country with Alexa Stirling, Elaine Rosenthal, and Perry Adair.

War Relief Matches at Baltusrol, Englewood, Siwanoy, and Garden City: he won three singles and two foursomes; lost one foursome with Perry Adair to Emmett French and Jack Dowling.

1919 (age 17)

Jones won first flight in the Yates-Gode tournament at East Lake.

He tied for second in the Canadian Open at Hamilton Golf Club, Ontario, Canada. J. Douglas Edgar shot 72-71-69-66—278, the lowest score returned in a national competition in any country at that time. Jones, Long Jim Barnes and Carl Keffer of Canada, tied for second, 16 strokes back.

He was a semifinalist in the Southern Amateur at New Orleans Country Club, losing to Nelson Whitney.

He shot 73-74-76-71—294 to finish second to Barnes in the Southern Open at East Lake. Barnes shot 293.

He and Edgar were defeated by Barnes and Leo Diegel on the 19th hole in an exhibition at East Lake.

He lost to Ned Sawyer in the first round of the Western Amateur at Sunset Hill Country Club, St. Louis.

1920 (age 18)

Jones won the Davis-Freeman tournament at East Lake, defeating Richard Hickey in the final, 4 and 2.

He was a semifinalist in the Georgia Amateur at Druid Hills, losing to C. V. Rainwater, 1 up. Jones, Milton Dargan, and Bowie Martin shared the medal with 77.

He won the Southern Amateur at Chattanooga, defeating Ewing Watkins in the final, 10 and 9. He was also medalist with 139.

He and Chick Evans defeated Harry Vardon and Ted Ray in a 36-hole exhibition, 10 and 9.

He was semifinalist in the Western Amateur at Memphis Country Club, losing to Evans, 1 up. He qualified with 69-70—139 to win the medal by eight strokes, the 69 being a new course record. He then defeated Frank Crager, 6 and 5; George McConnell, 2 up, and Clarence Hubby, 12 and 11.

He shot 78-78-74-74—304 to finish second to Edgar in the Southern Open at East Lake. Edgar shot 302, with a closing round of 70.

He and Oswald Kirby defeated Vardon and Ray at Englewood, New Jersey, in the morning; he and Cyril Walker defeated Vardon and Ray in the afternoon.

1922 (age 20)

Jones tied Joe Kirkwood for fourth place in the Western Open at Oakwood Country Club, Cleveland Heights, Ohio. Walter Hagen won with 287. Jones shot 295 after leading the field of 64 at the halfway mark with 69-70—139.

1922 (age 20)

Jones won the Southern Amateur at East Lake, defeating Frank Godchaux in the final, 8 and 7. Jones, Perry Adair, and T. W. Palmer shared the medal with 75s. Jones defeated W. G. Oehmig in the first round, 6 and 5, then D. T. McRitchie, 8 and 7; Chasteen Harris, 11 and 9; and Chris Brinke, 12 and 11. He was 10 under par for 123 holes. This was his final appearance in this championship.

He shot 31-32—63, nine under par, at East Lake, a 6,700-yard course, scoring nine birdies and nine pars. (He once scored 62 at Highland, North Carolina, Country Club.)

1923 (age 21)

Jones and Perry Adair defeated Jock Hutchison and Frank Godchaux in a 72-hole exhibition, at Atlanta and Nashville, 6 and 5. Jones shot 69-69-69-71.

1924 (age 22)

Jones lost to Arthur Havers, the British Open champion, in a 36-hole challenge match at East Lake. Jones, then U. S. Open champion, shot 78-71, Havers 76-72.

He and Perry Adair lost to Havers and Jimmy Ockenden, the French Open champion, at Augusta, 5 and 4. Havers shot 70 on the sand greens, Jones 75.

He and Cyril Tolley each shot 74 at East Lake in an exhibition, but at Druid Hills, Tolley edged Jones, 71 to 72. Tolley and Perry Adair defeated Jones and Tim Bradshaw at Druid Hills, 3 and 1.

He and Francis Ouimet lost to George Duncan and Abe Mitchell in a 36-hole exhibition at Asheville, North Carolina, 2 and 1.

1925 (age 23)

Jones shot 76-75-78-79—308 in the Florida West Coast Open at St. Petersburg—19 strokes behind the winner, Tommy Armour. This was his worst performance in a stroke-play event.

1926 (age 24)

Jones lost to Hagen in a special 72-hole match at Sarasota and St. Petersburg, Florida, 12 and 11.

He was second to Hagen in the West Coast of Florida Open at St. Petersburg, shooting 75-69-71-70—285 to Hagen's 283.

He and Tommy Armour defeated Hagen and Gil Nicholls, 4 and 3, in an exhibition at St. Petersburg.

He and Armour defeated Arnaud Massy and Archie Compston, 8 and 7, in an exhibition at Sarasota.

He and Armour defeated Gene Sarazen and Diegel, 3 and 2, in an exhibition at Sarasota.

He and Hagen defeated Abe Mitchell and Cyril Tolley, 4 and 2, in an exhibition at Moor Park, England.

1927 (age 25)

Jones won the Southern Open at East Lake with 72-66-71-72—281. Johnny Farrell was second, eight strokes back. The second round 66 included 32 putts and 11 4s, five 3s, one 2, and one 5.

He and Joe Kirkwood defeated Roger Wethered and Cyril Tolley, 1 up, in an exhibition at Epsom, England.

1928 (age 26)

Jones won the Warren K. Wood Memorial Cup with 37-30—67 at Flossmoor (Illinois) Country Club, scoring seven 3s in succession.

He and Watts Gunn tied Roland MacKenzie and Warren Corkran in an exhibition at Baltimore. MacKenzie shot 74, Jones 77.

He shot 69-67 in an exhibition with Farrell against Hagen and Sarazen at Woodland Golf Club, Newton, Massachusetts, but they were defeated 1 up.

1930 (age 28)

Jones was second to Horton Smith in the Savannah Open, scoring 67-75-65-72—279 to Smith's 278.

He then won the Southeastern Open at Augusta, Georgia, by 13 strokes with 72-72-69-71—284. Horton Smith finished second.

While abroad, he won the *Golf Illustrated* Gold Vase with 75-68—143 at Sunningdale, England. This was a record score for the 36-hole event.

He shot 68 in an exhibition with Ted Ray, Harry Vardon, and James Braid at Oxhey, England, Ray's home course.

He shot 70 at East Lake before 3,000 fans in a benefit for the 82nd Division Entertainment Fund.

He and Roland R. MacKenzie, another amateur, defeated Macdonald Smith and Fred McLeod, 1 up, in an 18-hole exhibition at Columbia Country Club, Chevy Chase, Maryland.

1935 (age 33)

Jones and Dorothy Kirby tied Joyce Wethered and Charles Yates in an exhibition at East Lake. Jones shot a par 71, Miss Wethered 74, Yates 76 and Miss Kirby (who was then 15 years of age), 84.

1936 (age 34)

Jones shot 32-39—71 in an informal round at St. Andrews before 6,000 people.

1941 (age 39)

Jones captained a team of challengers which defeated the United States Ryder Cup side at Detroit Golf Club. Jones won his single from Henry Picard, 2 and 1, but he and Gene Sarazen lost their foursome to Byron Nelson and Harold "Jug" McSpaden, 8 and 6.

He and Armour defeated Hagen and Sarazen in a Bahamas Red Cross exhibition, 3 and 2, being seven under par for 34 holes. Armour shot a one-under-par 70 the first day, Sarazen 72, Jones 73, Hagen 76.

1942 (*age 40*)

Jones tied for 35th in the Hale America National Open, a charity stand-in for the USGA National Open, with 70-75-72-73—290 at Ridgemoor Country Club, Chicago. He was a captain in the Air Force at the time.

1946 (*age 44*)

Jones played the first nine at East Lake in 29, six under par. He and Louise Suggs lost to Dick Garlington and Dorothy Kirby in an exhibition.

His Record as a Junior Player

1911 (*age 9*) Won Junior Championship Cup of the Atlanta Athletic Club.

1912 (*age 10*) Lost to Howard Thorne in the semifinals of the Atlanta Athletic Club Junior Championship.

1913 (*age 11*) Shot his first 80 on the East Lake course.

1915 (*age 13*) Lost in finals of the second flight, Montgomery Invitation. Won invitation tournament at Roebuck Springs, Birmingham. Won Davis and Freeman Cup at East Lake. Won East Lake and Druid Hills Club Championships.

1916 (*age 14*) Lost to Perry Adair in semifinals of first flight, Montgomery Invitation. Won Birmingham Country Club Invitation. Won Cherokee Club Invitation, Knoxville, Tennessee. Won East Lake Invitation tournament. Won Georgia State Amateur Championship at Brookhaven Country Club.

1917 (*age 15*) Lost to Louis Jacoby in the second round of the Druid Hills Invitation.

(Source: *Down the Fairway*, by Robert T. Jones, Jr., and O. B. Keeler, Minton, Balch & Company, New York, 1927.)